FINIS REI PUBLICAE

A TEXTBOOK FOR INTERMEDIATE LATIN

SECOND EDITION

FINIS REI PUBLICAE

EYEWITNESSES TO THE END OF THE ROMAN REPUBLIC

A TEXTBOOK FOR INTERMEDIATE LATIN

SECOND EDITION

ROBERT KNAPP

University of California, Berkeley

PAMELA VAUGHN

San Francisco State University

THE FOCUS CLASSICAL LIBRARY

Series Editors • James Clauss and Stephen Esposito

Aristophanes: Acharnians • Jeffrey Henderson • 1992 • 1-58510-087-0
Aristophanes: The Birds • Jeffrey Henderson • 1999 • 0-941051-87-0
Aristophanes: Clouds • Jeffrey Henderson • 1992 • 0-941051-24-2
Aristophanes: Lysistrata • Jeffrey Henderson • 1988 • 0-941051-02-1
Aristophanes: Three Comedies: Acharnians, Lysistrata, Clouds • Jeffrey Henderson • 1997 • 0-941051-58-7
Euripides: The Bacchae • Stephen Esposito • 1998 • 0-941051-42-0
Euripides: Four Plays: Medea, Hippolytus, Heracles, Bacchae • Stephen Esposito, ed. • 2003 • 1-58510-048-X
Euripides: Hecuba • Robin Mitchell-Boyask • 2006 • 1-58510-148-6
Euripides: Heracles • Michael R. Halleran • 1988 • 0-941051-01-3
Euripides: Hippolytus • Michael R. Halleran • 2001 • 0-941051-86-2
Euripides: Medea • Anthony Podlecki • 2005, Revised • 0-941051-10-2
Euripides: The Trojan Women • Diskin Clay • 2005 • 1-58510-111-7
Golden Verses: Poetry of the Augustan Age • Paul T. Alessi • 2003 • 1-58510-064-1
Golden Prose in the Age of Augustus • Paul T. Alessi • 2004 • 1-58510-125-7
Hesiod: Theogony • Richard Caldwell • 1987 • 0-941051-00-5
The Homeric Hymns • Susan Shelmerdine • 1995 • 1-58510-019-6
Ovid: Metamorphoses • Z. Philip Ambrose • 2004 • 1-58510-103-6
Sophocles: Antigone • Ruby Blondell • 1998 • 0-941051-25-0
Sophocles: King Oidipous • Ruby Blondell • 2002 • 1-58510-060-9
Sophocles: Oidipous at Colonus • Ruby Blondell • 2003 Revised • 1-58510-065-X
Sophocles: Philoktetes • Seth Schein • 2003 • 1-58510-086-2
Sophocles: The Theban Plays • Ruby Blondell • 2002 • 1-58510-037-4
Terence: Brothers (Adelphoe) • Charles Mercier • 1998 • 0-941051-72-2 [VHS • 0-941051-73-0]
Vergil: The Aeneid • Richard Caldwell • 2004 • 1-58510-077-3

ISBN 1-58510-079-X

Finis Rei Publicae Workbook ISBN 1-58510-080-3

10 9 8 7 6 5

Table of Contents

SECTION FORTY

APPENDICES

Acknowledgements

The creation of a text is perforce the work of many hands. We would like first of all to thank all the students who suffered through our work in various stages, from photocopied handouts to semi-final copy. Their comments and suggestions have been invaluable. We would also like to express our appreciation and gratitude to Sharon James (University of North Carolina, Chapel Hill) and to Kathleen McCarthy and Sarah Stroup (University of California, Berkeley), who used the book in a rather rough form in their Latin classes; again, both their encouragement and their ideas for improvements were most welcome. Finally, we would like to thank Ron Pullins and the folks at Focus Publishing who had faith in our work and helped us bring it to published fruition.

Robert Knapp   Pamela Vaughn
Berkeley   San Francisco

Introduction

The two years between about the middle of 50 BC and the middle of 48 BC saw a series of events that to contemporaries as to later observers seemed a watershed in the history of the Romans. Although the final battle for political control of the Roman state was not fought for another three years, and although the formalization of a new order did not take place for another half-generation, in these two years a dagger was driven through the heart of the Republican Roman political system. While the end of the political organization we call the "Republic" did not mean the end of much, even most, of Roman culture and society as it had developed over the previous two hundred years, it was a violent reordering of the power structure of the state: rule by an oligarchic aristocracy gave way to the rule of a single aristocratic warlord.

The "end of the Roman Republic" was in essence a political event. That is to say, the way the society was organized to rule itself was changed fundamentally. Although at the beginning of Roman history the state was ruled by kings who subordinated a kinship-based aristocracy to their wishes, that aristocracy grew tired of the constraints and abuses of the kings, and succeeded in driving the last king, Tarquin the Proud, into an exile from which he never returned. The Republic was the political order which the aristocracy then established to ensure their leadership in the Roman community, and to assure the survival of that community in the face of the unremitting hostility of its neighbors. As the success of the Roman military establishment moved the Roman state to a position of greater and greater preeminence in, first, Italy and then, later, the Mediterranean basin, the ruling oligarchic aristocracy began to suffer the strains of empire: the distribution of social capital in terms of prestige, glory, and fame became ever more uneven within the group, as did the distribution of the material benefits of successful war after successful war. In particular, after the defeat of Hannibal in the Second Punic War (202 BC), the aggrandizement of the Romans sowed the seeds of the destruction of the oligarchic governing system. As more and more wealth and power translated into more and more possibilities for the exercise by an individual of excessive power in society, the unified stance of the oligarchy against the emergence of a single or a few "great men" crumbled. Military exigencies and military reforms of the end of the second century BC created the agent for the emergence of warlords able to overcome opposition within the oligarchy in a drive for more and more personal prestige and power. Marius, Sulla, Pompey, Caesar—the names are familiar. These men outgrew and circumvented the constraints of the current oligarchic system, and when that system tried to thwart what they perceived as their just and proper deserts, they used the armies at their backs to establish their will in the state. Reeling from the ravages of Marius and Sulla in the eighties BC, the oligarchy had barely reestablished itself when first Pompey and then Caesar emerged as new threats. This time the battle was, as Cicero correctly perceived, over "who would be king." This time there was no re-establishment of the oligarchic way; this time the Republican governmental structure did, finally, come to an end in the fact of Caesar's overwhelming will and power.

Eyewitness accounts remain of this critical period in Roman history. The most spectacular is, of course, Caesar's own recounting of events in his *Bellum Civile (Civil War)*, supplemented by the "ghost written" material by his aide Aulus Hirtius in the final book of the *Bellum Gallicum (War in Gaul)*. To add to and somewhat control this material we have a number of letters from Cicero, including copies of letters of main actors like Pompey and Caesar themselves. But much has been lost. For example, Asinius Pollio, an eyewitness, wrote a history of the civil wars which has perished, although its contents are to some extent reflected in the later, second century AD, history by Appian. A myriad of letters and documents and accounts of course existed at one time, but no longer survive.

Finis Rei Publicae portrays the drama of the final years of the Republic from the material of the eyewitnesses. This approach produces a lively and challenging account which must be read with perception and care—but it rewards study with a new understanding of what men like Caesar and Cicero were about, what they were hoping for, fearing, and enduring during these crucial years. At the same time, the prose provides an excellent text to review and practice the principles of Latin grammar and syntax learned in an introduction to the language: Caesar is relatively straightforward and Cicero, while more difficult, is well worth the effort to read. The goal of *Finis Rei Publicae* is, therefore, to combine the intrigue and excitement of a critical moment in western history with a program for solidification of a reading knowledge of Latin prose. *Vale!*

The Organization of the Text

The material is presented in four ways:

First, the Latin Text is given. We have not used macrons as we believe that students in intermediate Latin should become used to reading Latin without them.

Second, to the right is a list of Vocabulary. These words are selected to facilitate translation; they are listed in the order in which they appear in the text.

Third, Grammar and Syntax appears below the vocabulary. In general, grammar which appears in the current section is highlighted, but sometimes additional material is brought up. In doing the entire text, all the important grammar points learned in elementary Latin are reviewed.[1]

Fourth, at the bottom of each page are notes designed to provide additional help with grammar and historical commentary on the text.

Macrons

A macron is the line above a long vowel used to distinguish those vowels from short vowels. The ancient Romans sometimes marked long vowels with a slanted stroke above the letter, called an apex (É= long E) or by a doubling (AA = long A) or, in the case of I, having the long vowel letter extend above the other letters of a line. But these uses were sporadic and unpredictable; no manner of indicating a long vowel ever came into regular use. It has become standard to use macrons in beginning Latin texts in order to allow students to tell immediately the quantity of a vowel. However, normal Latin texts (e.g., the Oxford and Teubner editions) do not mark quantities, as this is a modern habit (unlike Greek accentuation, which dates from the Hellenistic period). This text intends to serve as a first step toward reading normal Latin texts; thus, we have decided not to use macrons.

Abbreviations Used

AG = J.B. Greenough, et al. (eds.), *Allen and Greenough's New Latin Grammar for Schools and Colleges.* Boston 1931 [1888].

B = C.E. Bennett, *New Latin Grammar.* Boston 1960 [1895].

BC = Julius Caesar, *De bello civili.*

Carter = J.M. Carter. *Julius Caesar: The Civil War Books I & II.* Warminster UK 1991(?).

Green = J.C. Green, Jr., *Latin: Two Years.* New York 1959 [1927].

Peskett = A.G. Peskett, *Gai Iuli Caesaris commentariorum De bello civili, liber primus;* with introduction, notes and maps. Cambridge UK 1890.

Ruebel = J.S. Ruebel, ed., *Caesar and the Crisis of the Roman Aristocracy*: a civil war reader. Norman, Oklahoma 1994.

---

[1] J. C. Green, Jr., *Latin: Two Years* (new edition by H.E. Wedeck) (New York, 1959) presents a good summary and was used along with standard grammars in the preparation of this material.

Ancilla to Reading Latin Prose

On Using a Latin Dictionary

There are many types of Latin dictionaries available. As your reading, composition, and translation skills become more sophisticated, you will no doubt discover that having more than one dictionary is beneficial to your Latin studies. There are, of course, the always handy and easily portable paperback and pocket dictionaries with both Latin-English and English-Latin entries. There are intermediate dictionaries that provide in abbreviated format useful citations to particular authors and texts, variant forms, and linguistic root tables. Finally, there are the large unabridged dictionaries (Latin-English only!) that provide indispensable information on word history, linguistic roots, word variants, and citations to authors and texts. These unabridged dictionaries, used in conjunction with a good Latin grammar, are extremely valuable in helping you to perfect translation of and composition in Latin. We strongly recommend that you examine the types of Latin dictionaries (and grammars) available so that you are aware of the resources available to assist you in your translation and composition.

Pronunciation

If classical Latin is no longer spoken as a "native" language, how do we know how it should be pronounced? Studies of classical Latin pronunciation have been made since the Renaissance. In general, we follow the conclusions formulated by Erasmus, the leading classical scholar of that age (who thought, by the way, that his Latin was purer than Cicero's!). Although controversies remain, for which see Stephen Daitz, *The Pronunciation and Reading of Classical Latin* (1984), what follows is a generally accepted outline.

1. Vowels.

vowel	quantity	English equivalent	vowel	quantity	English equivalent
a	long	a in father	a	short	a in around
e	long	e in they	e	short	e in set
i	long	i in pique	i	short	i in sin
o	long	o in note	o	short	o in not
u	long	u in rude	u	short	u in dull

2. Diphthongs.

diphthong	English equivalent
ae	= ai in aisle
au	= ou in hour
ei	= ei in rein
eu	= eu in neuter
oe	= oi in boil, but when **o** is followed by long **e**, they are pronounced as two separate syllables, as in "po-e-ta"
ui	= wee

3. Consonants. Most Latin consonants are pronounced as in English. The few exceptions are:

c	= "k" in can	NOT = "s" in century
g	= "guh" in gun	NOT = "gheh" in gem
s	= "sis" in hiss	NOT = "z" in is
t	= "t" in native	NOT = "sh" in motion
v	= "w" in went	NOT = "v" in very
i-consonant	= "y" in yeti	NOT = "j" in jump

4. Peculiar consonants

"W" does not exist in Latin. However,

w-sound   appears with "u" when preceded by "q" so, **qui** = "kw-ee"

"I" exists in Latin in two forms, one as a consonant, the other as a vowel. "I" acts as a consonant when beginning a word and followed by a vowel (e.g., **iam** = "yam"), or within a word when the "i" falls between two other vowels (e.g., **huius** = huyus). Some dictionaries print entries under both the vowel and the consonant, listing the consonantal "i" words under "j" and the vowel "i" words under "i.". The "j" became a regular letter of the "Latin" alphabet only in the middle ages.

i-consonant	= "j"	= "y" in yeti
i-vowel	= "i"	= "ee" as in creep (long) or "eh" as in pit (short)

"U" in Latin has two sounds, one as a consonant, the other as a vowel. "U" acts as a consonant when beginning a word and followed by a vowel (e.g., uidi = vidi). Dictionaries print entries under both the vowel and the consonant, listing the consonantal "u" words under "v", the vowel words under "u." The "v" became a regular letter of the "Latin" alphabet only in the middle ages.

"H" is sounded in reading Latin. So, "**historia**," not "istoria." However, Latin speakers were unclear about this, as both forms of, e.g., "sand" appear: **harena** and **arena**. As the "h" does not affect such things as elision, it is probable that in common speech it was silent.

"R" is gently rolled.

Accent

In single syllable words, there is obviously no problem of accent. In two-syllable words, the accent is always on the first syllable. In other multi-syllabic words, the accent always falls on either the syllable second from the last (penult) or the syllable third from the last (antepenult)—NEVER ON THE FINAL SYLLABLE. Which syllable, the penult or the antepenult, is accented is determined by the quantity (long or short) of the penultimate syllable. The accent falls on the penult if it is long; if it is short, the accent falls on the antepenult. No Latin word has multiple accents.

1. Dipthongs. Diphthongs are two vowels standing together. Diphthongs have two characteristics important to accentuation.
    a. all dipthongs are long,
    b. dipthongs count as a single syllable.

    Although not actually a dipthong, the collocation of i+vowel/dipthong (e.g., **-ia**, **-ius**, **-iae**) at the end of a word, the two syllables formed (e.g., his-tor-**i-a**, dul-ci-**us**) count as one for purposes of accentuation. So, in **historia**, the accent is **histor'-ia**, NOT **histori'-a**.

2. Quantity of syllables.

    Syllables are LONG if
    a. the syllable has a diphthong (two vowels together),
    b. a short vowel is followed by two or more consonants, or
    c. a vowel long "by nature."

Natural long vowels are marked with a **macron** in beginning Latin texts; however, macrons are not part of the way the ancients wrote Latin (unlike the accents in Greek, which are ancient in origin). Thus, there are no macrons in this text. Long vowels are marked in Latin-English dictionaries, should you need to know a quantity.

Syllables are SHORT which are not long, i.e., short syllables are those whose vowel is not a dipthong, is not followed by two consonants together, and is not long by nature.

Examples:

Tum' Brū'tus (dĭ'cit): Orā tiō'nēs qui'dem Cae'saris mĭ'hĭ vehemen'ter probāban'tur.

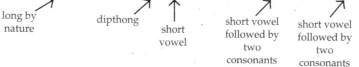

long by nature   dipthong   short vowel   short vowel followed by two consonants   short vowel followed by two consonants

Notice that elision (the running together of a vowel at the end of one word with a vowel at the beginning of the next word) affects pronounciation by turning the elided words into a single pronoucing unit:

Complūr'is au'tem lē'gi atque e'tiam commentār'iōs, quōs' ĭ'dem scrip'sit....

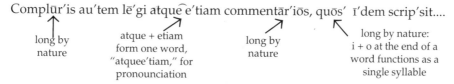

long by nature   atque + etiam form one word, "atquee'tiam," for pronounciation   long by nature   long by nature: i + o at the end of a word functions as a single syllable

Ni'hil est' e'nim in' histor'ia pūr'aet illus'tri brevitā'te dul'cius.

i+a at the ends of word function as single syllable   pura + et form one word, "pur'aet" for pronunciation   short vowel followed by three consonants   long by nature   i+u at the end of word function as single syllable

Strategies for Writing Latin

Composition in any language is an art that requires a great deal of practice. Writing well in any language must be accompanied by reading well, so the more Latin you read, and the greater the variety of Latin you read, the better your Latin compositions will become. It is very important to remember that your goal is to translate into Latin not words alone, but ideas. Frequently, you will need to interpret the English statement in order to understand its "true" meaning before ever attempting the Latin version. A brief example should be sufficient to illustrate this point: the English expression "Pompey is not winning the war" can best be rendered in Latin as "Pompeius victoriam non reportat" or even "Pompeius non vincit." A word-for-word translation of English into Latin would not carry any real meaning in the "Roman world."

In addition, it is equally important to remember that Latin, as a once living and evolving language, employs its own idioms and reveals a variety of expression depending on the style of a particular author, the literary genre, or the time period in which the literature was written. When we study "Latin composition," we are frequently trying to duplicate the rather artificial expressions learned in our beginning grammar lessons and to imitate the Latin of only one author or period. Because we have read only a few authors by this point in our study of Latin, we all too often assume that "real Latin" is the Latin of Cicero or Caesar and, as a result, overlook the great variety of expression inherent in a vibrant and evolving language.

As you progress through the workbook exercises, you will notice that we have included a number of sentences to be translated into Latin. Most of these sentences are designed to focus your attention on particular aspects of Latin syntax and do not require much exploration into the variety of Latin prose expression; their purpose is primarily to reinforce—through active expression of the Latin language—the points of grammar and syntax you have learned in your basic Latin courses. Yet, even these simple sentences can present opportunities for discussing and analyzing the differences between English and Latin and for expressing a single idea in a variety of ways. As an example, let us look at the following sentence:

When the troops had assembled, Caesar began to speak.

The first thing we must do is decide what the English sentence means: "when" could imply simply "at the time when," but it may imply "now that," "as soon as," or possibly "after." One could use an adverbial conjunction to introduce the subordinate clause:

Cum (quando? postquam?) copiae (milites? legiones? exercitus?) convenerant, Caesar dicere (loqui?) coepit (incepit?).

You will also notice that the variety of Latin vocabulary (some of the options are shown in parentheses) requires you to make additional decisions!

If we are interpreting the subordinate cum-clause as "circumstantial," then Latin asks that we employ the subjunctive rather than the indicative:

Cum copiae convenissent.....

But, of course, employing a subordinate clause is not the only option: we could make use of the ablative absolute:

Copiis conventis Caesar dicere coepit.

It is likely that, given its position at the beginning of the clause, the phrase "copiis conventis" will be read as an ablative; its form, however, could be another case: dative. Suppose, then, we change the word order:

Caesar copiis conventis dicere coepit.

It is now probable that we would translate this sentence as "Caesar began to speak to the assembled soldiers."

With these few examples – and more are possible – you can see that choice of vocabulary, word order, and syntax can make a great difference in the translation of ideas from one language to another. Observe what happens when we substitute "adloqui" for "dicere" in the last version:

Caesar copias conventas adloqui coepit.

"Adloqui" means "address" or "speak to," and it employs an accusative, rather than a dative, object. So, as you can see, unless we happen to be translating a basic idea like "vir canem mordet," Latin can offer us a variety of translation possibilities!

As you progress through the various sentences designed for composition practice, we urge you to discuss not only the points of grammar and syntax being reviewed in a particular unit, but the possibilities for interpretation and expression and how they may vary according to the choices you make in your Latin. Always try to ask yourself "how would a Roman say this?"

A word to the instructor: as you know, composition skills are greatly improved by asking students to translate extended prose passages into Latin. Rather than setting specific paragraphs for Latin composition, we encourage instructors to begin supplementing these simple exercises with English to Latin translations culled from magazines, newspapers, novels, current biographies, famous speeches, and the like. Extended narrative passages and historical speeches from Winston Churchill, Martin Luther King, Jr., John F. Kennedy, and others are especially useful in focusing attention on the translation of "ideas" rather than "words," and in gaining greater facility with the variety of Latin expression.

Strategies for Reading Latin

Latin is an inflected language. That is, the meaning of words is often determined by the endings of nouns, pronouns, adjectives, and verbs. Whereas English relies heavily on word order to give a sentence meaning, in Latin the self-contained nature of inflected words allows their position to be much less important to the meaning of a sentence. The trick is to learn to retain the various possiblities of a Latin word while forging ahead through a sentence or clause; as other words of the sentence come into play, the possibilities of earlier words can then be sorted out until the whole sentence makes sense. Following are some rules of thumb to help in this sorting out process.

The same rules of position and emphasis apply to clauses (i.e., mini-sentences embedded within a main sentence) as to sentences.

The most emphatic positions in Latin are at the beginning of a sentence or clause, and at its end. The subject or direct object often occupies the first, or nearly the first, position; the verb often the last.

Latin likes to connect a sentence to the previous one. Thus, even before the subject or direct object, a word or clause occurs which brings the reader from the previous sentence to the current one. This is why the following will often be first in a sentence:

- relative pronoun and its clause;
- ablative absolute;
- adverbial expressions of time or place;
- conjunction.

In the midst of the sentence, words closely connected with each other stand together.

- most words which modify (adjectives, genitives, etc.) usually follow their word;
- adjectives of number and quantity, as well as demonstrative pronouns, come before their word;
- adverbs and other words dependent on the verb come before their word;
- nouns in cases other than the nominative precede a word closely related (e.g., an adjective or a verb);
- prepositions come before their objects;
- adjectives precede nouns when there are other complementary words or phrases between them.

Like adjectives and adverbs, adjectival and adverbial clauses will stand close to their noun or verb.

Missing persons. Latin often assumes the reader can "supply" unexpressed words as s/he reads along. The most common "missing persons" are as follows:

- personal pronouns in general—because these are often contained in the verb ending;
- subject of impersonal verbs—because it is in the verb ending;
- subject of intransitive verbs used impersonally—because it is in the verb ending;
- forms of **sum** in compound verbs;
- the infinitive **esse**;
- nouns of substantive adjectives—the adjective alone assumes an understood noun, or a vague, neuter idea of "thing;"
- verbs that can be easily supposed from context—especially those expressing speaking, thinking, etc. and which, to add to the complexity, often introduce indirect discourse.

Orthographical traps. Latin spelling evolved into that used by authors such as Cicero and Caesar. However, there was no formal attempt to control or dictate "correct" orthography. As a result, there are a variety of ways to spell certain words and endings. For example:

- -es and -is: the older accusative plural ending is **-is**; often this is used instead of the often more "correct" **-es** (**complures** or **compluris**);
- -i- and -u-: so, maximus or **maxumus**;
- c- and q-: so **cum** or **quum**

Some specific hints.

- upon seeing a noun or adjective, keep an open mind about what the ending might be; avoid committing yourself until you have seen enough context to make a guess appropriate;
- upon seeing an accusative, remember that at least two possibilities need to be kept in mind—direct object AND indirect discourse, which generates the accusative and infinitive construction;
- upon seeing an infinitive, remember that it most likely will be complementary (look for a verb like **volo** or **possum**), or will be in the accusative and infinitive construction;
- nouns and verbs are often used multiple times, but expressed only once—sometimes even in a preceding sentence; remember to "carry down" such nouns and verbs in order to make later subjects, objects, and verbs make sense;
- indirect discourse is often launched into without any "sign" word such as **ut** or **quod**; watch for tell-tale accusative/infinitives to give it away.

Emphasis. Emphasis is achieved by messing with these general rules of position. The basic idea is that by putting a word outside its expected place, it is emphasized. Thus if a sentence has the verb first or the subject last, either is emphasized; if an adjective or adverb is removed far from its word, especially if removed to the beginning of the sentence, the adjective or adverb is emphasized.

Sentence structure. English is most usually written in short sentences which are coordinated into a paragraph. Latin can and does use such relatively brief, co-ordinated sentences. However, often Latin makes extensive use of subordination in order to bring the many aspects of a complex thought or description under the umbrella of a single sentence. Such complex sentences, made up of subordinate clauses woven around a core sentence, are called "periodic."

Passages to Practice Accentuation and Reading

1. CICERO: BRUTUS

In a reconstructed conversation about oratory and orators at Rome, Cicero has Brutus (later an assassin) speak about Caesar's accomplishment in writing his *commentarii*. Date: early 46 BC.

75 (262). Tum Brutus: Orationes quidem eius [sic., Caesaris] mihi vehementer probabantur. Compluris autem legi atque etiam commentarios, quos idem scripsit rerum suarum. Valde quidem, inquam, probandos; nudi enim sunt, recti et venusti, omni ornatu orationis tamquam veste detracta. Sed dum voluit alios habere parata, unde sumerent qui vellent scribere historiam, ineptis gratum fortasse fecit, qui illa volent calamistris inurere, sanos quidem homines a scribendo deterruit; nihil est enim in historia pura et illustri brevitate dulcius.

2. CICERO: LETTERS TO HIS FRIENDS *(Epistulae ad familiares)*

Gaius Matius writes to Cicero of his loyal friendship for his murdered friend, Caesar. Composed at Rome, the end of August, 43 BC

11.28.[1] Magnam voluptatem ex tuis litteris cepi, quod, quam speraram atque optaram, habere te de me opinionem, cognovi. De qua etsi non dubitabam, tamen, quia maximi aestimabam, ut incorrupta maneret, laborabam. Conscius autem mihi eram, nihil a me commissum esse, quod boni cuiusquam offenderet animum. ... [2] Nota enim mihi sunt, quae in me post Caesaris mortem contulerint. Vitio mihi dant, quod mortem hominis necessariii graviter fero, atque eum, quem dilexi, periisse indignor. Aiunt enim patriam amicitae praeponendam esse, proinde ac si iam vicerint, obitum eius reipublicae fuisse utilem.

3. MATIUS' LETTER CONTINUES....

Neque enim Caesarem in dissensione civili sum secutus; sed amicum, quamquam re offendebar, tamen non deserui: neque bellum umquam civile, aut etiam causam dissensionis probavi, quam etiam nascentem exstingui summe studui. ... Civibus victis ut parceretur, aeque ac pro mea salute laboravi. [3] Possum igitur, qui omnes voluerim incolumes, eum, a quo id impetratum est, periisse non indignari, cum praesertim iidem homines illi et invidiae et exitio fuerint?... [8][2] Sed mihi persuadeo ut tum meae vitae modestia magnum valitura sit in posterum contra falsos rumores, cum etiam ii, qui me non amant propter meam in Caesarem constantiam, non malint mei, quam sui similes amicos habere. ...

Letter *(epistula)* rolled and sealed, with address written on the outside. From a wall painting at Pompeii. The inscriptions reads:
MA(rco) LUCRETIO FLAM(ini) MARTIS DECURIONI POMPEI
"To Marcus Lucretius, flamen [priest] of Mars, decurion [town counsellor] of Pompeii"

---

[2] The original, using the somewhat confusing negative construction of **vereor**, is as follows: "Sed non vereor, ne aut meae vitae modestia parum valitura sit in posterum contra falsos rumores, aut ne etiam ii, qui me non amant propter meam in Caesarem constantiam, non malint mei, quam sui similes amicos habere."

VELLEIUS PATERCULUS:
Roman History (*Historia Romana*)[1]
January, 49 BC

Although Velleius Paterculus brings with him items of debatable perspective (adulation of Tiberius and Sejanus) and questionable style (labyrinthine sentences filled with less than artistic parentheses, ellipses and clauses), his work is still a very readable abridgement of some one thousand years of Roman history. He has an undeniable gift for breathing life into historical events by his focus on the people who made history; one editor in the early 20th century said he was more like a journalist than an historian. In the following passsage, which we have chosen because it gives us the point when "bellum civile exarsit,", you will encounter many of those stylistic difficulties alluded to above. For that reason, we urge you to read carefully the "Hints for Translation" and the grammar footnotes, as you tackle Velleius' prose.

2.49 [1] Lentulo et Marcello consulibus,[2] post urbem conditam annis septingentis et tribus,[3] et annos octo et septuaginta antequam tu, Marce Vinici, consulatum inires,[4] bellum civile exarsit. Alterius ducis causa melior videbatur, alterius erat firmior.[5]   *of the other*

Hints for Translation:

Asyndeton: literally, "without conjunction." Latin is fond of leaving out conjunctions where we might

Vocabulary

urbs, urbis, urbium (f.): city
condo, condere, condidi, conditus (3): build, found (a city)
tres, tres, tria: three
annus, -i (m.): year
octo (indeclinable): eight
antequam (or ante quam): before; note—ante and quam are often separated by another word
tu: you (m.)
consulatus, -us: consulship, the highest elective office at Rome
ineo, iniri, initus: begin
bellum, -i (n.): war
civilis, -e: civil
exardesco, exardescere, exarsi, exarsum (3): flame up, flare up
alter, -a, -um: the other of two; genitive = alterius; dative = alteri
alter...alter = the one ... the other
dux, ducis (m.): leader, general
causa, -ae (f.): cause (as in a political cause, faction, party); undertaking
melior, -ius: better
videor, videri, visum (2): seem, appear
firmus, -a, -um: strong; firm

Grammar and Syntax

1. Parts of Speech. The parts of speech encountered with regularity in Latin are nouns, adjectives, pronouns, verbs, adverbs, prepositions, and conjunctions. Review the basics of these categories by consulting the accompanying chart.

2. Vocative. The vocative is the case of direct address. It differs in form from the nominative only in the singular -**us** nouns of the second declension, where it is formed with -**e (Marce)**, and -**ius** nouns which become -**i (Vinici)** (B 17, 19.1, 25.1; AG 35, 38, 49, 110).

3. Exercise for this section.

expect them; this moves the narrative along more quickly and adds emphasis by juxtaposing items without a conjunction getting in the way. "Alterius ducis causa melior videbatur, [*sed*] alterius erat firmior. Hic omnia speciosa, [*sed*] illic valentia: Pompeium senatus auctoritas, [*sed*] Caesarem militum armavit fiducia. ... Nihil relictum a Caesare... [*et*] nihil receptum a Pompeianis, cum alter consul iusto esset ferocior, [*et*] Lentulus vero salva re publica salvus esse non posset. ... Vir antiquus et gravis Pompei partes laudaret magis, [*sed*] prudens sequeretur Caesaris, et illa gloriosiora, [*sed*] haec terribiliora duceret."

Forms of **sum** dropped: Very often **sum** in all its forms (conjugated, infinitive) is left to be understood by the reader. "Hic omnia speciosa [*erant*], illic valentia [*erant*] ... Nihil relictum a Caesare [*erat*], quod servandae pacis causa temptari posset, nihil receptum [*erat*] a Pompeianis, ... Marcus autem Cato moriendum [*esse*] antequam condicionum civis accipiendam [*esse*] rei publicae contenderet ...

Words repeated in sense, but not repeated in text: A word or words used once and then again in close proximity is often not repeated. To make this more of a challenge, the "repeated" word(s) often appear [continued on next page]

---

[1] Velleius Paterculus (ca. 19 BC - ca. AD 30) was not an "eyewitness" to events of the Civil War period, but wrote a historical sketch of Roman history which included treatment of that time. His paternal grandfather served loyally as a partisan of Pompey and, later, under Marcus Brutus (the assassin of Caesar); he himself served Rome under Augustus and Tiberius. Velleius had a particular interest in the Civil War, and had a monograph treating this period to his own day under preparation at his death.

[2] **Lentulo et Marcello:** Romans dated in two ways; this is one: the use of the names of the consuls from a given year. Lists were kept in order to be able to tell which names meant which year. It must have, in fact, been fairly awkward on a daily basis for dates some distance in the past. The date here = 49 BC.

[3] **annis septingentis et tribus:** This is the other way to designate a year: by counting years inclusively from the foundation of the city. In the Roman tradition, there are various dates for that founding, but Velleius uses Cato the Elder's date, 751 BC, not the more usual, Varronian, date of 753 BC. So 752 [in order to get the correct number, considering the Romans reckoned inclusively, one must begin with one year more than the actual foundation year] - 703 = 49 BC.

[4] M. Vinicius, consul in AD 30; 49 + 29 = 78; thus Velleius' number stops just 'antequam'—the year AD 29. **Inires** is subjunctive because **antequam** expresses anticipation (B 292; AG 551b).

[5] This assessment is directly reminiscent of Cicero's evaluation of the situation, which we will read shortly.

[handwritten top margin: perfect act. bestowed/have]

[handwritten left margin: Protecting the cause of peace]

[2] Hic omnia speciosa,[6] illic valentia: Pompeium[7] senatus auctoritas,[8] Caesarem militum armavit fiducia. Consules senatusque causae, non Pompeio, summam imperii[9] detulerunt.

[3] Nihil relictum a Caesare, quod servandae pacis causa temptari posset, nihil receptum[10] a Pompeianis, cum alter consul iusto esset ferocior, Lentulus vero salva re publica salvus esse non posset; Marcus autem Cato moriendum antequam ullam condicionem[11] civis accipiendam rei publicae contenderet.[12] Vir antiquus et gravis[13] Pompei partes[14] laudaret magis, prudens sequeretur[15] Caesaris, et illa gloriosiora, haec terribiliora duceret.

Vocabulary

hic (adv.): here, "on this side"
illic (adv.): there, "on that side"
fiducia, -ae (f.): good faith; + gen. = with reliance upon
defero, deferre, detuli, delatum (3): grant, bestow
relinquo, relinquere, reliqui, relictus (3): leave aside or behind
pax, pacis (f.): peace
causa, -ae (f.): constructed with the genitive, as here, it means "for the sake of." It is a very common usage in Caesar.
tempto, temptare, temptavi, temptatus (1): try, attempt
iustus, -a, -um: just, right
ferox, ferocis: fierce, savage, hostile
vero (adv.); however; indeed, in truth
salvus, -a, -um: safe, unharmed
autem (conj.): but, however
morior, mori, mortuus (3): die
pars, partis (f.): political faction, party
ullus, -a, -um: any
magis (adv.): more; rather
prudens, prudentis: prudent, cautious
duco, ducere, duxi, ductus (3): consider (along with many other meanings!)

[*Hints for Translation continued*] upon the second use. "Consules senatusque causae [*summam imperii detulerunt*], non Pompeio <u>summam imperii detulerunt</u>.... Vir antiquus et gravis Pompei <u>partes</u> laudaret magis, prudens sequeretur [*partes*] Caesaris...."

Neuter forms of nouns, pronouns, and adjectives often carry the understood meaning "thing" or "things." ....et illa gloriosiora, haec terribiliora duceret: "considered the former (things) the more glorious (things), the latter (things) the more frightening (things)."

Extended sentences, like the first one in section 3, are not unusual in Latin prose. Observe carefully the organization of the sentence, the main clauses and the subordinate clauses, the prepositional phrases, the nouns and their modifiers; mentally diagram your sentence and break it down into its basic components. Remember: these longer sentences are merely an accumulation of the basic types of clauses and phrases with which you are already familiar.

First, find the core sentence: **Nihil relictum [est] a Caesare...receptum [est] a Pompeianis...**

Then work out the subordinate clauses:

(1) Take note of the first subordinate clause, **quod servandae...posset**; what kind of clause, not in indirect statement, employs both a relative pronoun and a subjunctive?

(2) Now observe the **cum** clause, which has several subjects and verbs:

cum alter consul iusto esset ferocior
[cum] Lentulus vero salva re publica salvus esse non posset
[cum] Marcus autem Cato...contenderet (on contenderet, see also note 12)

You can now put together the main and subordinate clauses into a complete sentence.

---

[6] **speciosa**: splendid.

[7] **Pompeium**: The major player opposed to Caesar, Cn. Pompeius Magnus had risen swiftly and spectacularly to power in the Roman state since his youthful successes during Sulla's rule in the late 80's BC. He is now the greatest warlord, most influential political figure and wealthiest man in Rome. Until 54 BC, he and Caesar had cooperated; since then a gradual cooling of the relationship coupled with a rapprochement of Pompey to the senatorial faction opposed to Caesar has set the two strong-willed men on a collision course.

[8] **senatus auctoritas**: the majority of the senate supported Pompey.

[9] **summam imperii**: the "high command"; of course, a "cause" cannot be given "high command" like a person (Pompey) can; the point is that Pompey was appointed to the "high command" not because the senators favored *him* (there were many reasons to find him objectionable), but because they favored the cause he was willing to defend.

[10] **receptum**: accepted; that is, none of Caesar's overtures was accepted.

[11] **condicionem**: demand.

[12] **Marcus autem...**: Cato is the subject, **contenderet** is the verb introducing indirect discourse with **moriendum**, followed by the **antequam** clause. The **civis** is Caesar.

[13] **antiquus et gravis**: the Roman of old-time severity and sternness. **Gravitas** was perhaps the most prized trait for an **antiquus** Roman.

[14] **partes**: the political faction.

[15] **partes** is understood as the object of **sequeretur**; **sequeretur** as well as **laudaret** and **duceret** are potential subjunctives.

PARTS OF SPEECH

Seven English parts of speech are commonly used to describe Latin usage.[1]

Part of Speech	Definition	Example
Noun	name of a person, place, or thing	LENTULO et MARCELLO CONSULIBUS, post URBEM conditam ANNIS septingentis et tribus, et ANNOS octo et septuaginta antequam tu, M(ARCE) VINICI, CONSULATUM inires, BELLUM civile exarsit. Alterius DUCIS CAUSA melior videbatur, alterius erat firmior. [2] Hic OMNIA speciosa, illic valentia; POMPEIUM SENATUS AUCTORITAS, CAESAREM MILITUM armavit FIDUCIA. CONSULES SENATUSque CAUSAE, non POMPEIO, SUMMAM IMPERII detulerunt.
Adjective	used with a noun to limit or modify its meaning	Lentulo et Marcello consulibus, post urbem CONDITAM annis SEPTINGENTIS et TRIBUS, et annos OCTO et SEPTUAGINTA antequam tu, M(arce) Vinici, consulatum inires, bellum CIVILE exarsit. ALTERIUS ducis causa MELIOR videbatur, ALTERIUS erat FIRMIOR. [2] Hic omnia SPECIOSA, illic VALENTIA; Pompeium senatus auctoritas, Caesarem militum armavit fiducia. Consules senatusque causae, non Pompeio, summam imperii detulerunt.
Pronoun	takes the place of a noun	Lentulo et Marcello consulibus, post urbem conditam annis septingentis et tribus, et annos octo et septuaginta antequam TU, M(arce) Vinici, consulatum inires, bellum civile exarsit. Alterius ducis causa melior videbatur, alterius erat firmior. [2] Hic omnia speciosa, illic valentia; Pompeium senatus auctoritas, Caesarem militum armavit fiducia. Consules senatusque causae, non Pompeio, summam imperii detulerunt.
Verb	shows action or state of being	Lentulo et Marcello consulibus, post urbem conditam annis septingentis et tribus, et annos octo et septuaginta antequam tu, M(arce) Vinici, consulatum INIRES, bellum civile EXARSIT. Alterius ducis causa melior VIDEBATUR, alterius ERAT firmior. [2] Hic omnia speciosa, illic valentia; Pompeium senatus auctoritas, Caesarem militum ARMAVIT fiducia. Consules senatusque causae, non Pompeio, summam imperii DETULERUNT.
Adverb	limits the meaning of a verb, adjective, or other adverb	Lentulo et Marcello consulibus, post urbem conditam annis septingentis et tribus, et annos octo et septuaginta antequam tu, M(arce) Vinici, consulatum inires, bellum civile exarsit. Alterius ducis causa melior videbatur, alterius erat firmior. [2] HIC omnia speciosa, ILLIC valentia; Pompeium senatus auctoritas, Caesarem militum armavit fiducia. Consules senatusque causae, NON Pompeio, summam imperii detulerunt.
Conjunction	connects clauses, phrases, or words	Lentulo ET Marcello consulibus, post urbem conditam annis septingentis ET tribus, ET annos octo ET septuaginta ANTEQUAM tu, M(arce) Vinici, consulatum inires, bellum civile exarsit. Alterius ducis causa melior videbatur, alterius erat firmior. [2] Hic omnia speciosa, illic valentia; Pompeium senatus auctoritas, Caesarem militum armavit fiducia. Consules senatusQUE causae, non Pompeio, summam imperii detulerunt.
Preposition	shows the relation of a noun or pronoun to another word	Lentulo et Marcello consulibus, POST urbem conditam annis septingentis et tribus, et annos octo et septuaginta antequam tu, M(arce) Vinici, consulatum inires, bellum civile exarsit. Alterius ducis causa melior videbatur, alterius erat firmior. [2] Hic omnia speciosa, illic valentia; Pompeium senatus auctoritas, Caesarem militum armavit fiducia. Consules senatusque causae, non Pompeio, summam imperii detulerunt.

[1]The eighth, **interjection**, is found only rarely.

AULUS HIRTIUS: **The War in Gaul**
(De bello Gallico)
50 BC (late)

8.50 [1] Ipse[1], hibernis[2] peractis, contra consuetudinem in Italiam quam maximis itineribus[3] est profectus, ut municipia et colonias[4] appellaret quibus Marci Antoni[5], quaestoris[6] sui, commendaverat sacerdoti petitionem.[7] [2] Contendebat enim gratia,[8] cum libenter pro homine sibi coniunctissimo, quem paulo ante praemiserat ad petitionem, tum acriter contra factionem et potentiam paucorum,[9] qui Marci Antoni repulsa[10] Caesaris decedentis[11] gratiam convellere[12] cupiebant.

Hint for translation:

enim and **nam** (See Section 6) are commonly used to offer an explanation for what went just before. Translate, "for..."

An Historical Note...

Caesar, Pompey, and Crassus joined their political and financial resources in 60 BC to form the alliance known to us (but not to the Romans) as the "first triumvirate." One aspect of that arrangement was to award a significant military command to Caesar. Gaul eventually fell to him; at the point where we take up the story, he has been fighting there for eight years. His own *commentarii* cover the events through 52 BC; his lieutenant Aulus Hirtius completed the account down to the end of 50 BC. It is Hirtius who is writing now, consciously in the style of Caesar.

Vocabulary

ipse, ipsa, ipsum: self; very

perago, peragere, peregi, peractum (3): complete

contra: with acc.: against

consuetudo, consuetudinis (f.): custom, habit

quam: as possible (w/superl.); than (w/ compar.), how (w/ adj. or adv. in question or exclamation), correlative after tam = as...as possible (w/ superl.)

iter, itineris (n.): march; (a day's) journey; route

proficiscor, proficisci, profectum (dep.) (3): start, set out

appello, appellare, appellavi, appellatum (1): appeal to; call, name, address

contendo, contendere, contendi, contentum (3): exert oneself; hasten, march; contend

enim (conj.): for

cum...tum (conj.): with tum below = both...and

pro: with abl.: on behalf of

homo, hominis (m.): man, human being, person

coniungo, coniungere, coniunxi, coniunctum (3): unite

paulo (adv.): a little; (by) a little

ante (adv.): previously (also prep. w/ acc.)

praemitto, praemittere, praemisi, praemissum (3): send ahead

ad: with acc.: for the purpose of; also means to, toward, for, near

tum (conj.): with cum above = both...and

acer, acre: sharp, fierce; adv: acriter: forcefully

pauci, -ae, -a: few

cupio, cupere, cupivi, cupitum (3): desire

Grammar and Syntax
1. Endings of the first declension nouns (B 20-22; AG 40-44).
2. Ablative absolute (**hibernis peractis**).
3. Exercise for this section.

---

[1] Caesar.

[2] **hiberna**: time spent in winter quarters; troops were stationed in permanent camps or billeted on towns during the non-campaigning, winter months.

[3] **magna itinera**: "forced marches," usually covering 20-25 miles in a single day.

[4] **municipia et colonias**: two types of towns, the one a native town with the Roman citizenship , the other a colony founded by the Romans—although there were "honorary" **colonia** as well which had the juridical status, but not the actual origins, of a true colony.

[5] The soon-to-be famous Mark Antony, now just at the beginning of his political career as an ally of Caesar. Note that the genitive of **Antonius** is **-i**, not **-ii**.

[6] **quaestoris**: the quaestor is the financial officer of a legion or province.

[7] **petitio** (peto = seek): candidacy for office. Antony is a candidate for the priesthood (**sacerdotium**) of augur, and Caesar wishes to campaign for him—one of the obligations friends have to each other. Antony was, in the event, elected.

[8] **gratia**: a politically charged term. It means something like "favor," "influence;" here Caesar is concerned with both his private obligations of "favor"—helping his friend Antony—and his public condition—preventing his enemies from tearing down his influence.

[9] **paucorum**: Caesar brands his enemies as a small band (**pauci**) of nasty men, and constantly criticizes them as a tiny minority who act only in their own narrow self-interest.

[10] **repulsa**: from **repello**; here a noun, **repulsa** means defeat in an election.

[11] **decedentis**: decedo; "of Caesar suffering a set-back."

[12] **convellere**: from **convello** (shatter, break).

4

Ablative Absolute

The ablative absolute may consist of:

1. A noun or pronoun in the ablative case with the participle agreeing.

Translation: literally

Filia laudata, magistrum remunerati sunt.

The daughter having been praised, they rewarded the teacher.

Equo citante, cursum non vinxit.

With the horse galloping, he did not win the race.

2. A noun or pronoun in the ablative case with an adjective agreeing.

Translation: the verb "being" is understood

Matre volente, filia nubere potuit.

The mother being willing, her daughter could marry.

3. A noun or pronoun in the ablative case with another noun in apposition.

Translation: the verb "being" is understood

Patre milite, mater domum servavit.

The father being a soldier, the mother took care of the house.

A note on translation:

First step: a literal translation will often capture the basic meaning of the Latin.

Second step: the idea can then be expanded and translated more elegantly by using a subordinate clause or its equivalent. Note that you must decide what you think the ablative absolute means (causal, temporal, circumstantial, etc.); its grammar does not decide this for you!

Filia laudata, magistrum remunerati sunt.

After the daughter was praised, they rewarded the teacher.

Equo citante, cursum non vinxit.

Although the horse was galloping, he lost the race.

Matre libente, filia nubere potuit.

When the mother was willing, her daughter could marry.

Patre milite, mater domum servavit.

Because the father was a soldier, the mother took care of the house.

A Roman Mother watches her daughter
prepare to be wed.
(From a wall painting of Herculaneum).

AULUS HIRTIUS: **The War in Gaul**
(*De bello Gallico*)
50 BC (late)

Before the first (handwritten)

8.50[3] Hunc etsi augurem[1] prius factum quam[2] Italiam attingeret in itinere audierat[3], tamen non minus iustam sibi causam municipia et colonias adeundi[4] existimavit, ut eis gratias ageret quod frequentiam[5] atque officium suum Antonio praestitissent [4] simulque se et honorem suum sequentis anni commendaret petitione, propterea quod[6] insolenter adversarii sui gloriarentur[7] Lucium Lentulum et Gaium Marcellum[8] consules[9] creatos qui omnem honorem et dignitatem[10] Caesaris spoliarent, ereptum Servi Galbae[11] consulatum, cum is multo plus gratia suffragiisque[12] valuisset, quod sibi coniunctus et familiaritate et consuetudine legationis esset.[13]

augur romanus

Vocabulary

etsi (conj.): although
priusquam (conj.): before
facio, facere, feci, factum (3): do; make
attingo, attingere, attigi, attactus (3): reach, arrive in (+ acc.)
audio, audire, audivi, auditum (4): hear
tamen (adv.): nevertheless; yet, however
non (adv.): not
se (pron.—reflexive): self
causa, -ae (f.): reason for, cause (+ gen.)
existimo, existimare, existimavi, existimatum (1): think, believe
gratias ago: give thanks (takes dat.)
ago, agere, egi, actum (3): do; drive; discuss; live; spend
officium, offici (n.): allegiance
praesto, praestare, praestiti, praestitum (1): display; perform; offer
simulque (adv.) at the same time
honor, honoris (m.) public esteem, reputation
eripio, eripere, eripui, ereptum: snatch, take away
multus, -a, -um: much, many
plus: more (often with gen.)
et...et: both...and
legatio, legationis (f.): mission, embassy
spolio, spoliare, spoliavi, spoliatum: destroy, plunder

Denarius showing
Roman augur to left

Grammar and Syntax

1. Endings of the second declension nouns (B 23-27; AG 45-52).
2. Endings of the first declension adjectives, which are the same as those of first declension nouns (B 63-66; AG 110-113).
3. Endings of the second declension adjectives, which are the same as those for second declension nouns (B 63-66; AG 110-113).
4. Indirect speech and sequence of tenses (see explanations next pages).
5. Exercises for this section.

---

[1]There were twelve **augurs**, the priests who presided over the taking of the auspices at official ceremonies, functions, etc. Auspices had to be favorable, thereby showing that the gods approved of the action at hand.

[2]**prius ... quam**: before. Note that the two parts of this word are separable; so, too, **ante ... quam**, before.

[3]**audierat**: a shortened (sycopated) form; the full form is **audiverat**. Verbs with perfect forms in **-avi**, **-evi**, and **-ivi** (and related forms) can omit the **-ve** or **-vi** before **r** or **a**. (B116; AG 181).

[4]**adeundi**: from **adeo** (the verb) *Approach/reach* (handwritten)

[5]**frequentiam**: Literally, "crowded attendance."

[6]**propterea quod**: especially because

[7]**gloriarentur**: **glorior**, boast. The following clauses are in indirect discourse, accusative infinitive construction.

[8]Sworn enemies of Caesar.

[9]**consules**: the two consuls, elected each year by the army in assembly (the **comitia centuriata**), were the chief civil and military officials of the Roman state.

[10]**honorem et dignitatem**: **honor** is personal repute; **dignitas** is status, position. Both are charged words; the protection of one's **honor et dignitas** by a noble Roman could sometimes be as important as life itself.

[11]A political ally of Caesar.

[12]**suffragiis**: public support, approbation.

[13]**consuetudine legationis**: service as his subordinate commander; this was in Gaul, 58-56 BC.

Indirect Statement

An indirect quotation (*oratio obliqua*) reports the words or thoughts of a person, as opposed to quoting them directly (*oratio recta*). Latin uses the infinitive with subject accusative for such indirect speech. An indirect statement can follow expressions (explicit or implicit!) of saying, thinking, believing, reporting, announcing, writing, denying, perceiving, and so on. For example, *intelligimus eum esse bonum*, can be tendered with an English equivalent of the accusative-infinitive, "we understand him to be good," or the more common, "we understand that he is good"—but remember that Latin does not employ a word for "that"; it must be supplied in your translation.

Relative Time. In indirect statement, the infinitive in Latin does not express absolute time, but time *relative* to the tense of the main verb. In general, the present infinitive describes events contemporaneous with the main verb; the perfect infinitive describes events which occurred prior to the main verb; the future active infinitive describes events which will occur subsequent to the action of the main verb. The passive periphrastic can also be employed in indirect statement, and it still conveys the sense of obligation or necessity.

Examples:

> Magister **sentit** discipulos cogitare.
> *The teacher perceives that his students are thinking.*
> Magister **sensit** discipulos cogitare.
> *The teacher perceived that his students were thinking.*
> Magister **sentiet** discipulos cogitare.
> *The teacher will perceive that his students are thinking.*

Note that we need to adjust our English translation only when the main verb is a past tense. The same is true for our other infinitives in indirect statement:

Perfect:

> Magister **sentit** discipulos abisse.
> *The teacher perceives that his students have departed.*
> Magister **sensit** discipulos abisse.
> *The teacher perceived that his students had departed.*
> Magister **sentiet** discipulos abisse.
> *The teacher will perceive that his students have departed.*

Future active:

> Magister **sentit** discipulos multa intellecturos esse.
> *The teacher perceives that his students will understand many things.*
> Magister **sensit** discipulos multa intellecturos esse.
> *The teacher perceived that his students would understand many things.*
> Magister **sentiet** discipulos multa intellecturos esse.
> *The teacher will perceive that his students will understand many things.*

Passive Periphrastic:

> Magister **dicit** verba magna cum cura discenda esse.
> *The teacher says that the words must be learned very carefully.*
> Magister **dixit** verba magna cum cura discenda esse.
> *The teacher said that the words had to be learned very carefully.*
> Magister **dicet** verba magna cum cura discenda esse.
> *The teacher will say that the words have to be learned very carefully.*

A final note of caution: the expression which introduces an indirect statement is often to be inferred from the context and not explicitly stated; any time you are confronted with an accusative-infinitive construction, consider the possibility that you are dealing with an indirect statement. Likewise, "esse" is frequently omitted when the context clearly implies indirect statement: so you frequently may see "*magister sensit discipulos multa intellecturos*" or "*magister dixit verba magna cum cura discenda,*" in place of the complete version with "esse." The context makes it clear that an indirect statement is intended.

Sequence of Tenses

The term "sequence of tenses" is used to describe the general relationship between the subjunctive in a dependent clause and the main clause; that is, the tense of the subjunctive in a dependent clause expresses a time not absolute, but relative to the tense of the main clause. Before examining this phenomenon further, let's review the primary and secondary tenses:

In the **indicative mood**, the primary tenses refer to the present and future time, while the secondary tenses reflect past time:

Primary: Present, Future, Future Perfect
Secondary: Imperfect, Pluperfect, Perfect (*)

*The Perfect indicative generally functions as a secondary tense, but on occasion, remember, it can be primary (cf. English "present perfect") when the present time is clearly in the speaker's mind.

The imperative mood is also considered to be primary.
When we look at the **subjunctive mood**, we see the following arrangement of tenses:

Primary: Present, Perfect
Secondary: Imperfect, Pluperfect

It is this general association of primary tenses in "primary sequence" and secondary tenses in "secondary sequence" which helps explain what we observe in the various dependent uses of the subjunctive:

1. **Purpose Clauses:**
    Puer domum currit ut patrem videat. [The boy is running home so that he may see his father.]
    Pater discessit ne filium videret. [The father departed so that he might not see his son.]

    Relative clauses of Purpose (a relative pronoun may replace *ut* when there is an expressed antecedent):
    Milites misit qui hoc faceret. [He sent soldiers to do this.]

    Purpose clause with comparative (when there is a comparative in the purpose clause, *quo* may replace *ut*):
    Cucurrit quo canem facilius vitaret. [He ran so that he might more easily avoid the dog.]

2. **Conditions** (see Section 12).

3. **Indirect Questions** (seee Section 27).

4. **Clauses of Result**: In result clauses, the perfect subjunctive (rather than the imperfect) is regularly used to express the result in past (secondary) sequence. This actually makes a great deal of sense, when we consider the true nature of the "perfect," which is to stress completion of an action, i.e., the result. For example:

   Puer tam celeriter cucurrit ut fessus fuerit. [The boy ran so quickly that he was [as a result] tired.]

5. **Clauses of Characteristic** (also see Section 18):
   Nemo est qui isti credat. [There is no one who would trust *him*.]

6. **"Cum" clauses** (see Section 9).

7. **Indirect Command**:
   Hortata est ne discederemus. [She urged us not to depart.]
   Ille mihi non suadebit ut amicos tradam. [He will not persuade me to betray my friends.]

8. **Clauses of Fear** (see Section 13).

9. **Substantive result clauses/Noun clauses** (see Sections 5, 20):
   Accidit ut Caesar consul fieret. [It happened that Caesar became consul.]
   Evenit ut nemo domi sit. [It turns out that no one is at home.]

Remember to observe the sequence of tenses when you are composing in Latin or when you are translating!

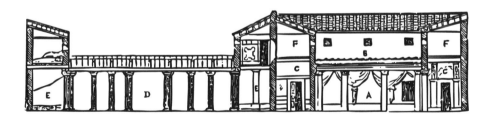

A House at Herculaneam

A = atrium; B = roof of atrium; C = corridors; D = peristylium; E = corridors; F = upper story

AULUS HIRTIUS: **The War in Gaul**
(De bello Gallico)
50 BC (late)

8.51 [1]Exceptus est Caesaris adventus ab omnibus municipiis et coloniis incredibili honore atque amore. [2] Tum primum enim veniebat ab[1] illo universae Galliae bello.[2] Nihil relinquebatur quod ad[3] ornatum portarum, itinerum, locorum omnium qua Caesar iturus erat excogitari poterat. [3] Cum liberis omnis multitudo obviam procedebat,[4] hostiae omnibus locis immolabantur,[5] tricliniis stratis[6] fora templaque occupabantur,[7] ut vel exspectatissimi triumphi[8] laetitia praecipi posset. Tanta erat magnificentia apud opulentiores, cupiditas apud humiliores.[9]

Hint for Translation:

When you see **tum**, remember that it can either be a simple adverb, "then", or a correlative, with a cum later in the sentence (= "both...and"); keep your mind open to both of these possibilities as you read beyond the **tum**.

sacrifice scene

Vocabulary

excipio, excipere, excepi, exceptum: receive
adventus, -us (m.): arrival
tum (adv): then
primum: for the first time
nihil: nothing (often with gen.)
relinquo, relinquere, reliqui, relictum (3): leave out
loca, -orum (n.): district, locality, place
qua (relative adv.): where
eo, ire, ii (or ivi), itum (irreg.): go
possum, posse, potui, — (irreg.): be able, can
liberi, -orum (m.): children
obviam (adv.): go out to meet
hostia, -ae (f.): sacrificial animals
-que: and (attached to the end of a word)
vel: assuredly, indeed; or (mostly with similar alternatives)
praecipio, praecipere, praecepi, praeceptum (3): anticipate
apud: with acc: among; at the house of, near
cupiditas, cupiditatis (f.): enthusiasm

lectisternium (from Eleusis)

Grammar and Syntax

1. Endings of third declension nouns (B 28-47; AG 53-87).
2. Endings of third declension adjectives (B 67-70; AG 114-119).
3. Exercises for this section.

---

[1] **ab** with ablative of time: after, since.

[2] **universae Galliae**: genitive of quality, see chart, Section 19. Caesar had been waging war in all Gaul from 58 BC, and most recently he had been active in putting down a revolt which encompassed tribes throughout Gaul.

[3] **ad**+ accusative = purpose in this case (cf. **ad petitionem** at 50.2 above).

[4] **obviam procedere**: go out to meet.

[5] The basic sacrifice in Roman religion was to burn something either animal or vegetable on an altar; the god(s) were thought to be able to "feed" on this burned material, for the fire made it rise to the heavens.

[6] Images of the gods were kept in the temples and shrines. For special occasions, the Romans brought them out, put them on dining couches (**triclinia**) draped with fancy coverlets, flowers, etc., and had them "participate directly" in the event at hand. Such a religious ceremony was called a **lectisternium** (**lectus** = couch).

[7] In ancient towns public open space was scarce. The spaces occupied by squares—both neighborhood and the main, central square—and the areas in front of and around temples would be the main open spaces available for general congregation.

[8] The triumph was a grand procession of a victorious general through Rome to the Capitolium to give thanks to Jupiter Optimus Maximus for success in war. Hirtius here subtly reminds his readers that Caesar deserves such a high honor for his recent conquest of Gaul.

[9] The wealthy can display their enthusiasm by "turning out" for the occasion (**magnificentia**); the humbler citizens have only their enthusiasm (**cupiditas**) to contribute to the spectacle.

AULUS HIRTIUS: **The War in Gaul**
(*De bello Gallico*)
50 BC (late)

8.52 [1] Cum omnis regiones Galliae togatae[1] Caesar percucurrisset, summa celeritate ad exercitum Nemetocennam[2] rediit, legionibusque ex omnibus hibernis ad finis Treverorum[3] evocatis[4] eo profectus est ibique exercitum lustravit[5]. [2] T(itum) Labienum[6] Galliae praefecit togatae, quo maiore commendatione conciliaretur ad consulatus petitionem.[7]

Hints for Translation:

i-stem nouns and adjectives can cause confusion in accusative plurals when **-is** is used instead of -**es**. Note that here **omnis** is an i-stem adjective with **regiones**; and that **finis** is an i-stem noun in the accusative plural.

The relative **quo** and, less frequently, the demonstrative **hoc**, are used with the comparative of an adjective or adverb (here, **maiore**) to express "degree of difference." Translate as "all the more..." (here, "in order that all the more by this significant support he might win over...").

Vocabulary

regio, regionis (f.): district, region
percurro, percurrere, percucuri, percursus: travel through
summus, -a, -um: greatest, highest, (the) top (of)
exercitus, -us (m.): army
redire, redii, reditum: go back
fines, finium (m.): territory; boundary
eo (adv.): to that place, there
lustro, lustrari, lustravi, lustratum: purify
praeficio, praeficere, praefeci, praefectum (3): put in charge (with acc. and dat.)
maior, -ius: quite important
concilior, conciliari, conciliatum: win over

Grammar and Syntax

Nouns: Fourth and Fifth Declensions; Purpose & Result Clauses; Correlatives
1. Fourth declension nouns (B 48-50; AG 88-94).
2. Fifth declension nouns (B 51-53; AG 95-98).
3. Expressing purpose and result with **ut** and with relative pronouns; see the explanation (B 282.1-2; AG 531.1-2).
4. Correlatives (**tantum...quantum; quamquam...tamen; neque...neque...**) ; see the explanation (B 341.3; AG 323e).
5. Exercise for this section.

consul romanus

---

[1]**Gallia togata** is another name for Cisalpine Gaul, today's northern Italy south of the Alps and north of the Apennines. It fell under Roman control and began to be colonized in the late third century BC. It was called "togata" because the people wore the Roman toga, not the trousers typical of Gauls beyond the Alps.

[2]**Nemetocenna** is a place in Belgic Gaul where troops were wintering. The form is accusative, expressing "place to which," without the preposition **ad** because it is a placename (B 182; AG 427).

[3]**Treverorum**: another people of Gaul; modern Trèves.

[4]**evocatis**: that is, called out of their **hiberna**.

[5]**lustravit**: an army had to be "purified," made sacrally ready for battle duty. This ceremony is called a **lustrum**.

[6]**Labienum**: a fascinating character. He fought well as Caesar's most trusted lieutenant during the Gallic wars. However, he had strong personal connections to Pompey and when civil war broke out he went over to his old patron. After the defeat of Pompey at Pharsalus (48 BC), Labienus continued to oppose Caesar until his death at the battle of Munda (45 BC). Caesar hated Labienus for what he viewed as his disloyalty in going over to Pompey, and later reserves some of his harshest criticism for his erstwhile right-hand man.

[7]This has been interpreted to mean that Caesar was going to support Labienus for the consulship of 48 BC, but, more probably, it means that Caesar was trying to treat Labienus well so that he would support Caesar in *his* bid for the consulship of 48 BC.

Ipse tantum[8] itinerum[9] faciebat quantum satis esse ad mutationem locorum propter salubritatem existimabat.[10] [3] Ibi quamquam crebro audiebat[11] Labienum ab inimicis suis sollicitari certiorque fiebat id agi paucorum consiliis, ut interposita senatus auctoritate aliqua parte[12] exercitus spoliaretur, tamen neque de Labieno credidit quicquam neque contra[13] senatus auctoritatem ut aliquid faceret adduci potuit. Iudicabat[14] enim liberis sententiis[15] patrum conscriptorum[16] causam[17] suam facile obtineri.

Hints for Translation:

certiorem facere = to inform; it is a very common construction introducing indirect speech in accusative/infinitive; learn to recognize it.

tantum...quantum is a correlative. Learn the most common correlatives (see next page) so that you can anticipate two coordinated clauses when you see the first correlative of a pair.

Vocabulary

tantus, -a, -um ... quantus, -a, -um: as great as
iter facere: to march
tantus...quantus: as great as
satis (indeclinable adj.): enough; sufficient; with gen., enough of
propter: with acc.: because of
quamquam (conj): although
crebro (adv.): frequently
inimicus, -i (m.): enemy (personal)
sollicito, sollicitare, sollicitavi, sollicitatum: agitate, egg on
certiorem facere: to inform
fio, fieri, factum (irreg.): become; happen; be made
consilium, -i (n.): advice, counsel; plan; meeting
auctoritas, auctoritatis (f.): influence, power
aliqui, aliqua, aliquod: some
pars, partis, partium (f.): part
neque...neque: neither...nor
neque or nec: and ... not, nor
credo, credere, credidi, creditum (3): believe; trust (with dat. of person)
quisquam, quisquam, quidquam or quicquam: anyone, anything (with negatives)
aliquis, aliquid: someone, something
adduco, adducere, adduxi, adductum (3): induce (with ut, etc.)
iudico, iudicare, iudicavi, iudicatum (1): judge
pater, patris (m.): father (pl.: senators)

Gaul at the time of Caesar

---

[8]**tantum**: the other half of this correlative, **quantum**, comes along a few words down the line.

[9]**itinerum**: "marches," i.e., training exercises. (Partitive genitive)

[10]**Ipse...existimabat**: "He himself made as many marches (by the troops) as he thought necessary for changing places (of encampment) in order to insure their good health."

[11]**audiebat** introduces indirect discourse in accusative-infinitive form (B 331; AG 580-582).

[12]Ablative of separation (B 214; AG 400) since **spoliaretur** has the sense of taking away something from someone. Translate the clause: "so that, with a recommendation of the senate passed, he might be despoiled of some part of the army...".

[13]**contra**: not "against," for a **senatus consultum** has not yet been passed; rather, "in opposition to...".

[14]Accusative—infinitive follows once more.

[15]**liberis sententiis**: "in free deliberation;" an ablative of attendant circumstance (B 221; AG 419, 420.5).

[16]**patres conscripti**: another name for members of the Roman senate.

[17]**causam**: "just cause," i.e., what he felt he deserved.

Result and Purpose with ut and Relative Pronouns

Ut Clause (*Purpose*)	ut/ne introduces subjunctive clause	"in order that..." "that..."	**Venit ut videat.** She comes in order that she may see.
Relative Clause (*Purpose*)	relative pronoun introduces subjunctive clause	"in order that..."	**Milites misit qui haec facerent.** He sent men in order that they would do these things.
Ut Clause (*Result*)	ut/ut non introduces subjunctive clause; There is often a word such as tantus, tot, tam, ita, sic, adeo, vel sim in the main clause which signals that a result clause is coming	"with the result that.." "so that..."	**Ita agit ut laudetur.** She so acts that she is praised.
Relative Clause (*Result*)	relative pronoun introduces subjunctive clause	"so that..."	**Filios castigat qui eum metuant.** He punishes the children so much that they fear him.

Correlative Conjunctions

Correlatives are two conjunctions or conjunction-phrases which function as a unit to bring together different but related elements of a sentence. The most common are:

et ... et	both ... and
neque (nec) ... neque (neque)	neither ... nor
cum ... tum	while ... at the same time
tum ... cum	both ... and
aut ... aut	either...or
vel ... vel	either...or
sive ... sive	whether...or
non modo (or **solum,** or **tantum) ... sed etiam**	not only...but also
tantum ... quantum	as great as
quamquam ... tamen	although ... nevertheless

AULUS HIRTIUS: **The War in Gaul**
(*De bello Gallico*)
50 BC (late)

8.52 [4] Nam Gaius [Scribonius] Curio,[1] tribunus plebis,[2] cum[3] Caesaris causam dignitatemque defendendam suscepisset, saepe erat senatui pollicitus,[4] si quem timor armorum Caesaris laederet,[5] et quoniam Pompei[6] dominatio[7] atque arma non minimum[8] terrorem foro[9] inferrent, discederet[10] uterque ab armis exercitusque dimitteret: fore[11] eo facto liberam et sui iuris[12] civitatem.

plebs romana

Vocabulary

nam (namque mostly before a vowel) (conj.): for
suscipio, suscipere, suscepi, susceptum (3): take up
saepe (adv.): often
polliceor, polliceri, —, pollicitum (dep.)(2): promise
si (conj.): in case; if
timor, timoris (m): fear
quoniam (conj.): seeing that; since
minor, -e: smaller
minimus, -a, -um: smallest, least
infero, inferre, intuli, illatum (irreg.): bring in or against
discedo, discedere, discessi, discessum (3): go away, depart
uterque, utraque, utrumque: each of the two (i.e., both)
dimitto, dimittere, dimisi, dimissum (3): send away, dismiss
liber, -era, -erum: free:
ius, iuris (n.): right(s), justice, law
civitas, civitatis (f.): community, state

Grammar and Syntax

Verbs: First Conjugation — Gerunds & Gerundives

1. Endings of first conjugation verbs, active and passive (B 101-102; AG 184).
2. Gerund (**morando**) and gerundive (**defendendam**). See the explanation.
3. Exercise for this section.

Tribunus Plebis

---

[1]An interesting fellow. A "gilded youth," he was a part of the circle of Clodia along with the poet Catullus. Caesar had offended him, and he had been elected as a tribune for 50 BC as an enemy of Caesar, but now, thanks to a huge bribe from Caesar, he has changed sides. He died in Africa in 49 BC fighting for Caesar against King Juba of Numidia.

[2]Originally held by protectors of the common people (**plebs**), the tribunate had become just another office to be held by aristocrats seeking power and prestige. There were ten; their greatest power came from the ability to introduce legislation and to stop the actions of any magistrates and of each other by simply declaring "**veto**" (i.e., "I forbid it").

[3]**cum**: causal; "since, because."

[4]**pollicitus**: Curio announced his intent to make a proposal to the senate; that proposal is contained in the **discederet...** and **dimitteret..** clauses below.

[5]**laederet**: laedo; here "trouble".

[6]Gaius Pompeius Magnus (106-48 BC) is the major player, along with Caesar himself, in the drama of the end of the Republic. First Caesar's mentor, then his ally, and now his rival, the other aristocrats are aligning themselves according to which powerful man they think will win out in this contest for power and prestige within the Roman aristocracy.

[7]**dominatio**: another charged word—being a "dominus," a "master," of others; hence the usual connotation of "tyranny." Aristocrats lived by the cultural/political assumption that they all were equal (although some might be more equal than others); domination by a single individual, or even a small group (**factio paucorum**), was anathema. To refer to a **dominatio Pompei** speaks of a tyranny of Pompey, and is a very negative thing to say about him.

[8]An example of **litotes**, the figure of speech which affirms one thing by denying its opposite.

[9]**foro**: the forum was the civic political and economic center of a Roman town and, a fortiori, of Rome itself. During the fifties BC armed men had been brought into the forum to intimidate political rivals.

[10]**erat pollicitus** introduces these two clauses, **discederet...dimitteret**; **ut** is understood after **pollicitus**.

[11]Indirect discourse. "He went on to say that...." is understood, but not expressed literally in the Latin. **fore = futuram esse**; this alternative form is *very* common.

[12]**sui iuris**: under its own laws, i.e., not under the control of another, a **dominus**. A state **libera** and **sui iuris** is good, one under a **dominatio** is bad.

[5] Neque hoc tantum[13] pollicitus est,[14] sed etiam senatus consultum per discessionem[15] facere coepit; quod ne fieret consules amicique Pompei intercesserunt,[16] atque ita rem morando discusserunt.[17]

An Historical Note...

Review the public structure of the Roman community by examining the chart on the next page.

Vocabulary

sed (conj.): but
etiam (adv. & conj.): also; even; still
per: with acc.: through
coepi, coepisse, coeptum (defective verb; perf. tenses only)
    (irreg.): to have begun, begin
ne (conj.): lest, for fear that (with subjunctive)
ita (adv.): so, thus, in such a way
res, rei (f.): thing; affair
moror, morari, ——, moratum (dep.) (1): delay

nummus cum
Capitolio descripto

templum Iovis Optimi Maximi
(reconstruction)

The Roman Forum of Caesar's day

---

[13]**non tantum...sed etiam**: like **non solum...sed etiam**, this means "not only...but also."

[14]**pollicitus est**: Again, he announced his intention to take a certain action.

[15]**discessionem**: a division of the house, i.e., a formal vote in the senate. The senate voted by senators literally moving in the senate chamber (**curia**) to the side of the person whose measure they favored.

[16]**intercesserunt**: **intercedo** can mean "veto," but here just means "intervene;" had the consuls actually vetoed Curio's motion, there would have been no need to try to thwart the action by delay (**morando**). However, the manuscript is corrupt here. This reading is the suggestion of Pantagathus, as given in the *apparatus criticus* of the OCT edition of the *Bellum Gallicum* by Du Pontet (1900).

[17]**discusserunt**: **discutio** = break up, bring to nothing; post-classical derivatives first acquire the meaning "discuss," which originally then meant "to separate mentally, dissect."

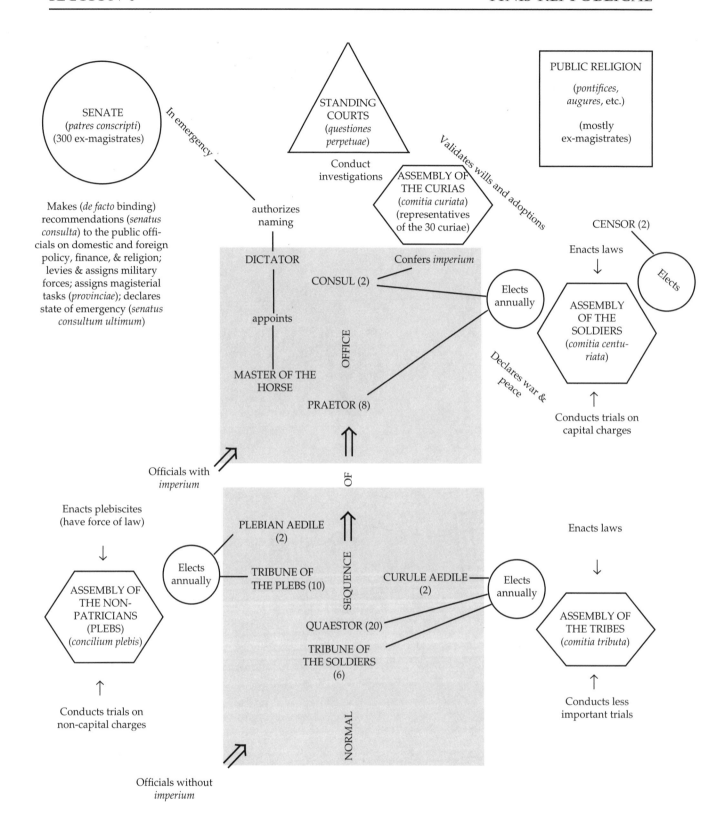

The Public Organization of the Roman Community in 49 BC

A Review of Gerundive and Gerund
Gerundive

The basic form which we have learned to identify as the "future passive participle" has two important uses:

1.   **Participle:** a simple verbal adjective (the **gerundive**); it is **passive** and carries the notion of worthiness, necessity or propriety:
     Poeta canticum suave <u>laudandumque</u> canebat.
     The poet was singing a charming song <u>worthy to be praised</u>.
     Ubi virum <u>laudandum</u> nunc inveniemus?
     Where will we now find a man <u>to be praised</u>? (i.e., a man whom we should praise)

2.   **Passive Periphrastic:** the **gerundive** working with a form of the verb *esse,* again carrying the notion of obligation or necessity:
     Credimus hoc canticum <u>laudandum esse</u>.
     We believe that this song <u>must be praised</u>. (Note: Agent for the passive periphrastic is regularly expressed by a "dative of agent." i.e., **Hoc canticum <u>nobis</u> laudandum est.** *This song must be praised <u>by us</u>.*)

Gerund

Verbal Noun (translated in the **active** voice), neuter and singular, in four cases only: genitive, dative, accusative and ablative:

genitive:	**<u>dicendi</u> amor,**	*a love <u>of speaking</u>*
dative:	**aptum <u>tegendo</u>,**	*suitable <u>for covering</u>*
accusative:	**missum ad <u>scribendum</u>,**	*sent <u>for writing</u>; sent <u>to write</u>*
ablative:	**<u>legendo</u> discimus,**	*we learn <u>by reading</u>*

(Note: The accusative is used only with prepositions.)

Gerundive-for-Gerund

When the gerund has an accusative object Latin prefers to substitute the gerundive for the gerund (here, the gerundive should be translated as if it were a gerund, an active verbal noun). Compare the following examples (noun-gerundive phrases standing for original gerunds with objects) with the examples just above (gerunds without objects):

   <u>veritatis dicendae</u> amor, *a love <u>of speaking the truth</u>*
   aptum <u>tegendis corporibus</u>, *suitable <u>for covering bodies</u>*
   missum <u>ad multas litteras scribendas</u>, *sent <u>for writing many letters</u>; sent <u>to write many letters</u>*
   <u>libris legendis</u> discimus, *we learn <u>by reading books</u>*

Note: From about the first century BC on, the Latin literary language preferred this gerundive-for-gerund construction. However, it is certain that the gerund continued to be used because the gerund (not the gerundive) survived into the Romance languages.

   Remember, too, that "purpose" can be expressed with **ad** and the accusative of the gerund or gerundive phrase and with **causa** or **gratia** and the genitive of the gerund or gerundive phrase:
   With Gerund:
      <u>simulandi</u> gratia, *in order <u>to deceive</u>* ("for the sake of deceiving")
   With Gerundive phrase:
      ad <u>conformandam audaciam</u>, *in order <u>to reinforce daring</u>* ("for reinforcing daring")

AULUS HIRTIUS: **The War in Gaul**
(*De bello Gallico*)
50 BC (late)

8.53 [1] Magnum hoc testimonium senatus erat universi conveniensque superiori facto[1]. [2] Nam Marcellus[2], proximo[3] anno, cum impugnaret Caesaris dignitatem, contra legem[4] Pompei et Crassi[5] rettulerat ante tempus[6] ad senatum de Caesaris provinciis, sententiisque[7] dictis, discessionem faciente Marcello, qui sibi omnem dignitatem[8] ex Caesaris invidia quaerebat, senatus frequens in alia omnia transiit.[9] Quibus non frangebantur animi inimicorum Caesaris sed admonebantur quo maiores pararent necessitates,[10] quibus cogi posset senatus id probare quod ipsi constituissent.

Vocabulary

convenio, convenire, conveni, conventum (4): agree, coincide with; assemble; meet (with dat.)

superior, -ius: earlier; higher

lex, legis (f.): law

refero, referre, rettuli, relatum (irreg.): put before (the senate); bring back; report

ante (with acc.): before

provincia, -ae (f.): province

dico, dicere, dixi, dictum (3): express, say

quaero, quaerere, quaesivi, quaesitum (3): try to get; inquire, seek

alius, alia, aliud: different; (an) other (of more than 2)

transeo, transire, transii, transitum (irreg.): cross (over); in alia transit = voted against

frango, frangere, fregi, fractum (3): break

animus, -i (m.): feeling; mind, spirit; sometimes pl. = courage

admoneo, admonere, admonui, admonitum (2): admonish, warn

paro, parare, paravi, paratum (1): prepare; obtain

cogo, cogere, coegi, coactum (3): collect, compel

constituo, constituere, constitui, constitutum (3): determine upon; decide, establish

Grammar and Syntax

1. Endings of second conjugation verbs, active and passive (B103-104; AG 185).
2. Ablative of Degree of Difference (**quo maiores**) (B223; AG 414b)
3. Exercises for this section.

Hints for Translation:

Latin narrative likes to connect a sentence with the thought which preceeds it. One very common way to do this is by using a relative pronoun as the first word of a sentence (as here, Quibus non frangebantur animi...). The use of this connecting relative (B 251.6; AG 308 f) moves the narrative along and connects ideas as well as words.

The pronoun is often best translated into English by a demonstrative pronoun (this, these, etc.), rather than by a relative pronoun. So, here, Quibus non frangebantur animi inimicorum is better translated "The enemies' spirits were not broken by these events..." rather than with "By which things the enemies' spirits were not broken...".

Think of **quo maiores** as "**ut eo maiores pararent necessitates**," "to make ready compulsions greater by this much (**eo**)", i.e., "even greater compulsions...". **eo** is an ablative of degree of difference.

---

[1] **Magnum...facto**: "This was very clear (literally, 'great') evidence of how the whole senate felt and was in agreement with its earlier action."

[2] **Marcellus** Marcus Claudius Marcellus was a consul in 51 BC and a bitter enemy of Caesar. His cousin, Gaius Claudius Marcellus, was consul in 50 and was aggressively Pompeian, but remained neutral in the ensuing civil war; married to Octavia, Caesar's niece, he was the step-father of the future emperor Augustus.

[3] **proximo**: the one next to another, so "next," or "previous"; here = "previous".

[4] **legem**: In 55 BC Pompey and Crassus as consuls had passed a law protecting Caesar's position as military governor (proconsul) in Gaul. The law had forbidden discussion of Caesar's provincial command before late 50 BC or, perhaps, early 49 BC (the issue is a hotly debated one!). Marcellus in 51 BC had nevertheless raised the issue (illegally: **ante tempus**), and had attempted to have Caesar's recall discussed as early as March of 51 BC.

[5] **Crassi**: Marcus Licinius Crassus (115-53 BC) was the wealthiest man of his day. He harbored great personal ambition and had had a long and successful political career culminating in his alliance with Caesar and Pompey in the First Triumvirate. He was killed fighting the Parthians in 53 BC.

[6] **ante tempus**: before the time appointed by the **lex Pompeia et Cassia**—and so, illegally.

[7] **sententiis**: **sententiae** are the opinions expressed in the course of the debate. The **sententia** of the senate as a whole as determined by a vote is a "decree," also called a **senatus consultum**.

[8] **omnem dignitatem**: Translate, "great influence."

[9] **in alia omnia transiit**: "voted overwhelmingly against it."

[10] **necessitates**: here, "compulsions."

AULUS HIRTIUS: **The War in Gaul**
(*De bello Gallico*)
50 BC (late)

8.54 [1] Fit deinde senatus consultum, ut ad bellum Parthicum[1] legio[2] una a Gnaeo Pompeio, altera a Gaio Caesare mitteretur; neque obscure duae legiones uni[3] detrahuntur.[4] [2] Nam Gnaeus Pompeius legionem primam,[5] quam ad Caesarem miserat, confectam ex dilectu[6] provinciae Caesaris,[7] eam tamquam ex suo numero dedit.

milites romani

Vocabulary

consulo, consulere, consului, consultum (3): consult; take thought for (with dat.); senatus consultum = decree of the senate
unus, -a, -um: one; only; irregular in genitive and dative
alter, altera, alterum: one of two; the other
mitto, mittere, misi, missum (3): send, let go
duo, duae, duo: two
primus, -a, -um: first
conficio, conficere, confeci, confectum (3): bring together; finish, complete
tamquam (conj.): just as if, as though
do, dare, dedi, datum (irreg.): give

Grammar and Syntax

1. Endings of third conjugation verbs, active and passive (B 105-106; AG 186).
2. Ordinal numbers (**primam; quintum; decimam; teriam; quinta**); see the chart (B 78.I, 79; AG 133-135).
3. Declension of irregular adjectives alius, alter, nullus, totus, ullus, unus (**uni**) (B 66; AG 113).
4. Exercises for this section.

Hints for Translation: Historical Present

Often the present tense is used, as here, to express past action; this is called the Historical Present. This use creates a much more vivid narrative. Notice that up to now all the narrative has been in the true past tenses; now, by switching into the historical present, the action takes on more life, and the sentence is emphasized because of this. The historical present is sometimes treated as a primary and sometimes as a secondary tense, as here with **mitteretur** (B 268.3; AG 485.e).

---

[1]**bellum Parthicum**: Crassus had been killed in war against the Parthians in 53 BC; now Romans sought revenge for that humiliating defeat. The Parthians were an Indo-European people of the Iranian plateau whose empire at times stretched from India to the Euphrates; it was at the Euphrates that the two empires clashed.

[2]**legio**: a legion is the basic unit of the Roman army. Technically made up of 6,000 infantrymen and additional supporting cavalry and troops, most legions fought under strength, at about 4,500 men.

[3]**uni**: dative of separation (B 188.2.d; AG 381; see section 21).

[4]**duae**: Pompey as proconsul for Spain loaned Caesar a legion in 53 BC. When the Parthians continued to cause trouble for the Romans in the East after the defeat and death of Crassus at their hands in 53 BC, it was decided that both Pompey and Caesar should contribute a legion to an army to be sent against this enemy. Pompey cleverly (from his standpoint) or treacherously (from Caesar's) offered the legion he had loaned to Caesar. In effect, therefore, Caesar lost two legions, Pompey none. This maneuver stuck in Caesar's craw like few others; he will constantly refer to it as typifying Pompey's unfair treatment of him.

[5]**primam**: legions were numbered according to the order in which they were recruited for a campaign. Legions were disbanded after a campaign, and new ones were recruited, with a new numbering system. So, this was Pompey's first-recruited legion of his current proconsulship, whereas Caesar makes note of the 13th and 15th which he had recruited for his use in Gaul. At the height of the Empire, Rome had 28-30 legions under arms at one time, but many fewer were in the field at this date.

[6]**dilectu**: a **dilectus** is the recruitment of a legion; also referred to as a conscription, or as a levy.

[7]Not only did Pompey commit the loaned legion, but that very legion had been recruited (**confectam ex dilectu**, recruited by a conscription) in a province under Caesar's authority, Cisalpine Gaul.

[3] Caesar tamen, cum de voluntate minime dubium esset adversariorum suorum, Pompeio legionem remisit et suo nomine quintam decimam, quam in Gallia citeriore[8] habuerat ex senatus consulto iubet tradi. In eius locum tertiam decimam legionem in Italiam[9] mittit quae praesidia[10] tueretur, ex quibus praesidiis quinta decima deducebatur.

Vocabulary

voluntas, voluntatis (f.): intention, wish, inclination
minime (adv.): least of all
nomen, nominis (n.): name
habeo, habere, habui, habitum (2): have; hold; consider
iubeo, iubere, iussi, iussum (2): order; bid, tell (to do something)
trado, tradere, tradidi, traditum (3): hand over
tertius, -a, -um: third
decimus, -a, -um: tenth (here, tertiam decimam = thirteenth)
praesidium, -i (n.): garrison post
tueor, tueri, —, tuitus/tutus sum (dep.) (2): guard; watch
quintus, -a, -um: fifth (here, quinta decima = fifteenth)
deduco, deducere, deduxi, deductum (3): withdraw; lead away

Irregular Adjectives

There are a few adjectives which irregularly form the genitive singular in -ius and the dative singular in -i. Plural forms are regular. Here are six of the most common.

Singular						
nominative	alius, -a, -um	alter, -a, -um	nullus, -a, -um	totus, -a, -um	ullus, -a, -um	unus, -a, -um
genitive	alterius	alterius	nullius	totius	ullius	unius
dative	alii	alterio	nulli	toti	ulli	uni
accusative	alium, -am, -um	alterum, -am, -um	nullum, -am, -um	totum, -am, -um	ullum, -am, -um	unum, -am, -um
ablative	alio, -a, -o	altero, -a, -o	nullo, -a, -o	toto, -a, -o	ullo, -a, -o	uno, -a, -o

Plural is regular

The Ordinal Numbers

Numbers used to express the order of things. All ordinal numbers are first/second declension adjectives (-us, -a, -um).

first	primus	eleventh	undecimus
second	secundus	twelfth	duodecimus
third	tertius	thirteenth	tertius decimus
fourth	quartus	fourteenth	quartus decimus
fifth	quintus	fifteenth	quintus decimus
sixth	sextus	sixteenth	sextus decimus
seventh	septimus	seventeenth	septimus decimus
eighth	octavus	eighteen	duodevicesimus
ninth	nonus	nineteenth	undevicesimus
tenth	decimus	twentieth	vicesimus

---

[8]**Gallia citeriore**: another name for Cisalpine Gaul, Italy north of the Apennines.

[9]**in Italiam**: that is, from Gaul to northern Italy.

[10]**praesidia**: there were legionary garrison posts in various of the Cisalpine towns as an advance protection against possible incursions from beyond the Alps by hostile peoples.

AULUS HIRTIUS: **The War in Gaul**
(*De bello Gallico*)
50 BC (late)

8.54 [4] Ipse exercitui distribuit hiberna: Gaium Trebonium[1] cum legionibus IIII in Belgio collocat, Gaium Fabium[2] cum totidem in Aeduos[3] deducit. [5] Sic enim existimabat tutissimam fore Galliam, si Belgae, quorum maxima virtus, Aedui, quorum auctoritas[4] summa esset, exercitibus continerentur. Ipse in Italiam profectus est.

8.55 [1] Quo[5] cum venisset, cognoscit per[6] Gaium Marcellum consulem legiones duas ab se remissas, quae ex senatus consulto deberent ad Parthicum bellum duci, Gnaeo Pompeio traditas atque in Italia retentas esse.[7] [2] Hoc facto quamquam nulli erat dubium quidnam[8] contra Caesarem pararetur, tamen Caesar omnia patienda esse statuit, quoad[9] sibi spes aliqua relinqueretur iure potius disceptandi quam belli gerendi.

Vocabulary

totidem: (indeclin.) the same number, just so many
sic (adv.): so, thus, in such a way
tutus, -a, -um: safe (irreg. adj. in -ius, -i — see Section 8)
virtus, virtutis (f.): courage; merit
contineo, continere, continui, contentum (2): contain, restrain
cognosco, cognoscere, cognovi, cognitum (3): find out, learn
debeo, debere, debui, debitum (2): owe, be obliged
duco, ducere, duxi, ductum (3): lead; take (someone) with you
retineo, retinere, retinui, retentum (2): hold back
quamquam: although
nullus, -a, -um: no...at all (irreg. adj. in -ius, -i — see Section 8)
patior, pati, —, passum (dep.) (3): endure; allow (with infin.)
statuo, statuere, statui, statutum (3): set up; decide
spes, spei (f.): hope(s) (often with gen. = "hope of...")
potius (adv.): rather; more; potius...quam = rather..than, more...than
discepto, discepare, disceptavi, disceptatum (1): settle; decide; debate

Grammar and Syntax

1. Endings of third conjugation "i-stem" verbs, active and passive (B 109-111; AG 188).
2. Clauses using **cum** (**cum...deducit; cum venisset**). See the explanation below.
3. Gerund and gerundive (**patienda, disceptandi, gerendi**); see Section 6.
4. Exercises for this section.

---

[1]A staunch Caesarian, he had, as a tribune of the people, sponsored the **lex Pompeia et Cassia**, giving Pompey his Spanish, Crassus his Syrian, command; he then was rewarded by being named a **legatus** (lieutenant general) under Caesar in Gaul from 55 to 50 BC. Trebonius fell out with Caesar and ultimately in 44 BC joined the conspiracy to kill him, playing the role of drawing Antony from Caesar's side as Caesar entered the theater of Pompey.

[2]Another firm ally of Caesar, he was a successful lieutenant general in Gaul and later served against the legates of Pompey in Spain, where he died in 49 BC.

[3]An important tribe of Gaul, they inhabited east central France, modern Burgundy; the Aedui had joined the revolt of Vercingetorix in 52 BC. See map, Section 5.

[4]**auctoritas**: another important, charged word. It means "authority"— that prestige, standing, importance, "presence" which makes others do what you want them to do.

[5]**quo**: adverbial; = "to which place; there."

[6]**per**: expresses agency and takes the accusative; here = "through the efforts of...".

[7]Cornelius Bibulus, Caesar's colleague in the consulship in 59 BC, had been sent to Syria to avenge Crassus' defeat and death in 53 BC at the hands of the Parthians. He returned in 50 BC for a **supplicatio**, or lesser triumph, as a result of his minor successes. Scipio, Pompey's son-in-law, was assigned Syria for 49 BC and so, presumably, he was intended to continue attacks on the Parthians. But the war against the Parthians did not take place as civil strife intervened.

[8]**quidnam**: the interrogative pronoun **quinam, quaenam, quidnam**; = "what," and introduces an indirect question subordinate clause after **nulli erat dubium**.

[9]**quoad**: "as long as."

"CUM" CLAUSES

Cum is not only a preposition, but also a subordinating conjunction with the various meanings "when," "after," "since," and "although." The verb in such clauses is most often in the subjunctive, its tense determined by the rules for sequence of tenses after the main verb. The meaning of **cum** in such clauses must be determined by context.

I. TEMPORAL AND CIRCUMSTANTIAL CLAUSES (B 288-290; AG 545-548)

- When the **cum** refers strictly to time and its action is coordinate with that of the main verb, it is a temporal clause, and **cum** is translated "when." Such clauses have their verbs in the **INDICATIVE**.

Cum te videbo, felix ero.	(at the very time) When I [will] see you, I shall be happy.
Cum te vidi, felix eram.	(at the very time) When I saw you, I was happy.

- If the **cum** clause states the circumstances in which the action of the main verb takes place, it is called a "circumstantial cum clause," and **cum** is translated "when" or "after." When the action in such clauses refers to present or future time, the **INDICATIVE** is used.

Cum te videbo, felix ero.	When I [will] see you, I shall be happy.
	After I [will] see you, I shall be happy.

- When the action in the circumstantial **cum** clause is past time, the verb is **SUBJUNCTIVE**. Note, however, that the English translation employs the **INDICATIVE**.

Cum te viderem, felix eram.	When I *saw* you, I was happy.
	(emphasizing the *seeing*, not the *when*)

II. CAUSAL CLAUSES (B 286.2; AG 549)

- When **cum** is translated as "since" or "because," the clause is causal. The verb is always in the **SUBJUNCTIVE**. Note, however, that the English translation employs the **INDICATIVE.**

Cum te videam, felix sum.	Since I see you, I am happy.
Cum te viderim, felix sum.	Since I have seen you, I am happy.
Cum te viderem, felix eram.	Since I saw you, I was happy.
Cum te vidissem, felix eram.	Since I had seen you, I was happy.

(Notice the **sequence of tenses** in the above examples.)

III. CONCESSIVE CLAUSES (B 309; AG 549)

- When **cum** translates "although," the clause is concessive. Frequently the word **tamen** ("nevertheless") in the main clause is an indication that the **cum** clause is concessive, but **tamen** is not always there. Concessive **cum** clauses always use the **SUBJUNCTIVE**. Here, too, the English translation employs the **indicative.**

Cum te videam, felix sum.	Although I see you, I am (still) happy.
Cum te viderim, felix sum.	Although I have seen you, I am happy.
Cum te viderem, felix eram.	Although I saw you, I was happy.
Cum te vidissem, felix eram.	Although I had seen you, I was happy.

(Note the **sequence of tenses** in the above examples.)

We can thus produce the following chart, which reflects potential usage in Latin:

CUM	PRIMARY SEQUENCE	SECONDARY SEQUENCE
Temporal	Indicative	Indicative
Circumstantial	Indicative	Subjunctive
Causal	Subjunctive	Subjunctive
Concessive	Subjunctive	Subjunctive

IV. **"CUM" MEANING "WHENEVER"** (B 288.3; AG 545 n. 2; 548)
- If **cum** means "whenever," it takes a perfect indicative when the main verb is present, and a pluperfect indicative when the main verb is imperfect.

Cum te vidi, felix sum.	Whenever I see you, I am happy.
	[literally, whenever I have seen you...]
Cum te videram, felix eram.	Whenever I saw you, I was happy.
	[literally, whenever I had seen you...]

Knowing these variations will be an aid in translation!

The indicative mood is restricted only to certain types of meaning, the subjunctive to others. There will be many cases when more than one possibility exists, as you should be able to observe from the examples. In the final analysis, CONTEXT will be your best guide.

CICERO: **Letters to Atticus**
(*Epistulae ad Atticum*)
ca. December 10, 50 BC

7.4 [1]Pompeium vidi IIII (die quarto) (ante) Idus Decembres.[1] Fuimus una horas duas[2] fortasse. Magna laetitia mihi visus est[3] adfici meo adventu; de triumpho[4] hortari,[5] suscipere partis suas,[6] monere[7] ne ante in senatum accederem quam rem confecissem, ne dicendis sententis[8] aliquem tribunum alienarem. Quid quaeris?[9] In hoc officio sermonis[10] nihil potuit esse prolixius.[11] De re publica[12] autem ita[13] mecum locutus est quasi non dubium[14] bellum haberemus, nihil ad spem concordiae[15].

Vocabulary

quattuor (indecl.): four; quartus, -a, -um, fourth
una (adv.): together
fortasse (adv.): perhaps
laetitia, -ae (f.): joy, elation
adficio, adficere, adfeci, adfectum (3): move, impress; also "aff-"
adventus, -us (m): arrival
hortor, horari, —, hortatum (dep.) (1): encourage
suscipio, suscipere, suscepi, susceptum (3): support, take up
pars, partis, partium (f.): role, part
cedo, cedere, cessi, cessum (3): yield; here accedo = come near, approach
sermo, sermonis (m): conversation, talk, discourse
loquor, loquari, —, locutum (dep.) (1): speak, say

Grammar and Syntax

1. Endings of fourth conjugation verbs, active and passive (B 107-108; AG 187).
2. Infinitives (**adfici,** etc.). See the chart, page 26.
3. Exercises for this section.

Hints for Translation:

The historical infinitive is an alternate way to express ongoing action in the past; this can also be expresssed by the imperfect tense. Here **hortari, suscipere...monere** are historical infinitives, used to narrate Pompey's actions (B 335; AG 463). Historical infinitives are common in narration.

Separable adverbs: Be alert to the separable nature of common adverbs such as **antequam**, **priusquam**, and **postquam**. As here, they often appear in two pieces, first **ante-**, **prius-**, or **post-**, then some other words in the sentence, then the **-quam**.

triumph scene (Boscoreale Cup)

---

[1]Four days before the Ides of December = December 10th. For an explanation of the Roman calendar see B 371-372; AG 630-31.

[2]**horas duas**: accusative of duration of time (B 181; AG 423).

[3]**visus** from **video, videre**; the subject is Pompeius.

[4]**triumpho**: Cicero was sent unwillingly to be military governor of Cilicia, in southern Asia Minor, in 51 BC. There he beat around some hill tribes, and now having returned to Rome, wishes to be awarded a triumph for this action. Alas for Cicero, because of the chaos of the ensuing civil war, it never happens. For Cicero's narrative of his adventures in Cilicia, see *Ad Familiares* 15.4; for Cato's response, *Ad Familiares* 15.5.

[5]**hortari, suscipere...monere**: these are historical infinitives, used to narrate Pompey's actions; see B 335; AG 463. "He encouraged...he promised to take up...he warned..."

[6]**partis suas**: that is, his own (Pompey's) proper role. **Pars** is an -i stem noun; hence the accusative plural can be **partes**, or **partis** (B 40; AG 66, 67).

[7]**monere** takes a negative command clause here, **ne...**, followed by a negative purpose clause, **ne...**

[8]Gerundive for gerund construction (B 339; AG 503): "by speaking my mind."

[9]**quid quaeris**: an interjection with many translations. Try "Need I say more?" here.

[10]**officio sermonis**: "in the courtesy (**officium**) of his words."

[11]**prolixius**: "more obliging."

[12]**re publica**: the code word for the current governmental system in which an oligarchy of wealthy landowners controlled the state. Translate, "about matters of state."

[13]**ita...quasi**: "just as if."

[14]**non dubium**: adjective with bellum: "certain."

[15]**nihil...**: understand "**haberemus**."

[2] Plane[16] illum[17] a se[18] alienatum cum[19] ante intellegeret, tum vero proxime[20] iudicasse. Venisse[21] Hirtium a Caesare, qui[22] esset illi familiarissimus; ad se non accessisse[23] et, cum ille[24] ante diem VIII (octavum) Idus Decembris[25] vesperi venisset, Balbus de tota re[26] constituisset[27] ante diem VII (septimum) ad Scipionem[28] ante lucem venire, multa de nocte[29] eum profectum esse ad Caesarem. Hoc illi[30] τεκμηριῶδες[31] videbatur esse alienationis.

Vocabulary

plane (adv.): clearly, evidently

intellego, intellegere, intellexi, intellectum (3): understand, recognize

familiaris, -e: as adj., familiar, intimate; as noun, friend, companion

octo (indecl.): eight; octavus, -a, -um: eighth

vesper, vesperi OR vesperis (m.): evening

septem (indecl.): seven

lux, lucis (f.): light

nox, noctis, noctium (f.): night

CALENDAR FOR THE PRE-JULIAN YEAR

Days of the Month	March, May, July, October		January, August, December		April, June, September, November		February.	
1	KALENDĪS.[1]		KALENDĪS.		KALENDĪS.		KALENDĪS.	
2	VI.	Nōnās.[1]	IV.	Nōnās.	IV.	Nōnās.	IV.	Nōnās.
3	V.	"	III.	"	III.	"	III.	"
4	IV.	"	Prīdiē Nōnās.		Prīdiē Nōnās.		Prīdiē Nōnās.	
5	III.	"	NŌNĪS.		NŌNĪS.		NŌNĪS.	
6	Prīdiē Nōnās.		VIII.	Īdūs.	VIII.	Īdūs.	VIII.	Īdūs.
7	NŌNĪS.		VII.	"	VII.	"	VII.	"
8	VIII.	Īdūs.	VI.	"	VI.	"	VI.	"
9	VII.	"	V.	"	V.	"	V.	"
10	VI.	"	IV.	"	IV.	"	IV.	"
11	V.	"	III.	"	III.	"	III.	"
12	IV.	"	Prīdiē Īdūs.		Prīdiē Īdūs.		Prīdiē Īdūs.	
13	III.	"	ĪDIBUS.		ĪDIBUS.		ĪDIBUS.	
14	Prīdiē Īdūs.		XIX.	Kalend.[2]	XVIII.	Kalend.[2]	XVI.	Kalend.[2]
15	ĪDIBUS.		XVIII.	"	XVII.	"	XV.	"
16	XVII.	Kalend.[2]	XVII.	"	XVI.	"	XIV.	"
17	XVI.	"	XVI.	"	XV.	"	XIII.	"
18	XV.	"	XV.	"	XIV.	"	XII.	"
19	XIV.	"	XIV.	"	XIII.	"	XI.	"
20	XIII.	"	XIII.	"	XII.	"	X.	"
21	XII.	"	XII.	"	XI.	"	IX.	"
22	XI.	"	XI.	"	X.	"	VIII.	"
23	X.	"	X.	"	IX.	"	VII.	"
24	IX.	"	IX.	"	VIII.	"	VI.	"
25	VIII.	"	VIII.	"	VII.	"	V. (VI.)[3]	"
26	VII.	"	VII.	"	VI.	"	IV. (V.)	"
27	VI.	"	VI.	"	V.	"	III. (IV.)	"
28	V.	"	V.	"	IV.	"	Prīd. Kal. (III. Kal.)	
29	IV.	"	Prīdiē Kalend.		Prīdiē Kalend.		(Prīd. Kal.)	
30	III.	"						
31	Prīdiē Kalend.							

---

[16]**plane** introduces the idea of "it was clear that," which then drives the substantive clause **(ut) intellegeret...** and the indirect discourse **judicasse... illum a se alienatum** is accusative/infinitive indirect discourse depending on **intellegeret** and **judicasse.** The first means "learn of," the second, "judge for oneself." Note the syncopated form of **judicasse,** for **judicavisse.**

[17]**illum**: Caesar.

[18]**se**: Pompey.

[19]**cum...tum**: "although ... then."

[20]**proxime**: "just recently."

[21]**venisse**: indirect discourse continues; understand, "Pompey continued, saying that..."

[22]**qui** = Hirtius.

[23]**accessisse**: **accedo** again; here, "gone to see."

[24]**ille** = Hirtius.

[25]December 6th.

[26]**de tota re**: "to talk about the entire situation."

[27]**constituisset...venire**: "had arranged that he come to Scipio's house the next day before dawn;" "Balbus" (presumably with Hirtius) is the understood subject of **venire.**

[28]**Scipionem**: Quintus Caecilius Metellus Pius Scipio, usually referred to as "Scipio." He was the scion of illustrious families. He married his daughter to Pompey after Julia's demise. Supported to the consulship in the chaotic year 52 BC by Pompey, he spearheaded the political and military confrontation with Caesar in 49 BC and remained a resolute anti-Caesarian until his death fighting Caesarian forces in Africa in 46 BC.

[29]**multa de nocte**: "in the middle of the night;" i.e., he left before the early morning meeting.

[30]**illi**: Pompey.

[31]**"Tekmeriodes"** is a Greek word meaning "clear evidence."

Infinitives

The "complete" Latin verb has six infinitive forms. Example:

	Active		**Passive**	
present	vincere	"to conquer"	vinci	"to be conquered"
perfect	vicisse	"to have conquered"	victum esse	"to have been conquered"
future	victurum esse	"to be going to conquer"	victum iri	"to be going to be conquered"

Deponent verbs have three infinitive forms:

  insequi, "to pursue"
  insecutum esse, "to have pursued"
  insecuturum esse, "to be going to pursue"

The infinitive can be used to "complete" the meaning of a verb (the "complementary infinitive"):

Illud credere possum.   I can believe that.

The infinitive can be used, usually with a form of esse, as a subject or predicate (the "subject infinitive"):

Caesari vincere non est difficile.

To conquer is not difficult for Caesar

Note that the infinitive, when used as a noun, is neuter. This form frequently can be translated with an English gerund or substantive: "conquering is not difficult," "conquest is not difficult."

The infinitive is the verb of an indirect statement, with subject accusative ("infinitive in indirect discourse"):

Urbs audivit Caesarem Pompeianos vicisse. The city heard that Caesar had conquered the Pompeians.

The infinitive is used by many historians as a descriptive verb, standing for the imperfect indicative with subject nominative (the "historical infinitive'):

Alii insequi, alii cedere, sed nos vincere.   Some were giving pursuit and others yielding ground, but we were prevailing.

These are among the most common uses of the infinitive. Consult your grammar for others.

CICERO: **Letters to Atticus**
(Epistulae ad Atticum)
ca. December 10, 50 BC

7.4 [3] Quid multa?[1] Nihil me aliud consolatur nisi quod illum,[2] cui etiam inimici alterum consulatum, Fortuna summam potentiam dederit, non arbitror fore tam[3] amentem ut haec in discrimen adducat. Quod si ruere coeperit, ne[4] ego multa timeo quae non audeo scribere. Sed ut nunc est, ante diem III (tertium) Nonas Januarias[5] ad urbem cogito.[6] [4] De re publica cottidie magis timeo. Non enim boni, ut putantur,[7] consentiunt. Quos[8] ego equites Romanos,[9] quos senatores video, qui acerrime cum[10] cetera tum hoc iter Pompei vituperarent!

Hint for Translation:

If you see **ne** as the first word of a clause or a sentence, think first that it is the interjection, not the subordinating conjunction introducing a result clause, purpose clause, etc.

Fortuna

Vocabulary

consolor, consolari, —, consolatus (1) (dep.): comfort, encourage, relieve
nisi (conj.): unless, except
tam (adv.): so
amens, amentis: mad; foolish, stupid
arbitror, arbitrari, —, arbitratus (dep.) (1): think, consider
discrimen, discriminis (n.): critical moment; crisis
adduco, adducere, adduxi, adductum (3): bring
quod si (also quodsi) (conj.): but if
ruo, ruere, rui, rutum (3): rush (to ruin)
ne (interj.): truly; indeed, certainly
timeo, timere, timui, — (3): fear, be afraid
audeo, audere, —, ausum (2): dare
ut (conj.): as
tertius, -a, -um: third
cottidie (adv.): daily
qui, quae, quod (interrogative): what? what kind of?
eques, equitis (m.): equestrian, the second noble group at Rome; cavalryman

Grammar and Syntax

1. Endings of deponent verbs, active and passive (**consolatus, iocari**) (B 112-114; AG 190-192).
2. Uses of **ut**.
3. Exercise for this section.

senator romanus

---

[1]**Quid multa:** "why (do I need to say) many things," i.e., "Need I say more?".
[2]**illum:** the subject of accusative/infinitive indirect discourse after **non arbitror**. Who *is* **illum**?
[3]**tam...ut:** watch for **tam** as an anticipator of the **ut**; = "so...that."
[4]**ne:** this is very tricky; remember that **ne** can be an emphasizing particle as well as a subordinator; translate, "truly."
[5]As the nones fall on January 5th, this would be January 3rd.
[6]Understand **ire** after **cogito**; translate, "I'm making plans for town."
[7]A snide remark: "as they think (of themselves)."
[8]**quos:** the interrogative pronoun (B 90; AG 148). Translate, "what kind of...what kind of...."
[9]**equites Romanos:** the equites were the "second élite" at Rome. Dedicated to a non-political life, often engaged in commerce or banking, these men were wealthy—and a very important political constituency. They are here distinguished from the "first elite," the **senatores**.
[10]**cum** is displaced for emphasis; read **qui cum acerrime cetera tum hoc iter**...

Pace[11] opus est. Ex victoria cum multa mala, tum certe tyrannus[12] exsistet. Sed haec prope diem coram. Iam plane mihi deest quod ad te scribam; nec enim de re publica, quod uterque nostrum[13] scit eadem, et domestica nota sunt ambobus.[14] [5] Reliquum est iocari,[15] si hic[16] sinat. Nam ego is sum qui illi concedi putem[17] utilius esse quod postulat quam[18] signa conferri.[19] Sero enim resistimus ei quem per annos decem aluimus contra nos. "Quid senties igitur?" inquis. Nihil scilicet nisi de sententia tua nec prius quidem quam nostrum negotium[20] confecerimus aut deposuerimus.[21] Cura igitur ut[22] valeas.

Vocabulary

opus est: there is need for (with abl.)
malus, -a, -um: bad, evil
exsisto, exsistere, exstiti, exstitum (3): arise, emerge
prope diem (adv.): very soon, presently
coram (adv.): face-to-face; in the presence of
iam (adv.): now; already
desum, deesse, defui, defuturus: fail; be missing; lack (with dat.)
uter, -ra, -um: each of two; also = uterque
ambo, ambae, ambo: both, the two
iocor, iocari, —, iocatus (dep.) (1): joke
sino, sinere, sivi/sii, situm (3): allow
sero (adv.): too late
alo, aluere, alui, alitum (3): nourish; support; promote
sentio, sentire, sensi, sensum (4): think, sense
igitur (adv.): therefore
inquam: say (defective: see B 134 or AG 206b for forms)
scilicet (adv): of course; (ironically) naturally; that is to say
quidem (adv.): certainly, indeed
curo, curare, curavi, curatum (1): see to it; take care

---

[11]**pace**: **opus est** takes an ablative to express the thing there is need of; the person in need is in the dative. So, e.g., **Pace Pompeio opus est.** = "Pompey has need of peace."

[12]**tyrannus**: the rule of one man is anathema to the ruling oligarchic elite. A **tyrannus** is a ruler who has seized power unconstitutionally.

[13]**nostrum**: this form can either be nominative/accusative singular, or genitive plural (for **nostrorum**). Here, it is the partitive genitive with **uterque**.

[14]**ambobus**: **ambo** is declined like **duo**.

[15]**iocari**: an infinitive as subject of **est**; the infinitive as noun is always neuter.

[16]**hic**: Caesar?; or Pompey?.

[17]**putem**: introduces accusative/infinitive indirect discourse, **utilius esse**.

[18]**utilius...quam**: comparative with **quam**, "than."

[19]**signa conferri**: "come to a pitched battle." The **signa** (military standards) which are brought together are the standards of opposing armies.

[20]**nostrum negotium**: "my own concerns," i.e., the matter of whether Cicero would be granted a triumph.

[21]**confecerimus...deposuerimus**: epistolary tenses. "In letters the writer often uses tenses which are not appropriate at the time of writing, but which will be so at the time when his letter is received; he thus employs the imperfect and the perfect for the present, and the pluperfect for the present perfect." (B 265; AG 479).

[22]**cura ut**: "see to it that..."

Uses of Ut

Part of Speech	Description	Examples
Subordinating Conjunction	1. **Ut**, *that* (negative **ne** = *that not, lest*) • purpose clause • subjunctive • adverb: answers such questions as "why?" "to what end?"	**Laborant ut vincant.** *They strive in order to win.* **Fugiunt ne capiantur.** *They flee lest they be captured.*
	2. **Ut**, *that* (negative **ut non**, *that not*) • result clause • subjunctive • noun: answers the question, "what?"	**Ita agit ut omnes eum laudent.** *She acts so that all praise her.* **Tam fortes sunt ut non timeant.** *They are so brave that they do not fear.*
	3. **Ut**, *that* (negative **ne**, *that not*) • substantive clause (also called substantive purpose clause or jussive noun clause) • subjunctive • noun: answers the question, "what?"	**Postulavit ut haec fierent.** *He demanded that these things be done.* **Eum moneo ne veniat.** *I advise him not to come.*
	4. **Ut** (*that not, lest*) (negative **ne**, *that*) • fearing clause • subjunctive • noun: answers the question, "what?"	**Timet ut morer.** *She fears that I not delay.* **Timet ne morer.** *She fears that I delay.*
	5. **Ut**, *when, after* • temporal clause • indicative	**Ut venator venit, cervae fugerunt.** *When the hunter came, the deer fled.*
	6. **Ut**, *as, as if* • manner clause • indicative	**Ut constitutum est, ab urbe discessit.** *As was determined, he withdrew from the city.*
Interrogative Adverb	**Ut**, *how?* direct question = indicative indirect question = subjunctive	**Ut mater tua est?** *How is your mother?* **Docuit ut mater sua fuisset.** *He learned how his mother had been.*

CAESAR: **The Civil War**
(*De bello civili*)
January 1, 49 BC[1]

1.1 [1] Litteris[2] Caii Caesaris consulibus redditis,[3] aegre ab his[4] impetratum est summa tribunorum plebis contentione,[5] ut in senatu recitarentur—ut vero ex litteris ad senatum referretur,[6] impetrari non potuit. [2] Referunt consules de re publica infinite.[7] Lucius Lentulus consul[8] senatui rei publicae se non defuturum pollicetur,[9] si audacter ac fortiter sententias dicere vellent;[10] [3] sin Caesarem respiciant atque eius gratiam sequantur, ut[11] superioribus fecerint temporibus,[12] se sibi consilium capturum neque senatus auctoritati obtemperaturum; habere se quoque ad Caesaris gratiam atque amicitiam receptum.[13]

Vocabulary

reddo, reddere, reddidi, redditum (3): deliver
aegre (adv.): scarcely; with difficulty
impetro, impetrare, impetravi, impetratum (1): to ask and gain the request.
verus, -a, -um: true; vero = however; truly, certainly
audacter (adv.): boldly
fortis, -e: brave; fortiter (adv.) = strongly, bravely
volo, velle, volui, — (irreg.): be willing, want, wish
sin (conj.): but if
respicio, respicere, respexi, respectum (3): look to
tempus, temporis (n.): time
capio, capere, cepi, captum (3): take; capture
obtempero, obtemperare, obtemperavi, obtemperatum (1): obey (+dat)
quoque (adv.): also
gratia, -ae (f.): favor; friendship; influence
amicitia, -ae (f.): friendship

Grammar and Syntax

1. Endings of sum and possum (B 100, 125-126; AG 170, 198b).
2. Conditions (see explanation and B 301-307; AG 513-525).
3. Exercise for this section.

Roman writing tablets

---

[1]The new consuls take office on January first, and waste no time dealing with Caesar.

[2]**Litteris**: litterae = a single communication, letter.

[3]**litteris...redditis**: an ablative absolute. Caesar has sent his proposal for a peaceful resolution via letter to the senate; he proposes mutual disarmament for himself and Pompey.

[4]**his**: the consuls of 49 BC, Lucius Lentulus and Gaius Marcellus. Ablative of separation, see Section 20.

[5]Caesar leaves the impression that many of the tribunes stood up for him; in fact only two did, Mark Antony and Quintus Cassius Longinus. Longinus was a particularly unsavory character who distinguished himself by rapaciously governing Further Spain (Andalucía) not once, but twice, in his rather brief public career.

[6]**referretur**: to put a question to the house for discussion. Perhaps Peskett ad loc. is correct to suppose that the tribunes shouted **refer! refer!** (cf. Cicero, *In Catilinam* 1.20).

[7]**infinite**: " in general." The manuscripts give **in civitate**; **infinite** has been suggested as an improvement. The idea is that the consuls were willing to put the matter up for general discussion, but were unwilling to put Caesar's specific proposal to a vote, for they knew that the vast majority of senators wished both warlords to give up their armies. Peskett, however, ad loc., denies that **infinite** is a classical usage and prefers simply to delete the words **in civitate**.

[8]Lentulus consul: L. Cornelius Lentulus Crus, brother of the consul of 57 BC and consul with Marcellus in 49 BC. He seems to have been an uninspiring person given to luxurious living. As senior consul (i.e., the one elected first in the balloting of the previous year) Lentulus had the right to speak first.

[9]**pollicetur**: followed by indirect discourse in the accusative/infinitive construction.

[10]**vellent**: note that **senatus** is taken as a group noun, and so the verb is in the plural.

[11]**ut**: "as"

[12]**superioribus temporibus**: an allusion to the senate's capitulation to Caesar's demands earlier in the 50s.

[13]**receptum**: a place of retreat, refuge; here constructed with **ad** = "a refuge in Caesar's...."

Conditional Sentences

Conditional sentences are composed of two parts: (a) **the condition**, a subordinate clause (also called the **protasis**) introduced by one of the following:

> If = *si*
> Unless = *nisi*
> But if = *quod si*, or *sin*

[note: after si, nisi, num or ne, every ali- drops away from aliquis, aliquid, etc.]

and (b) **the conclusion,** the main clause of the sentence (also called the **apodosis**). "Conditions" can be expressed with either indicative or subjunctive verbs in Latin.

1. General (or "simple") conditions (where "if" is best translated "whenever") employ the indicative in the protasis, and the indicative, imperative, or independent subjunctive in the apodosis, as appropriate.

   Si ille dicet, audite! If he speaks (lit. "will speak"), listen!

   Si ille dicet, audiamus. If he speaks, let us listen.

   Si ille dixerit, audiemus. If he speaks (lit. "will have spoken), we shall listen.

   Si ille dicebat, audiebamus. Whenever he spoke, we used to listen.

2. Ideal or "future less vivid" conditions employ the present subjunctive in both clauses; compared to the general condition, the ideal condition expresses real doubt as to whether the condition will be fulfilled.

   Si ille dicat, audiamus. If he should speak (which is not likely), we would listen.

3. Contrary-to-fact conditions express unfulfilled conditions in present or past time; the present contrary-to-fact employs the imperfect subjunctive in both clauses; the past contrary-to-fact, the pluperfect subjunctive in both clauses.

   Si ille diceret, audiremus. If he were speaking (but he is not), we would be listening.

   Si ille dixisset, audivissemus. If he had spoken (but he did not), we would have listened.

   It is possible for a past contrary-to-fact condition to have a present contrary-to-fact conclusion (this is sometimes called a "mixed" condition):

   Si Caesar venisset, beati essemus. If Caesar had come (but he did not), we would (now) be happy (but we aren't!).

   Often, when the verb of the conclusion of a contrary-to-fact conditional sentence is a form of *possum* or expresses *necessity* (as with *debeo* or a passive periphrastic), that verb takes the indicative, not subjunctive, form. In this usage, we see the imperfect indicative replacing the imperfect subjunctive, and the perfect indicative replacing the pluperfect subjunctive:

   Si Caesar adesset, laudandus erat. [If Caesar were present, he ought to be praised.]

   Si Caesar venisset, superare potuit. [If Caesar had come, he could have won.]

Conditional sentences in indirect statement. The protasis, as a subordinate clause, is **always** in the subjunctive; the apodosis regularly in the infinitive. With limited infinitives to use, we are faced with a loss of distinction between types of conditions in some instances: (1) there is no distinction between future general (more vivid) and future ideal (less vivid) conditions in indirect statement; (2) the apodosis of present and past conditions contrary-to-fact is identical, and only the protasis may keep them distinct. Frequently, your best guide to deciphering the nature of a conditional sentence in indirect statement is the context of the passage and the logic inherent in the narrative.

CAESAR: **The Civil War**
(*De bello civili*)
January 1, 49 BC

1.1. [4] In eandem sententiam loquitur Scipio:[1] Pompeio[2] esse in animo rei publicae non deesse, si senatus sequatur; si cunctetur atque agat lenius, nequiquam eius auxilium, si postea velit, senatum imploraturum.

1.2. [1] Haec Scipionis oratio, quod senatus in urbe habebatur[3] Pompeiusque aderat,[4] ex ipsius ore Pompei mitti[5] videbatur. [2] Dixerat aliquis[6] leniorem sententiam, ut primo[7] Marcus Marcellus,[8] ingressus in eam orationem,[9] non oportere ante de ea re ad senatum referri, quam dilectus tota Italia habiti et exercitus conscripti essent,

An historical note...

All of our classical texts originated in manuscripts. These were transcribed originally and then copied over and over, by hand; we have nothing like an "original" ("autograph") manuscript for any ancient work. It was relatively easy for corruptions to slip in during this copying. The manuscripts for the works of Caesar and Cicero all date, at the earliest, from the eighth to ninth centuries AD; most are a couple of centuries or more later. One of the tasks of classical scholars is to determine the most reliable (i.e., most likely to be genuine) text of a work by comparing various manuscripts and making educated guesses about what possible corruptions have slipped in during the centuries of copying; this process is called "textual criticism."

Vocabulary

sequor, sequi, —, secutum (dep.) (3): follow, go (along) with
cunctor, cunctari, —, cunctatum (dep.) (1): delay, hesitate
lenis, -e: gentle; mild
nequiquam (adv.): to no purpose, to no avail
auxilium, -i (n.): help
postea (adv.): afterwards, later
adsum, adesse, adfui (irreg.): be near, at hand; be present
os, oris (n.): mouth; lips
ingredior, ingredi, —, ingressum (dep.) (3): enter, undertake; begin
oratio, orationis (f.): speech
oportet, oportere, oportuit (impersonal) (3): it is right, proper
dilectus, -us (m.): levy of troops; conscription
totus, -a, -um: (the) whole (of)

Grammar and Syntax

1. The endings of fero and volo, active and passive (B 129, 130; AG 199, 200).
2. The rules of sequence of tenses (see material in section 3 and B 267-68; AG 482-85).
3. Dative of possession (**Pompeio**) (B. 190; AG 373).
4. Uses of quod (**quod ... habebatur**).
5. Clauses of fearing (with timeo, etc.; **timere ... ne**) (B. 296.2; AG 564). See explanation below.
6. Exercise for this section.

Pompeius Magnus

---

[1] **Scipio** is Pompey's father-in-law. His full name is Quintus Caecilius Metellus Pius Scipio. He was born a Cornelius and adopted by a Caecilius Metellus. Hence his daughter, Pompey's wife at this time, is named Cornelia. She, by the way, had previously been married to Licinius Crassus, the triumvir killed at Carrhae in 53 B.C.

[2] **Pompeio**: dative of possession, with esse.

[3] The senate was meeting in the **curia hostilia**, in the forum, and therefore within the core boundaries of Rome, marked by the **pomerium**.

[4] Pompey was a general with **imperium** and therefore could not enter the core city (marked by the **pomerium**). He was, however, in the part of the city just outside the **pomerium**, and so nearby (**aderat**).

[5] **mitti**: Carter ad loc. suggests that this is a military metaphor: "launch," as one would hurl forth a spear or other missile.

[6] **aliquis**: i.e., another speaker; in fact it is a sequence of other speakers, but the Latin thinks of them one at a time, and so **aliquis** is in the singular. Three exemplary speakers are given: Marcellus, then Calidius, and then Rufus.

[7] **primo**: he later changes his tune; see below.

[8] M. Marcellus is the brother of the current consul and was himself consul in 51 BC. He had previously raised the issue of recalling Caesar before the legal time.

[9] The verbal notion of **orationem**, "giving an argument," provides the impetus for the following indirect discourse in accusative/infinitive construction.

quo praesidio tuto et libere senatus quae vellet decernere auderet; [3] ut Marcus Calidius,[10] qui censebat ut Pompeius in suas provincias[11] proficisceretur, ne qua[12] esset armorum causa; timere[13] Caesarem, ereptis ab eo[14] duabus legionibus, ne ad eius periculum reservare et retinere eas ad urbem[15] Pompeius videretur; ut[16] Marcus Rufus,[17] qui sententiam Calidi paucis fere mutatis verbis sequebatur.

Vocabulary

tuto (adv.): safely
libere (adv.): freely
decerno, decernere, decrevi, decretum (3): decree
censeo, censere, censui, censum (2): give an opinion
proficiscor, proficisci, —, profectum: set out
periculum, -i (n.): danger
fere (adv.): almost, practically; only
muto, mutare, mutavi, mutatum (1): change
verbum, -i (n.): word

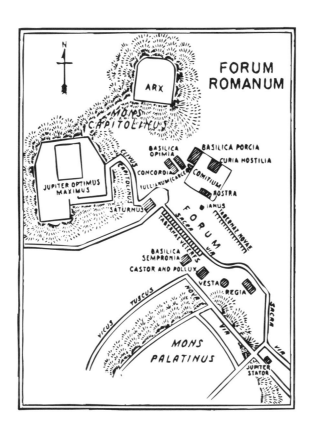

Forum et Comitium

---

[10]**Calidius**: a Caesarian.

[11]**suas provincias**: the Spanish provinces voted him in 55 BC, but which he had been governing through lieutenants (**legati**) rather than leave Rome himself.

[12]**ne qua**: = negative purpose clause; **qua** = **aliqua**.

[13]Caesarem is the subject of **timere** in this accusative/infinitive construction.

[14]**ab eo**: either Pompey (the legions were taken by Pompey), or Caesar (they were taken from Caesar). The grammar does not allow a secure choice.

[15]**ad urbem**: near the city

[16]Note the anaphora of the repeated **ut...ut...ut.** For anaphora, see B 350.11.b; AG 598.f.

[17]This is the well-known M. Caelius Rufus who participated in the murder of Clodius in 52 BC. He has by now jumped to the Caesarian side.

Uses of Quod

Part of Speech	In the form...	Introduces	Translated	Examples
Relative Pronoun	neuter nominative or accusative singular	relative clause	"that" "which"	**Bellum confecimus quod suscepisti.** *We have finished the war that you began.* **Fecisti id quod pollicitus es.** *You did that which you promised.*
Interrogative Adjective	neuter nominative or accusative singular	direct or indirect question	"what"	**Quod bellum gerunt?** *What war are they waging?* **Rogat quod bellum gerant.** *He asks what war they are waging.*
Subordinating Conjunction (1)	quod-as-conjunction	causal clause indicative or subjunctive (if the reason of another)	"because"	**Timemus quod haec fecisti.** *We fear because you have done these things.*
Subordinating Conjunction (2)	quod-as-conjunction	substantive clause (indicative)	"(as to) the fact that"	**Hoc praetereo, quod Manilium occidit.** *I pass over this, the fact that he killed Manilius.* **Quod id fecisti, nos eo despicere noli.** *As to the fact that you have done this, do not despise us on that account.*

Clauses of Fear

Verbs or expressions of fearing take subjunctive clauses introduced by **ne** for the positive and **ut** for the negative.   (Sometimes **ne non** is used instead of **ut**.) This development is actually quite logical, since the subordination developed from originally paratactic (non-subordinated) ideas: an expression of fear, and a wish.

Example: Timeo. Ne veniant. [paratactic]
                         I am afraid. May they not come!
                         Timeo ne veniant. [hypotactic, or subordinate]
                         I am afraid that they may come.

CAESAR: **The Civil War**
(*De bello civili*)
January 1, 49 BC

1.2 [4] Hi omnes[1] convicio Luci Lentuli consulis correpti exagitabantur.[2] [5] Lentulus sententiam Calidi pronuntiaturum[3] se omnino negavit, Marcellus perterritus[4] conviciis a sua sententia discessit.[5] [6] Sic vocibus[6] consulis, terrore praesentis exercitus,[7] minis amicorum Pompei plerique compulsi, inviti et coacti Scipionis sententiam sequuntur:[8] uti[9] ante certam diem[10]Caesar exercitum dimittat; si non faciat, eum adversus rem publicam facturum videri.[11][7] Intercedit Marcus Antonius, Quintus Cassius, tribuni plebis. Refertur confestim de intercessione tribunorum.[12][8] Dicuntur sententiae graves; ut quisque acerbissime crudelissimeque dixit, ita maxime ab inimicis Caesaris collaudatur.[13]

Vocabulary

convicium, -i (n.): insult; jeers; cry of protest
corripio, corripere, corripui, correptum (3): attack; reproach
omnino (adv.): altogether, completely, wholly
perterreo, perterrere, perterrui, perterritum (2): frighten, terrify
vox, vocis (f.): word; expression; voice; cry
praesens, praesentis: present, at hand
minae, -arum (f.): threats
plerique, pleraeque, pleraque: the majority of; most
cogo, cogere, coegi, coactum (3): compel, force; bring together
dies, diei (m. or f.): day
confestim (adv.): immediately, suddenly
gravis, -e (adv.): serious, severe; heavy
quisque, quaeque, quidque and quodque: each, each one
crudelis, -e: cruel

Grammar and Syntax

1. Endings of eo and fio, active and passive (B 131, 132; AG 203, 204).
2. Exercises for this section.

---

[1]**omnes**: all the previous speakers, whether moderates (Marcellus), or Caesarians (Calidius and Rufus).

[2]**exagitabantur**: were being intimidated, scared off.

[3]**pronuntiaturum**: put to a vote.

[4]**perterritus**: a propagandistic word for Caesar. His enemies often show themselves **perterriti**; his own men, seldom.

[5]**discessit**: so Marcellus **primo** said one thing, but now changes his line under threats from Lentulus.

[6]**vocibus**: Peskett ad loc. notes that the plural of **vox** is used to indicate a remarkable utterance of some kind.

[7]It is not clear how "nearby" the army was; certainly in Campania, to the south. But Pompey probably had some troops stationed closer to Rome itself.

[8]Naturally, implies Caesar, men would not have voted against his modest proposal unless they had been **compulsi, inviti,** and **coacti**...

[9]**uti**: an alternative form of **ut.**

[10]**certam diem**: probably the end of February, when Caesar's command was due to lapse and his army disband. Note the feminine form of **dies, diei**: Normally it is masculine, but is feminine when, as here, it means an appointed day (B 53: AG 97).

[11]A circumlocutious way of saying "commit treason."

[12]Although tribunes could not be prevented from vetoing actions, there were ways around this power, and options were now discussed in the senate. With the veto standing the senate could still vote an "auctoritas"—recommendation, but a "consultum"—decree, was impossible.

[13]Probably Pompeians tried to intimidate the tribunes, to get them to withdraw their vetos. Plutarch **Caes**. 30 says that ultimately the senate adjourned with no measure passed.

CAESAR: **The Civil War**
(*De bello civili*)
January 2-5, 49 BC
January 2nd

1.3 [1] Misso ad vesperum senatu[1] omnes qui sunt eius ordinis a Pompeio evocantur.[2] Laudat Pompeius atque in posterum confirmat, segniores castigat atque incitat. [2] Multi undique ex veteribus Pompei exercitibus spe praemiorum atque ordinum evocantur, multi ex duabus legionibus, quae sunt traditae a Caesare, arcessuntur.[3] [3] Completur urbs, clivus,[4] comitium[5] tribunis,[6] centurionibus, evocatis.[7]

Vocabulary

ordo, ordinis (m.): order, rank
ordo senatus = senatorial order
laudo, laudare, laudavi, laudatum (1): praise
posterus, -a, -um: later, next following; in posterum = for the future
confirmo, confirmare, confirmavi, confirmatum (1): strengthen; declare
segnis, -e: slow, sluggish
castigo, castigare, castigavi, castigatum (1): punish
incito, incitare, incitavi, incitatum (1): urge on
undique (adv.): from (on) all sides
vetus, veteris: old, long-standing
praemium, -i (n.): reward, prize
arcesso, arcessere, arcessivi, arcessitum (3): summon
compleo, complere, complevi, completum (2): fill
centurio, centurionis (m.): centurion
evocatus, -i (m.): recalled veteran soldier

Grammar and Syntax

1. Ablative of attendant circumstances (**misso senatu**) (B 221, 227.2.e; AG 419, 420.5 generally) (see chart Section 20 below).
2. Possessive genitive (**eius ordinis; consulum; Pompei; eorum; quorum;**) (B 198; AG 343; see chart Section 19 below).
3. Partitive genitive (genitive of the whole (**spatii**) (B 201; AG 346).
4. potestas is constructed with the genitive (**decernendi potestas**).
5. Review again three ways to express purpose:
   (a) ut clauses (negative, ne) (**ut mittantur**) ; look at section 5 again (B 282; AG 529-33).
   (b) relative clauses intoduced by qui, quae, quod (**qui proponant**) (B 282.2; AG 531, with 533).
   (c) ad is often used with a gerundive for gerund to express purpose (**ad eam rem conficiendam**) (B 338.3; AG 506).
6. ad is often used to express "toward," "in the vicinity of." (**ad vesperum; ad urbem**, BC 1.1.3).
7. Exercise for this section.

---

[1] The senate could not meet after sundown.

[2] **evocantur**: that is, summoned beyond the Pomerium, where Pompey had to remain since he was a general on active duty; perhaps to the Temple of Bellona, which was often the meetingplace of the senate when it needed to meet outside the Pomerium.

[3] Perhaps an exaggeration, or a desire to mention those pesky two legions: they were stationed in southern Italy, and so not near Rome at this time.

[4] **clivus**: the mss. are corrupt here, reading **et ius**. **Ipsum** is an attractive suggestion, but **clivus** has been suggested as an emendation (see the OCT ad loc.) since this provides a nice tripartite parallel between the civil ("comitium, urbs, clivus [sic. Capitolinus, beside the forum])" and the military ("tribunis, centurionibus, evocatis").

[5] **comitium**: the location for the civil assemblies of the Roman state, in the forum next to the senate house and rostra. It was therefore all the more horrible that this symbol of the rule of law was now overrun by military men.

[6] **tribunis**: tribuni militum, tribunes of the solders (staff officer of a legion), not the **tribuni plebis**. There is a certain irony here in the word order, for the **tribuni plebis** would have held their civil assembly, the **concilium plebis**, in the **comitium**, which is now being taken over by the **tribuni militum**.

[7] **evocatis**: recalled veterans. These were a valuable addition to any army because of their loyalty and experience.

January 5th[8]

1.3 [4] Omnes amici consulum, necessarii Pompei atque eorum, qui veteres inimicitias cum Caesare gerebant, in senatum coguntur; [5] quorum vocibus et concursu terrentur infirmiores, dubii confirmantur, plerisque vero libere decernendi potestas eripitur. [6] Pollicetur Lucius Piso[9] censor,[10] sese iturum ad Caesarem, item Lucius Roscius praetor, qui de his rebus eum doceant; sex dies ad eam rem conficiendam spatii postulant.[11] [7] Dicuntur etiam ab nonnullis sententiae, ut legati[12] ad Caesarem mittantur, qui voluntatem senatus ei proponant.

Vocabulary

necessarius, -i: close connection, friend
gero, gerere, gessi, gestum (3): carry on, engage in; wear
concursus, -us (4): clash
infirmus, -a, -um: weak; inconstant
decerno, decernere, decrevi, decretum (3): decide, determine; decree, resolve
eripio, eripere, eripui, ereptum (3): snatch away
doceo, docere, docui, doctum (2): reveal; teach
spatium, -i (n.): time; space, room
postulo, postulare, postulavi, postulatum (1): demand
nonnullus, -a, -um: some, many
legatus, -i (m.): emissary; lieutenant commander
propono, proponere, proposui, propositum (3): put forward, propose; report

His rebus gestis omni Gallia pacata, tan-
ta huius belli ad barbaros opinio perlata est uti ab iis nationibus quae
trans Rhenum incolerent legationes ad Caesarem mitterentur, quae se obsides
daturas, imperata facturas pollicerentur. Quas legationes Caesar, quod
in Italiam Illyricumque properabat, inita proxima aestate ad se reverti
iussit. Ipse in Carnutes, Andes, Turonos quaeque civitates propinquae iis locis
erant ubi bellum gesserat, legionibus in hiberna deductis, in Italiam
profectus est. Ob easque res ex litteris Caesaris dierum XV supplicatio
decreta est, quod ante id tempus accidit nulli

A Latin manuscript of a passage from Caesar's *De bello Gallico*

---

[8] January 3rd and 4th were religious days when the senate could not be in session.
[9] **Piso**: Caesar's father-in-law since 59 BC. Consul in 58 BC and now censor, he was a strong partisan of Caesar.
[10] **censor**: every five years (supposedly) two men were elected to review the register of the citizens and their property worth, let state contracts for public building, etc., and to express an opinion regarding the moral fitness of citizens. It was a very coveted and prestigious post.
[11] As Caesar is near Ravenna, in northern Italy, the journey there and back in six days would mean extremely swift travel.
[12] **legati**: official emissaries of the state; contrasted to Piso and Roscius, who wanted to go in a private capacity.

CAESAR: **The Civil War**
(*De bello civili*)
January 5, 49 BC

1.4 [1] Omnibus his resistitur omnibusque oratio consulis, Scipionis, Catonis[1] opponitur. Catonem veteres inimicitiae[2] Caesaris incitant et dolor repulsae.[3] [2] Lentulus aeris alieni[4] magnitudine et spe exercitus ac provinciarum et regum appellandorum[5] largitionibus movetur, seque alterum fore Sullam[6] inter suos gloriatur, ad quem summa imperii[7] redeat. [3] Scipionem eadem spes provinciae atque exercituum impellit, quos se pro necessitudine partiturum cum Pompeio arbitratur, simul iudiciorum[8] metus, adulatio atque ostentatio sui et potentium, qui in re publica iudiciisque tum plurimum pollebant.

senatus romanus

Vocabulary

resisto, resistere, restiti, — (3): stand up (to), resist (with dat.)
oppono, oponere, opponui, oppositum (3): oppose
dolor, doloris (m.): pain; distress; resentment
rex, regis (m.): king
appello, appellare, appellavi, appellatum (1): name; appoint
largitio, largitionis (f.): bribery; generosity
moveo, movere, movi, motum (2): move
inter: with acc.: between, among
glorior, gloriari, —, gloriatum (dep.) (1): boast (about)
idem, eadem, idem: same
impello, impellere, impuli, impulsus (3): stimulate; push, drive
necessitudo, necessitudinis (f.): friendship, relationship; necessity, need; , bond
partio, partire, partivi, partitum (4): share
simul (adv.): at the same time (as)
metus, metus (m.): fear
potens, potentis: powerful
plurimus, -a, -um: most
polleo, pollere, —, — (2): be powerful, be strong

Grammar and Syntax

1. Objective genitive (**exercitus; provinciarum; regum; provinciae; exercituum; Caesaris**) (B 200; AG 347-48; see chart Section 19 below).
2. Exercise for this section.

Hints for Translation:

et, ac, and **-que**: **ac** is a stronger conjunction than **et**, while **-que** tends to join larger pieces into a whole. So, here, **ac** joins with emphasis two related words (**exercitus** and **provinciarum**) within a series joined by **et** (**et spe...et regum...**). **-que** then joins two large segments (**Lentulus aeris alienum...and se alterum fore...**) into a whole (B 324; AG 324 a-c).

---

[1]**Catonis**: Marcus Porcius Cato, a staunch opponent of Caesar and representative of the most radical of the Pompeians.

[2]**veteres inimicitiae**: If Sallust is to be trusted, these enmities go back at least to 63 BC and the Catilinarian Conspiracy.

[3]**dolor repulsae**: anguish, resentment at having lost an election. Cato had failed of election to the consulship in 51 BC and Caesar says that he had taken this very badly, blaming Caesar himself. On the contrary, Plutarch (*Cat.* 49) says that Cato bore his defeat well.

[4]**aeris alieni**: aes alienum is debt—literally, **aes** (bronze=money) which belongs to someone else.

[5]**regum appellandorum**: bribes which would come from aspirants to thrones; the Romans regularly installed rulers in petty kingdoms.

[6]**Sullam**: Cornelius Sulla had seized power in Rome in 82 BC and ruled with bloody fervor for a number of years. For his enemies, his name was synonymous with tyrannical rule. To have another Cornelius boast that he would be the "next Sulla" did not sound very appealing to most Romans.

[7]**imperii**: that is, supreme power in the state.

[8]**iudiciorum**: the law courts, where political battles were often waged.

1.4 [4] Ipse Pompeius, ab inimicis Caesaris incitatus et quod neminem dignitate secum exaequari volebat,[9] totum se ab eius amicitia averterat et cum communibus inimicis in gratiam redierat, quorum ipse maximam partem illo affinitatis tempore[10] iniunxerat Caesari; [5] simul infamia duarum legionum permotus, quas ab itinere Asiae Syriaeque[11] ad suam potentiam dominatumque converterat, rem ad arma deduci studebat.

Vocabulary

nemo, neminis (m./f.): no one
exaequo, exaequare, exaequavi, exaequatum (1): equal
averto, avertere, averti, aversum (3): turn away; alienate
communis, -e: general
affinitas, affinitatis (f.); relationship by marriage
iniungo, iniungere, iniunxi, iniunctum (3): join; inflict on; impose
infamia, -ae (f.): disgrace, scandal
permoveo, permovere, permovi, permotum (2) affect deeply
studeo, studere, studui, — (2): be eager (with dat. or infin.)

Sulla seizes Rome (82 BC)

---

[9]Note the two unpraiseworthy motivations for Pompey: following the lead of Caesar's personal enemies, and being jealous of Caesar's greatness.

[10]**affinitatis tempore**: when Pompey was married to Caesar's daughter, Julia—59-54 BC.

[11]**Asiae Syriaeque**: a strange construction, probably to be taken as genitives describing the route: " from the march to Asia and Syria."

CAESAR: **The Civil War**
(*De bello civili*)
January 7, 49 BC

1. 5 [1] His de causis aguntur omnia raptim atque turbate. Nec docendi[1] Caesaris propinquis eius[2] spatium datur, nec tribunis plebis sui periculi deprecandi[3] neque etiam extremi iuris[4] intercessione retinendi, quod Lucius Sulla reliquerat,[5] facultas tribuitur, [2] sed de sua salute septimo die[6] cogitare coguntur, quod illi turbulentissimi superioribus temporibus tribuni plebis post octo denique menses[7] variarum actionum respicere ac timere consuerant.[8]

Sulla the Dictator

Vocabulary

raptim (adv.): hurriedly, suddenly
propinquus, -i: relative
deprecor, deprecari, deprecari, —, deprecatum (1) (dep.): avert by prayer; intercede on behalf of
extremus, -a, -um: most basic; outermost, last
facultas, facultatis (f.): leave to do, opportunity (+gen.)
salus, salutis (f.): health, safety, welfare
septimus, -a, -um: seventh
cogito, cogitare, cogitavi, cogitatum (1): think through, ponder
post; with acc.: after, behind; adv. = afterwards
denique (adv.): finally
mensis, mensis (m.): month
consuesco, consuescere, consuevi, consuetum (3): become accustomed

Grammar and Syntax

1. Nouns which take the genitive (**spatium**, **facultas**)
2. Genitive of the whole ("partitive genitive") (**quid detrimenti**) (B 201; AG 346).
3. Accusative of duration of time (**octo...menses**) (B 181; AG 423-24).
4. Impersonal verbs (**decurritur**; **descensum est**) (see explanation below and B138; AG 207-208.)
5. Exercise for this section.

Hints for Translation...

Note the word order of **His de causis** and **quo ex die**. Latin does not like to begin a sentence or a subordinate clause with a preposition. In addition, it is usual to find a preposition surrounded by a noun and its modifier, e.g., "magna cum laude."

dare operam means to exert oneself, make an effort; it is a common idiomatic expression.

Coins of Sulla

---

[1]**docendi**: here are two excellent examples of gerundives (**docendi**; also **deprecandi** and **retinendi** just below). See the grammatical material in Section 6.
[2]**propinquis eius**: specifically, Calpurnius Piso, censor and Caesar's father-in-law.
[3]**deprecandi**: making entreaty to avoid the danger to themselves.
[4]**extremi iuris**: their most basic, fundamental right.
[5]**reliquerat**: Sulla had indeed left the tribunate as an office, but had decreed that no one who held it could ever hold higher office—thus cleverly gutting the position of any political importance.
[6]**septimo die**: that is, since the new consuls took office on January 1st.
[7]This is a difficult passage to interpret. The reference must be to the eight months between tribunes taking office (December 10th) and the following July elections for the next year's tribunes. It was at the time of re-election that violent opposition had previously surfaced.
[8]**consuerant**: a syncopated form. The unsyncopated form here would be **consue-ve-rant**.

1.5 [3] Decurritur ad illud extremum atque ultimum senatus consultum, quo nisi paene in ipso urbis incendio atque in desperatione omnium salutis,[9] latorum[10] audacia, numquam ante descensum est: dent operam consules, praetores, tribuni plebis, quique pro consulibus sint ad urbem, ne quid res publica detrimenti capiat.[11] [4] Haec senatus consulto perscribuntur[12] ante diem VII Idus Ianuarias. Itaque V primis diebus,[13] quibus haberi senatus potuit, quo ex die consulatum iniit Lentulus, biduo excepto comitiali,[14] et de imperio Caesaris et de amplissimis viris, tribunis plebis, gravissime acerbissimeque decernitur. [5] Profugiunt statim ex urbe tribuni plebis seseque ad Caesarem conferunt. Is eo tempore erat Ravennae[15] expectabatque suis lenissimis postulatis[16] responsa, si qua hominum aequitate res ad otium deduci posset.

Vocabulary

decurro, decurrere, decurri, decursum (3): rush headlong to; pass over; have recourse to
paene (adv.): almost, nearly, practically
audacia, -ae (f.): boldness, courage (positive sense); recklessness, audacity (negative sense)
dare operam: exert oneself
res publica (f.): government, state, constitution
itaque (adv.): and so
amplus, -a, -um: distinguished, honorable; glorious
vir, -i (m.): man; great man, hero; husband
profugio, profugere, profugi, — (3): flee, escape from
statim (adv.): immediately
confero, conferre, contuli, conlatum (irreg.): join, compare
expecto, expectare, expectavi, expectatum (1): wait for, wait

Northern Italy about Ravenna

---

[9]**paene...salutis**: Reference to the threat of the Catilinarian conspirators in 63 BC to burn the city.

[10]**latorum**: so the mss. The meaning would be "the audacity of men proposing laws." Emendations have been proposed, e.g., **senatorum**, or **sceleratorum**, but see Carter ad loc.

[11]**dent...capiat**: a direct quotation of the **senatus consultum**.

[12]**perscribuntur**: perscribo is the technical term for approving an s.c.; witnesses signed at the end to validate the accuracy of the decree.

[13]**primis diebus**: ablative of time.

[14]**comitiali**: of the seven days since January 1st, two had been comitial days, i.e., days on which public assemblies could be held and so, according to Roman law, days on which the senate could not meet.

[15]**Ravennae**: the major Roman town nearest to the border between Italy and Caesar's province, the Rubicon river. The case is locative.

[16]**lenissimis postulatis**: right, well, at least from Caesar's perspective. These proposals were presumably contained in the letter noted at the beginning of *Civil War* Book 1.

Impersonal Verbs

Latin, in general, seems to make more use of the passive voice and impersonal expressions (active and passive) than does English; for example, **decurritur** and **descensum est** in Section 17.

Some verbs, because of their meaning, appear only in the third person singular, infinitive and gerund in all tenses and are called "impersonal verbs" and translated with the subject "it." Grammatically, however, the real subject of the impersonal verb is an infinitive or noun clause.

1. Verbs which take the **infinitive** as subject can express an agent of the action in either dative or accusative:

    Libet and **placet** regularly take the dative:

Mihi nunc meminisse placet.	*literally*—To remember is pleasing for me now.
	better—It is pleasing for me to remember now.
Gloriari regi libet.	*literally*—To boast is pleasing to the king.
	better—The king likes to boast.

    Oportet, **piget** and **pudet** regularly take the accusative with an infinitive

Me oportet meminisse.	*literally*—To remember suits me.
	better—It is proper that I remember.
Pudet me meminisse.	*literally*—To remember shames me.
	better—I am ashamed to remember.
Bellum gerere illam piget.	*literally*—Waging war disgusts her.
	better—She is disgusted to wage war.

    Licet, **decet** and **necesse est** can take either dative or accusative and infinitive:

Mihi necesse est meminisse.	*literally*—To remember is necessary for me.
	better—It is necessary for me to remember.
Me meminisse non decet.	*literally*—To remember does not become me.
	better—It is not fitting that I remember.

2. Impersonal verbs which deal with **emotion or feeling** regularly use the accusative to express the person affected by the emotion and the objective genitive (or infinitive, as above) for the source of the emotion. These verbs include **miseret**, **piget**, **pudet**, **taedet, paenitet**:

Erroris me paenitet.	I regret my error.
Audaciae suae se piget.	Her own recklessness annoys her.
Amoris pecuniae se pudet.	Love of money shames him.
Conviciorum plebis te taedet.	The insults of the people irk you.

3. Other impersonal verbs frequently use a subjunctive noun clause as their subject. These include verbs such as **accidit**, **fit**, **convenit**, **contingit**, **obvenit**, and others (many of which are also used personally).

Accidit ut Caesar Romam rediret.	It happened that Caesar returned to Rome.
Contingit ut Caesar imperator sit.	It turns out that Caesar is the commander.

CAESAR: **The Civil War**
(*De bello civili*)
January 8-9, 49 BC

1.6 [1] Proximis diebus habetur extra urbem[1] senatus. Pompeius eadem illa, quae per Scipionem ostenderat, agit, senatus virtutem constantiamque collaudat, copias suas exponit: legiones habere sese paratas X;[2] [2] praeterea cognitum compertumque[3] sibi, alieno esse animo[4] in Caesarem milites neque eis posse persuaderi, uti eum defendant aut sequantur saltem.[5] [3] De reliquis rebus ad senatum refertur: tota Italia delectus habeatur; Faustus Sulla[6] propere in Mauritaniam[7] mittatur; pecunia uti ex aerario[8] Pompeio detur.

Vocabulary

ostendo, ostendere, ostendi, ostentum (3): show, make clear
copia, -ae (f.): supply, abundance
copiae, -arum (f.) (pl.): troops, forces
praeterea (adv.): besides, moreover
comperio, comperire, comperi, compertum (4): learn, ascertain; with dat. = known to...
alienus, -a, -um: hostile; strange; another's
miles, militis (m.): soldier, the soldiery
aut (conj.): or (mostly with contrasted alternative)
saltem (adv.): at least; in any event
reliquus, -a, -um: remaining
delectus, -us (m.): conscription, levy
propere (adv.): quickly, hastily
utor, uti, —, usum (dep.) (3): use (with abl.)

Grammar and Syntax

1. Ablative of time when (**proximis diebus**) (B 230; AG 423-24).
2. Ablative of description (**alieno...animo**) (B 224 [called "of quality"]; AG 415): an ablative is used with a modifying adjective to describe something about a noun.
3. **Cum** with adversative subjunctive (**cum cuperem**) (B 309.3; AG 549).
4. Double dative (**impedimento mihi fuerunt**) (B 191; AG 382): the first dative expresses purpose or end, while the second expresses the person affected.
5. Subjunctive in dependent clauses of characteristic (**cupiant**) (B 283; AG 534, 535).
6. Exercises for this section.

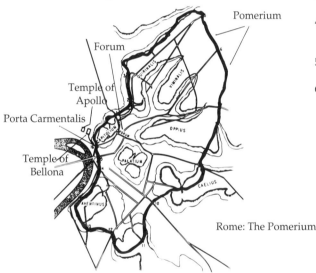

Rome: The Pomerium

coin of King Juba I

---

[1]**extra urbem**: in the temple of Apollo (Cic. ad Att. 15.3), outside the **porta Carmentalis**.

[2]**legiones X**: this turns out to be a gross miscalculation on Pompey's part. Apparently he is thinking of his seven in Spain and the two **traditae ab Caesare** for the Parthian war; the tenth legion is not directly attested, but probably turns up with Domitius at Corfinium, later in the story (see Reubel 52 n. 47 and Carter ad loc. for other speculation). But the legions in Italy turn out to be unreliable, and his legions in Spain were further from Rome than Caesar's in Gaul. Pompey had boasted a month before that he had only to stamp on the earth for legions to rise up—an allusion to his veterans settled in Italy who he supposed, would rush to his standards. No such thing happened.

[3]**cognitum compertumque**: "acknowledged and well known."

[4]**alieno ... animo**: ablative of description (see grammar for this section).

[5]**alieno...animo...etc.**: another serious failure either of Pompeian intelligence or perspicacity, as events demonstrate. Could this false information have come from Labienus, recently gone over to Pompey, and wishing to ingratiate himself?

[6]**Faustus**: The son of Sulla the Dictator. Sulla took the cognomen "Felix," "blessed by good fortune," and named his son Faustus and the twin sister Fausta, "Lucky." He was married to Pompey's daughter but never rose beyond the office of quaestor. He remained a Pompeian until his death in battle in 46 BC.

[7]**Mauritaniam**: a native kingdom still, Faustus was supposed to organize support for Pompey on this flank of the Mediterranean by winning over the pro-Caesarian rulers, Bocchus and Bogud.

[8]**aerario**: the treasury of Rome, kept in the temple of Saturn next to the Forum. It was all in cash and bullion.

1. 6 [4] Refertur etiam de rege Iuba,[9] ut socius sit atque amicus;[10] Marcellus[11] vero passurum in praesentia negat. De Fausto impedit Philippus[12] tribunus plebis. [5] De reliquis rebus[13] senatus consulta perscribuntur. Provinciae privatis decernuntur, duae consulares, reliquae praetoriae. Scipioni[14] obvenit Syria, Lucio Domitio[15] Gallia. Philippus[16] et Cotta[17] privato consilio praetereuntur; neque eorum sortes deiciuntur.[18] [6] In reliquas provincias praetorii mittuntur. Neque exspectant, quod superioribus annis acciderat, ut de eorum imperio ad populum feratur, paludatique votis nuncupatis exeunt, quod ante id tempus accidit numquam.[19]

Vocabulary

socius, -i (m.): ally
impedio, impedire, impedivi, impeditum (4): hinder
privatus, -i (m.): a private citizen, i.e., one not holding public office
obvenio, obvenire, obveni, obventum (4): be alotted to; happen
praetereo, praeterire, praeterii, praeteritum (irreg.): pass over in silence, neglect
sors, sortis (f.): lot
deicio, deicere, deieci, deiectum (3): throw down into [the urn]
imperium, -i (n.): command; chief power
populus, -i (m.): the people of Rome; a tribe or nation
fero, ferre, tuli, latum (irreg.): put to a vote; bring; endure; assert
nuncupo, nuncupare, nuncupavi, nuncupatum (1): make (a vow); proclaim publicly
accido, accidere, accidi, — (3): happen, occur
obviam prodire: go out to meet (with dat.)
sic ... ut (correlatives): such ... that
ornatus, -a, -um: adorned, illustrious, excellent
potius (adv.): rather
medeor, mederi, —, — (dep.) (2): heal, remedy (with dat.)
pugno, pugnare, pugnavi, pugnatum (1): fight

CICERO: **Letter to his friend Tiro**
(Epistulae ad familiares 16.11)
January 5, 49 BC

1 Ego ad urbem accessi pridie Nonas Januarias. Obviam mihi sic proditum est ut nihil possit fieri ornatius; sed incidi in ipsam flammam discordiae vel potius belli. Cui cum cuperem mederi et, ut arbitror, possem, cupiditates certorum hominum (nam ex utraque parte sunt qui pugnare cupiant) impedimento mihi fuerunt.

general in
paludamentum

sortitio

---

[9]**Iuba**: king of Numidia and a friend of Pompey.

[10]**socius et amicus**: Diplomatic recognition of political friendship. The titles were often used to flatter client rulers.

[11]**Marcellus**: the other consul, with Lentulus.

[12]**Philippus**: L. Marcius Philippus, a Caesarian, and son of the Philippus mentioned below.

[13]**reliquis rebus**: three of these were illegal: Scipio and Domitius were ineligible for provincial commands because five years had not passed since they had been consuls, a requirement of the Lex Pompeia of 52 BC; men should not be passed over in the casting of lots; magistrates need the approval of the people before becoming officially inaugurated. Caesar paints a picture of hasty and/or illegal action on the part of his enemies.

[14]**Scipioni**: consul in 52 BC.

[15]**Domitio**: consul in 54 BC. His assigned province is ... Caesar's Gaul.

[16]**Philippus**: the father of the tribune mentioned above, he had been consul in 56 BC. He was married to Caesar's niece, Atia, and was the stepfather of Octavius, the later emperor Augustus.

[17](Aurelius) **Cotta**: consul in 65 BC, by now an old man; possibly he was considered to be a Caesarian—he was related to Caesar's mother, an Aurelia.

[18]**sortes**: assignments were determined by drawing names from a hat or, in the Roman situation, an urn. The gods then were making the choice. The lots could be fixed in various ingenious ways; to simply refuse to put the tokens of two men in the urn was pretty blatant, even by ancient standards.

[19]Magistrates entitled to **imperium** (see chart, section 6) acquired that power through a vote of the **comita curiata**; thus Marcellus and Lentulus have acted with gross illegality by taking up their **imperium** without this pro forma, but none-the-less necessary, sanctioning of that power.

CICERO: **Letter to his friend Tiro**
(Epistulae ad familiares 16.11)
January 5, 49 BC

2 (cont.) Omnino et ipse Caesar, amicus noster, minacis ad senatum et acerbas litteras miserat et erat adhuc impudens, qui exercitum et provinciam, invito senatu, teneret, et Curio meus illum incitat; Antonius quidem noster[1] et Quintus Cassius, nulla vi expulsi, ad Caesarem cum Curione profecti erant, posteaquam senatus consulibus, praetoribus, tribunis plebis et nobis, qui pro consulibus sumus, negotium dederat ut curaremus ne quid res publica detrimenti caperet.[2]

3 Numquam maiore in periculo civitas fuit; numquam improbi cives habuerunt paratiorem ducem.[3] Omnino ex hac quoque parte[4] diligentissime comparatur. Id fit auctoritate et studio Pompei nostri qui Caesarem sero coepit timere.

Nobis inter has turbas senatus tamen frequens flagitavit triumphum;[5] sed Lentulus consul, quo maius suum beneficium faceret, simul atque expedisset quae essent necessaria de re publica dixit se relaturum. Nos agimus nihil cupide[6] eoque est nostra pluris auctoritas. Italiae regiones descriptae sunt,[7] quam quisque partem tueretur. Nos Capuam[8] sumpsimus.

Haec te scire volui. Tu etiam atque etiam cura ut valeas litterasque ad me mittas, quotienscumque habebis cui des. Etiam atque etiam vale. Data pridie Idus Ianuarias.

Vocabulary

omnino (adv.): to be sure
minax, minacis (adj.): threatening, menacing
acerbus, -a, -um: bitter; harsh; troublesome
adhuc (adv.): to this point (leading to a result clause); besides, moreover
impudens, -entis: shameless
invitus, -a, -um: unwilling
teneo, tenere, tenui, tentum (2): hold
posteaquam (adv.):after
negotium, -i (n.): charge, assignment; business
studium, -i (n.): zeal, eagerness
sero (adv.): late, too late
flagito, flagitare, flagitavi, flagitatum (1): demand
simul atque (or ac or et) (conj.): as soon as
expedio, expedire, expedii, expeditum (4): clear the way, 'expedite,' arrange, settle
necessarius, -a, -um: necessary; related
sumo, sumere, sumpsi, sumptum (3): take up, begin
scio, scire, scivi, scitum (4): know
etiam atque etiam (adv.): again and again
quotienscumque (adv.): however often

Grammar and Syntax

1. Genitive of price or value (**pluris**) (B 283.3.a; AG 417). This is similar to the more general "genitive of description." See chart below.
2. Subjective genitive (B 199; AG 343 and note). Just as the genitive can express the OBJECT of the action inherent in a noun, so, too, the genitive can express the SUBJECT, the DOER of that action. So, here, **auctoritate Pompei**: the authority Pompey is able to command and **studio Pompei**, the zeal Pompey evinces.
3. Review these and other uses of the genitive, such as:
   a. possession (in this section, **tribunis plebis, studio Pompei**, etc.)
   b. partitive (in this section, **quid detrimenti**)
   c. subjective (**Pompei**)
   d. objective (in another context, **auctoritate et studio Pompei** might be such a genitive)
   e. quality
   f. with special verbs
   g. with special adjectives
   h. price or value (similar to "description," but the genitive often stands as a single word) (in this section, **pluris**).
4. Exercise for this section.

---

[1]**noster**: "our friend," here used sarcastically.
[2]**ut...caperet**: again, the phraseology of the **senatus consultum ultimum** that Caesar has told us was passed.
[3]**ducem**: Caesar.
[4]**hac parte**: the Pompeians.
[5]**triumphus**: ah, yes, that triumph over the Cilicians which was, in the end, never realized.
[6]**cupide**: ambitiously.
[7]**descriptae sunt**: assigned.
[8]**Capuam**: a major city in Campania, south of Rome.

CAESAR: **The Civil War**
(*De bello civili*)
January 18, 49 BC

1.6 [7] Consul[ar]es, quod ante id tempus accidit numquam, ex urbe proficiscuntur, lictoresque habent in urbe et Capitolio privati contra omnia vetustatis exempla.[9] [8] Tota Italia delectus habentur, arma imperantur, pecuniae a municipiis exiguntur, a fanis tolluntur, omnia divina humanaque iura permiscentur.

Vocabulary

impero, imperare, imperavi, imperatum (1): order up; give orders (with dat.)

tollo, tollere, sustuli, sublatum (irreg.): take away; lift.

permisceo, permiscere, permiscui, permixtum (3): confuse, mix up, throw into chaos

Hints for Translation...

Note the remarkable asyndeton of **Tota Italia... arma...pecuniae...a fanis...omnia** which reflects and emphasizes the final verb, **permiscentur**.

---

[9]**Consules...exempla**: this passage has been obelised, i.e., marked as unresolvably corrupt, in the OCT, deleted from other editions of the text and tortuously explained by commentators. A simple solution presents itself: emend **consules** to **consulares**. Thus, the reference is to Scipio and Domitius, the **consulares**, who fail to have their **imperium** authorized by the people and so are technically **privati**.

Subjective, Possessive, and Objective Genitive

The subjective genitive is properly a subdivision of the possessive genitive, and often indistinguishable from it: e.g., *coniuratio Catilinae.* The subjective genitive is, however, usually so described when it is associated with a verbal noun or with a noun implying activity; then the genitive with that noun can be used to denote the author of the activity. So the phrase *coniuratio Catilinae* could be interpreted, as a subjective genitive, as "Catiline **has started** a conspiracy"; as a possessive genitive, the phrase would be interpreted as "the conspiracy **belongs to** Catiline." One can see — especially from this example — that the author or source of an event may also be regarded as its possessor.

The objective genitive, on the other hand, emphasizes not the author of an activity, but its recipient: *metum Romanorum.* "a fear of the Romans."

When translating, one way to distinguish between the three types is to rephrase the statement:

> **Example: iniuria populi Romani**
>
> Are these injustices caused by the Roman people?
>
> > If yes, then this is a subjective genitive.
>
> Are these injustices committed against the Roman people?
>
> > If yes, then this is an objective genitive.
>
> Do these injustices belong to the Roman people?
>
> > If yes, then this is a possessive genitive.

Uses of the Genitive Case Reviewed in *FRP*

Name	Explanation	Environment Note: no genitive is governed by prepositions	Examples	Grammar Reference
Possession	Indicates the possessor.		**Caesaris vocem audio.** I hear *Caesar's* voice.	B 198; AG 343
Partitive	Notes the whole of which a part is given (i.e., the *whole* is in the genitive).		**Hominum tres sustulit.** She took away three *of the men.*	B 201; AG 346
Subjective	Expresses the agent of verbal action implied in a noun or adjective.		*Filiae amor patris* **magnus est.** A *father's* love of his daughter is great.	B 199; AG 343
Objective	Expresses the recipient of verbal action implied in a noun or adjective.		*Filiae amor* **patris magnus est.** A father's love *of his daughter* is great.	B 200; AG 347-348
Quality	A noun modified by an adjective describes or qualifies.		**Est domina magnae virtutis.** She is a mistress *of great virtue.*	B 203; AG 345
With Verbs	Certain verbs MAY take the genitive. (e.g., memini, obliviscor)		**Ipse sui meminerat.** He was mindful *of himself.* (See B & AG for the full variety of possibilities, which is great)	B 205-212; AG 350-358
With Adjectives	Certain adjectives take the genitive in order to limit them; see also "subjective" and "objective" above.		**Mendicus est peritus obsecrandi.** He is a beggar skilled *in begging.* (For the full variety, see B)	B 204; AG 349
Price/Value	Expresses what something costs or is worth.		**Margarita magni pretii est.** It is a pearl *of great price.*	B 203.4; AG 417

CAESAR: **The Civil War**
(De bello civili)
January 11, 49 BC

1.7 [1] Quibus rebus cognitis Caesar apud milites contionatur.[1] Omnium temporum iniurias inimicorum in se commemorat; a quibus deductum ac depravatum Pompeium queritur invidia atque obtrectatione laudis suae,[2] cuius ipse honori et dignitati semper faverit adiutorque fuerit. [2] Novum in rem publicam introductum exemplum queritur, ut tribunicia intercessio armis notaretur atque opprimeretur, quae superioribus annis armis[3] esset restituta. [3] Sullam nudata omnibus rebus tribunicia potestate tamen intercessionem liberam reliquisse; [4] Pompeium, qui amissa restituisse videatur[4] bona, etiam, quae ante habuerint, ademisse. [5] Quotienscumque sit decretum, darent operam magistratus, ne quid res publica detrimenti caperet, qua voce et quo senatus consulto populus Romanus ad arma sit vocatus, factum in perniciosis legibus, in vi tribunicia, in secessione populi, templis locisque ditioribus occupatis; atque haec superioris aetatis exempla

general seated on his *suggestum*

Vocabulary

contionor, contionari, —, contionatum (dep.) (1): speak at a rally; speak before the troops; harangue
iniuria, -ae (f.): injustice; injury
queror, queri, —, questum (dep.) (3): complain
invidia, -ae (f.): envy
obtrectatio, -onis (f.): disparagement
semper (adv.): always
faveo, favere, favi, fautum (2) (with dat.): favor
novus, -a, -um: new, recent
noto, notare, notavi, notatum (1): repress; mark down; censure
potestas, -tatis (f.): power; permission
amitto, amittere, amisi, amissum (3): lose, mislay
restituo, restituere, restitui, restitutum (3): restore
bonus, -a, -um: good
adimo, adimere, ademi, ademptum (3): take away
magistratus, us (m.): magistrate
detrimentum, -i (n.): damage, harm
voco, vocare, vocavi, vocatum: call; invite; name
vis, vim (gen. not used) (f.): violence, force

Grammar and Syntax

1. Uses of the ablative case, especially the two types below. See the explanatory page (p. 51).
   a. the ablative of separation (**omnibus rebus**) (B 214; AG 400).
   b. the ablative of time within which/duration (**VIIII annis**): often duration of time is expressed with the accusative, but the ablative can do this, too (B 231; AG 423).
2. Genitive of quality (**omnium temporum, superioris aetatis exempla**) (B 203.2; AG 345).
3. Uses of **ne** we have learned so far:
   a. with the subjunctive in subordinate clauses
      (1) negative purpose clauses (B 282; AG 531)
      (2) fearing clauses (B 296.2; AG 564)
      (3) negative substantive noun clause (B 295; cf. AG 563).
   b. independent uses
      (1) intensifier: "indeed"
      (2) **ne ... quidem**: "not even"
      (3) **-ne** enclitic introduces a question with no predisposition to either a "yes" or "no" answer (**nonne** = expects a "yes"; **num** = expects a "no").
4. Exercise for this section.

---

[1] The general addressing his troops was a reality in the ancient world. Think of the scene in *Patton* in which George C. Scott must speak to his assembled men, and you have some sense of the normal situation for the Romans in arms. The general had a **suggestum**, a raised platform, in the center of the legionary camp, from which he could address the men, usually before an important engagement.

[2] **laudis suae**: Caesar's merit.

[3] **annis armis**: there is no sign of corruption in the manuscripts, but some editors deleted the whole phrase "quae...restituta" and others have deleted "armis" on the grounds that some copyist added the word or whole phrase under the influence of carelessness or the preceeding "armis notaretur." But the tribunes ultimately defended their **sacrosanctitas** by the willingness of the plebs to use force to protect their bodily safety. So Caesar is referring back to the early days of the tribunate, when the tribunes had been, according to tradition, defended by arms from the patricians who sought to kill them.

[4] **videatur**: "gave the appearance of having..." The reference is to Pompey's role in the restoration of the tribunes' rights in 70 BC, after Sulla had gutted the office of political importance.

expiata Saturnini[6] atque Gracchorum[7] casibus[8] docet; quarum rerum illo tempore nihil factum, ne cogitatum quidem [: nulla lex promulgata, non cum populo agi coeptum,[9] nulla secessio facta].[10] [6] Hortatur,[11] cuius imperatoris ductu VIIII annis[12] rem publicam felicissime gesserint plurimaque proelia secunda fecerint, omnem Galliam Germaniamque pacaverint, ut eius existimationem dignitatemque ab inimicis defendant. [7] Conclamant legionis XIII, quae aderat, milites (hanc enim initio tumultus[13] evocaverat; reliquae nondum venerant), sese paratos esse imperatoris sui tribunorumque plebis iniurias defendere.[14]

January 12, 49 BC

8. [1] Cognita militum voluntate Ariminum[15] cum ea legione proficiscitur ibique tribunos plebis qui ad eum confugerant, convenit;[16] reliquas legiones ex hibernis evocat et subsequi iubet.

coin of Ariminum

Vocabulary

ne ... quidem (adv.): not even; emphasises the word between the ne and the quidem (B 347.1; 2)
hortor, hortari, —, hortatum (dep.) (1): urge on, encourage
imperator, imperatoris (m.): commander, general
proelium, -i (n.): battle
secundus, -a, -um: successful
initium, -i (n.): beginning
nondum (adv.): not yet

melancholy end of Tiberius Gracchus

---

[6]**Saturnini**: C. Appuleius Saturninus, **tribunus plebis** in 100 BC, when he was killed in rioting.

[7]**Gracchorum**: Ti. Gracchus was killed by a mob in 133 BC; his brother, Gaius, in a riot of 121 BC—however, Caesar stretches things a bit here, for the S.C.U. was first used against Gaius, not Tiberius.

[8]**casibus**: "the fates," that is, the violent deaths of Saturninus and the Gracchi.

[9]**non...coeptum**: "no undertaking was carried out in alliance with the commons."

[10]**nulla...facta**: deleted by some editors of Caesar's text. The difficulty is that the text shifts here unnaturally (according to some) into **oratio recta**.

[11]**Hortatur...**: a complicated sentence. Try reading in this order: **Hortatur ut [imperatoris], cuius ductu VIIII annis rem publicam felicissme gesserint plurimaque proelia secunda fecerint, omnem Galliam Germaniamque pacaverint, eius existimationem dignitatemque ab inimicis defendant**. The **imperatoris** has been attracted inside the relative clause, and the **eius** is repetitious, for emphasis.

[12]**VIIII annis**: 58-50 BC.

[13]**tumultus**: a technical term refering to a disturbance in Italy south of the Alps, as opposed to a **bellum**, a foreign war. Its "beginning" was apparently in December 50, when Caesar realized there would probably be war: in early December the then-consul Marcellus had called upon Pompey to raise an army to defend the state (Plutarch, **Pompeius** 59).

[14]**defendere**: here = ward off, beat off.

[15]**Ariminum**: the first town in Italy, across the Rubicon from Gallia Cisalpina, one of Caesar's provinces.

[16]**convenit**: "awaits."

Plutarch has a dramatic description of this critical moment:

At this time there were with Caesar not more than three hundred cavalry and five thousand infantry, for the rest of his army had been left on the other side of the Alps and was going to be brought over by those whom he had sent to do so. But he realized that the initiation of his undertaking and its first stage did not, for the present, require a large force; that more could be obtained by unexpected boldness and swift seizure of the opportune moment, for the opposing forces would be panicked more readily by him doing something unanticipated than if he were to overpower them by making an attack after due preparation. So he ordered his centurions and officers, with no other weapons except their swords, to occupy the large Gallic city of Ariminum, avoiding as much as possible bloodshed and mayhem. He put Hortensius in charge of this force, while he himself spent the day in public giving his attention to watching the gladiators at their exercises. Then a little before evening he bathed and changed and went into the banqueting hall. After brief conversations with the dinner guests, and just as it was growing dark he got up and left, although he had kind words for some and asked them to wait until he returned. But to a few of his friends he had already given instructions earlier to follow him, not all by the same route, but some by one way and some by another. Caesar himself got into one of the hired carts and first drove along some other road and then turned towards Ariminum. When he came to the river—it is called the Rubicon—which divides Cisalpine Gaul from the rest of Italy, he slowed his course as he took into account the fact that he was coming nearer the awful moment and found himself wavering at the magnitude of his ventures. Then he halted and reflected much, alone and in silence, wavering between his two options. His purpose changed many times during this period. He also discussed his many doubts with those of his friends who were present, including Asinius Pollio. Caesar calculated the suffering which his crossing of the river would bring to humanity, as well as how they would leave to future generations the tale of that crossing. Finally, with some burst of emotional energy, as if freeing himself from calculated reasoning and abandoning himself to whatever the future held, Caesar uttered that expression so often used by those about to commit themselves to desperate and chancy undertakings, "let the die be cast," and rushed headlong across the river.

(Translation by P. Vaughn)

Uses of the Ablative Case Reviewed in FRP

Name	Explanation	Environment	Examples	Grammar Reference
Instrument	The means or THING (not a person) by which something is done.	without preposition	**His libris commoti sunt.** They are aroused by these books.	B 218; AG 409
Agent	The PERSON (not means or thing) by whom something is done.	with preposition **a (ab)** used with passive verbs	**A nostris militibus id factum est.** It was done by our soldiers.	B 216; AG 405
Place Where	Indicates where something takes place.	with preposition **in**	**In domo vivimus.** We lived in the house.	B 228; AG 421
Place from Which	Indicates from what place something occurs.	with one of three prepositions meaning "from": **-(ab)**: away from **-e (ex)**: out of **-de**: down from	**Filium ex oppido eiecit.** He cast the son from the town.	B 229; AG 426
Accompani-ment	A person (rarely, a thing) with whom something is done.	with preposition **cum**	**Cum Cornelia iter facit.** He travels with Cornelia.	B 220; AG 413
Manner	Indicates in what way something is done.	with preposition **cum**	**Cum studio laborat.** He works with zeal.	B 220; AG 412
Attendant Circumstance	A noun modified by an adjective spells out the circumstances of act	without a preposition	**Malis auspiciis bellum gerebat.** He waged the war under bad auspices.	B 221; AG 419, 420.5
Cause	Indicates the cause of an action.	without preposition	**Inopia pecuniae ibi mansit.** She stays there because of a lack of money.	B 219; AG 404
Time When	Indicates time when or within which.	without preposition	**Secundo die veniet.** He will come on the second day.	B 230-231; AG 423
Description	A noun modified by an adjective describes or qualifies someone or something.	without preposition	**Est vir magna virtute.** He is a man of great excellence.	B 224; AG 415
Separation	Some verbs expressing separation take an ablative; other verbs take the dative (see that chart)	without preposition OR with **a (ab)**, depending on the verb	(variety makes a single example unhelpful; see B 214; AG 400)	B 214; AG 400
Ablative Absolute	A noun and (usually) a participle tell something about the rest of the sentence.	without preposition	**Femina laudata, ex aula excedit.** Having praised the woman, he withdrew from the room.	B 227; AG 419-420
Comparison	Used with a comparative noun to express "than"	without preposition	**Frigidior inferis hic est.** It is colder than hell here.	B 217; AG 406
Degree of Difference	Used with an idea of comparison to express "by how much"	without preposition	**Multo stultior est.** He is much stupider.	B 223; AG 414
Specification	Indicates in what respect something is so.	without preposition	**Ingenio melior est.** She is better with respect to intelligence.	B 226; AG 418

CAESAR: **The Civil War**
(*De bello civili*)
January 17, 49 BC

1.8 [2] Eo Lucius Caesar adulescens venit, cuius pater Caesaris erat legatus.[1] Is reliquo sermone confecto, cuius rei[2] causa venerat, habere se a Pompeio ad eum privati officii mandata demonstrat: [3] Velle Pompeium se Caesari purgatum,[3] ne ea, quae rei publicae causa egerit, in suam contumeliam vertat. Semper se rei publicae commoda privatis necessitudinibus habuisse potiora. Caesarem quoque pro sua dignitate debere et studium et iracundiam suam rei publicae dimittere neque adeo graviter irasci inimicis, ut, cum illis nocere se speret, rei publicae noceat. [4] Pauca eiusdem generis addit cum excusatione Pompei coniuncta. Eadem fere atque eisdem verbis praetor Roscius[4] agit cum Caesare sibique Pompeium commemorasse[5] demonstrat.

legatus legionis

Vocabulary

adulescens, adulescentis (m.): "the younger"; young man
mandatum, -i (n.): command; plural = instructions, communications
demonstro, demonstrare, demonstravi, demonstratum (1): point out, explain
contumelia, -ae (f.): insult
verto, vertere, verti, versum (3): turn
commodus, -a, -um: suitable, advantageous
potior, potius: preferable, more important (comparative of potis)
iracunia, -ae (f.): anger
adeo ... ut: so ... that
graviter (adv.): severely
irascor, irasci, —, iratum (dep.) (3): get angry (with dative)
noceo, nocere, nocui, nocitum (2): harm (with dative)
spero, sperare, speravi, speratum (1): hope; hope for
genus, generis (n.): kind; lineage; tribe
excusatio, -onis (f.): apology for; excuse (with gen.)
commemoro, commemorare, commemoravi, commemoratum (1) (dep.): mention, relate

Grammar and Syntax

1. Uses of the dative case: See chart.
   a. dative of reference (**Velle Pompeium se Caesari purgatum**...; **rei publicae**): indicates a person or thing to which an action refers (...Pompey wished himself to be justified *in Caesar's eyes*...) (B 188; AG 376-379).
   b. dative with adjectives (**rei publicae commoda**): adjectives as well as verbs can have an "indirect object" usage to show to whom or to what the implicit action of an adjective applies (B 192; AG 383-385).

continued next page...

---

[1]**Lucius Iulius Caesar** the father was consul in 64 BC, Caesar's legate in Gaul from 52-49 BC, and remained neutral in the civil war; the family is only distantly related to the more famous Iulii Caesares. The son had done nothing to distinguish himself, but here seems to be used because of his (distant) relationship to Caesar to carry a message.

[2]**cuius rei causa**: that is, "for the sake of which thing."

[3]**purgatum**: **purgo** = "exculpate," "justify." **se** is Pompey; the dative expresses the person to whom he wishes himself justified, in whose eyes he wishes to be exculpated.

[4]Remember that at *BC* 1.3.6 Calpurnius Piso, Caesar's father-in-law, was also to be sent on an embassy to Caesar. For some reason, he has changed his mind, for he is not mentioned here—unless he went on a separate mission, not noticed here by Caesar.

[5]**commemorasse**: syncopated form.

1.9 [1] Quae res etsi nihil ad levandas iniurias pertinere videbantur, tamen idoneos nactus homines per quos ea quae vellet ad eum perferrentur, petit ab utroque, quoniam Pompei mandata ad se detulerint, ne graventur sua quoque ad eum postulata deferre, si parvo labore magnas controversias tollere atque omnem Italiam metu liberare possint.

Vocabulary

levo, levare, levavi, levatum (1): lessen, lighten
pertineo, pertinere, pertinui, pertentum (2): concern, have to do with (with ad)
idoneus, -a, -um: suitable
nanciscor, nancisci, —, na(n)ctum (dep.) (3): chance upon, obtain
perfero, perferre, pertuli, perlatum (irreg.): endure to the end; bring news
defero, deferre, detuli, delatum (irreg.): carry away; report
gravor, gravari, —, gravatum (1) (dep.): refuse; feel annoyed at
parvus, -a, -um: small, little
labor, laboris (m.): toil, work, effort
metus, -us (m.): fear

Civis Romanus sum.

Grammar and Syntax, continued

c. dative of indirect object (the most frequent usage)
   (1) with transitive verbs (**sibi**) (B 187.I; AG 362-65)
   (2) with intransitive verbs (**irasci inimicis**) (B 187.II; cf. AG 366-69)
d. dative of purpose or tendency (**iracundiam suam rei publicae dimittere**: "...put away his anger for the sake of the community..."). (B 191; AG 382)
e. double dative (already reviewed) (B 191.2; AG 369)
f. dative of possession: constructed with a form of **esse** (B 190; AG 373)
g. dative of agent: mostly with the passive periphrastic (already reviewed) (B 189; AG 374)
h. dative with specific verbs (**illis nocere...rei publicae noceat** (B 187; AG 367, 370)
i. dative of separation is used with verbs compounded of ab, de, ex, and ad when a person is involved or, less frequently, a thing (B 188.2.; AG 381).
2. Exercise for this section.

A general before his troops

Uses of the Dative Case Reviewed in *FRP*

Name	Explanation	Environment NOTE: no dative is governed by prepositions	Examples	Grammar Reference
Indirect Object	The person to whom something is done, given, or said		**Pompeio haec narravit.** He told these things to Pompey.	B 187; AG 362-365
With Verbs	Some verbs are constructed with the dative		(variety makes a single example unhelpful)	B 187.III; AG 367, 370
Reference	Denotes the person or thing some action refers to.		**Fortunam magnam nobis fecit.** He made a great fortune for us.	B 188; AG 376-381
Advantage/ Disadvantage ("Ethical")	Expresses a loose connection between a person and a clause		**Mihi tota perdita sunt.** As far as I am concerned, all is lost.	B 188.2.b; AG 380
Separation	Expresses separation from a person or (less often) thing	verbs compounded of **ab, ad, de, ex**	**Oves lupo eripuit.** He snatched the sheep from the wolf.	B 188.2d AG 381
Agent	Indicates personal agency.	usual with gerundive; less commonly with passive	**Carthago nobis delenda est.** Carthage must be destroyed by us.	B 189; AG 374
Possession	Indicates who or what owns something.	with **esse** only	**Sella est ei.** It is her chair.	B 190; AG 373
Purpose	Indicates the reason or purpose for something.		**Legiones praesidio conscribent.** They draft legions for their protection.	B 191; AG 382
Double Dative	A dative of purpose combines with a personal indirect object.		**Panem eis cibo dat.** He gives bread to them for food.	B 191.2; AG 382 & note
With Adjectives	Some adjectives are constructed with the dative		(variety makes a single example unhelpful; see B, AG)	B 192; AG 383-384

Cæsar as an Author.

CAESAR: **The Civil War**
(*De bello civili*)
January 17, 49 BC

1.9 [2] Sibi semper primam fuisse dignitatem vitaque potiorem. Doluisse se, quod populi Romani beneficium[1] sibi[2] per contumeliam ab inimicis extorqueretur, ereptoque semestri imperio[3] in urbem retraheretur, cuius absentis rationem[4] haberi proximis comitiis populus iussisset. [3] Tamen hanc iacturam honoris sui rei publicae causa aequo animo tulisse; cum litteras ad senatum miserit, ut omnes ab exercitibus discederent,[5] ne id quidem impetravisse.[6] [4] Tota Italia delectus haberi, retineri legiones II quae ab se simulatione Parthici belli sint abductae,[7] civitatem esse in armis. Quonam haec omnia nisi ad suam perniciem pertinere?[8]

Vocabulary

doleo, dolere, dolui, dolitum (2): hurt; take offence
extorqueo, extorquere, extorsi, extortum (3): wrench, wrest (from); extort
semestris, semestre: half a year
retraho, retrahere, retraxi, retractum (3): drag back
ratio, rationis (f.): reason; plan; account; here = candidacy for office
iactura, -ae (f.): loss, sacrifice
aequus, -a, -um: calm, fair
litterae, litterarum (f.): letter, message; literature
simulatio, -onis (f.): pretense
quonam (adv.): where (i.e., whither); to what end
pernicies, perniciei (f.): ruin, destruction

Grammar and Syntax

1. Comparison of adjectives (**potiorem**)(B 71-75; AG 120) & adverbs (**facilius, proprius**) (B 76-77; AG 218). The terms used are the "positive" degree (the basic application of the adjective), the "comparative" degree (the greater of two things), and the "superlative" degree (the greatest of three or more things).

   a. Forms of comparison of regular adjectives (see summary).

     (1) remember: comparative forms are adjectives of TWO endings, one for M&F, one for N. Unlike most third declension adjectives, they are NOT i-stem. Thus, the ablative singular is -e, not -i; the genitive plural is -um, not -ium; the neuter nominative and accusative plural is -a, not -ia.

     (2) ending of the positive and superlative forms are those of the first and second declension, and are perfectly regular.

continued on next page....

---

[1]**beneficium**: the Law of the Ten Tribunes (52 BC) by which Caesar was allowed to stand for the consulship of 48 BC (i.e., at the elections held in summer, 49 BC) **in absentia**.

[2]**sibi**: dative of separation (see section 21).

[3]**semestri imperio**: once elected, Caesar would be protected from prosecution; the "half year" which he complains about is the time between middle July, when he would have to give up his command and come to Rome to stand in person for the consulship in elections, and the end of 49, until which time he would have been able to hold his command, if he were allowed to stand for the consulship **in absentia**.

[4]**absentis rationem**: **ratio** = candidacy for office; his "right" to become a candidate for office while absent from Rome is another **beneficium** bestowed by the Law of the Ten Tribunes.

[5]Curio reported this offer to Cicero in December, 48: "fert tamen (Caesar) illam condicionem ut ambo exercitus tradant" (Cicero **Ad Familiares**. 8.14.2).

[6]**litteras...impetravisse**: an echo of the opening lines of the **BC**.

[7]**legiones II**: those Parthian legions, *again*.

[8]**pertinere**: historical infinitive.

9. [5] Sed tamen ad omnia se descendere paratum atque omnia pati rei publicae causa. Proficiscatur Pompeius in suas provincias,[9] ipsi exercitus dimittant; discedant in Italia omnes ab armis, metus e civitate tollatur, libera comitia atque omnis res publica senatui populoque Romano permittatur.[10][6] Haec quo[11] facilius certisque condicionibus fiant et iure iurando sanciantur, aut ipse propius accedat aut se patiatur accedere; fore, uti per colloquia omnes controversiae componantur.[12]

Vocabulary

descendo, descendere, descendi, descensum (3): descend, sink

permitto, permittere, permisi, permissum (3): permit, entrust to (with dat.)

condicio, condicionis (f.): terms, condition(s)

iuro, iurare, iuravi, iuratum (1): swear; swear by

sancio, sancire, sanxi, sanctum (4): consecrate, make inviolable

aut...aut (correlative): either...or

accedo, accedere, accessi, accessum (3): approach; to be added to (with ad, in)

colloquium, -i (n.): conference

compono, componere, composui, compositum (3): arrange, settle

Grammar and Syntax, continued

  b. Ways to express comparison
    (1) with the ablative of comparison (**vita potiorem**)(B 217; AG 406)
    (2) with quam (B 217.2; AG 407).
  c. Forms of comparison of adverbs **facilius...proprius**) (see summary).
  d. meaning of the comparative forms
    (1) there is no special meaning for the positive form
    (2) the comparative form can mean "too," "rather"
    (3) the superlative can mean "very."
2. Exercises for this section.

coin with portrait of Pompey the Great

---

[9]**suas provincias**: that is, to the two Spanish provinces.

[10]**libera...Romano**: Caesar continues to represent his proposal as designed to free the Romans from the coercive threat of the Pompeians; of course the Pompeians thought that Caesar was the threat... Note how the asyndeton here—the sequential statement of events without a conjunction—makes the narrative rapid and effective.

[11]**quo**: think of this as "ut eo;" the **eo** is an ablative of degree of difference with **facilius** = "in order that these things (**haec**) might be done by this much the more easily...," i.e., "the more easily."

[12]**componantur**: Caesar continues to be convinced that he could solve all problems if Pompey would just meet him, face-to-face. This is the LAST thing the Pompeians want, given Caesar's proof of his persuasive powers over Pompey before.

Comparison of Adjectives
(B 71-75; AG 120-131)

Latin, like English, has three basic levels of description:
- positive (the basic quality: "long" — "a long road")
- comparative (more than the basic quality, often in relation to another entity: "longer, rather long, too long" — "a rather long road," "a road too long," "a road longer than the river")
- superlative (a very high level of the basic quality: "longest, very long, most long" — "the longest road")

In addition, Latin offers a fourth level of description by the addition of *quam* to the superlative: "as long as possible, the longest possible" — "the longest possible road"

> Note: *Quam* can be used with all levels of comparison, with varying results:
>
> **Quam** longa via est! "How long the road is!"
> Illa via est longior **quam** haec. "That road is longer than this."
> In viam **quam** longissimam ingressi sumus. "We embarked upon the longest possible road."

Review the formation of the comparative and superlative adjective (remember to build on the **stem** of the positive degree):

Positive	Comparative	Superlative
longus, -a, -um	longior (m/f), longius (n)	longissimus, -a, -um
dulcis, -e	dulcior, dulcius	dulcissimus, -a, -um
pulcher, -a, -um	pulchrior, pulchrius	pulcherrimus, -a, -um*

> *adjectives ending in **-er** in the *masculine nominative* form of the positive degree form their superlative by adding **-rimus, -a, -um** to the entire positive degree masculine nominative form

Six third declension adjectives ending in **-lis** in the masculine and feminine form their superlative by adding **-limus, -a, -um** to the stem of the adjective:

facilis, -e	facilior, facilius	facillimus, -a, -um
difficilis, -e	difficilior, difficilius	difficillimus, -a, -um
similis, -e	similior, similius	simillimus, -a, -um
dissimilis, -e	dissimilior, dissimilius	dissimillimus,-a, -um
gracilis, -e	gracilior, gracilius	gracillimus,-a, -um
humilis, -e	humilior, humilius	humillimus,-a, -um

> Note that the comparative degree of these six adjectives is regular; the superlative of all other -lis adjectives is formed in the "usual" way, by adding **-issimus, -a, -um**, e.g. naturalis, -e — naturalissimus, -a, -um

REVIEW the comparison of irregular adjectives:

bonus, -a, -um	melior, melius	optimus, -a, -um
malus, -a, -um	peior, peius	pessimus, -a, -um
magnus, -a, -um	maior, maius	maximus, -a, -um
parvus, -a, -um	minor, minus	minimus, -a, -um
multus, -a, -um	___, plus	plurimus, -a, -um
[prae, pro]	prior, prius	primus, -a, -um
superus, -a, -um	superior, superius	summus, -a, -um
		supremus, -a, -um

Comparison of Adverbs
(B 76-77; AG 218)

As in English, in Latin there are three degrees of comparison:
- the positive (no comparison);
- the comparative (two items compared);
- the superlative (three or more items compared).

Degree	Formation	Examples
Positive	simple adverb without change	**longe** **fortiter**
Comparative	neuter singular comparative of the adjective: add **-ius** to the positive stem	**longius** **fortius**
Superlative	superlative of the adjective: add **-e** to the superlative stem	**longissime** **fortissime** **facillime** **acerrime**

Some adverbs are not derived from adjectives; nevertheless, they follow the same comparison formation: **saepe, saepius, saepissime.**

IRREGULAR COMPARISON

Category		Positive	Comparative	Superlative
Specific irregulars				
	bene	bene	melius	optime
	male	male	peius	pessime
	parum	parum	minus	minime
	magnopere	magnopere	magis	maxime
	multum	multum	plus	plurimum

CAESAR: **The Civil War**
(*De bello civili*)
January 25-27, 49 BC

1.10 [1] Acceptis mandatis Roscius a Caesare Capuam pervenit ibique consules Pompeiumque invenit;[1] postulata Caesaris renuntiat. [2] Illi deliberata re respondent scriptaque ad eum mandata remittunt, quorum haec erat summa: [3] Caesar in Galliam[2] reverteretur, Arimino excederet[3], exercitus dimitteret;[4] quae si fecisset, Pompeium in Hispanias iturum. [4] Interea, quoad fides esset data, Caesarem facturum, quae polliceretur, non intermissuro consules Pompeiumque delectus.

Julius Caesar

Vocabulary

accipio, accipere, accepi, acceptum (3): receive
pervenio, pervenire, perveni, perventum (4): come through; arrive
invenio, invenire, inveni, inventum (4): find, come upon
renuntio, renuntiare, renuntiavi, renuntiatum (1): report, announce
respondeo, respondere, respondi, responsum (2): reply, answer
scribo, scribere, scripsi, scriptum (3): write (to = ad)
remitto, remittere, remisi, remissum (3): send back; slacken
summa, -ae (f.): chief point, substance
revertor, reverti, —, reversum (dep.) (3): return, go back
excedo, excedere, excessi, excessum (3): withdraw, depart
interea (adv.): meanwhile
quoad: until
fides, fidei (f.): pledge; trust, belief; honor, loyalty; assurance
intermitto, intermittere, intermisi, intermissum (3): interrupt

Grammar and Syntax

1. Uses of the accusative case: See chart and note especially:
  a. accusative as direct object (**consules Pompeiumque, postulata**, etc.) (B 172-176; AG 387-389)
  b. accusative in indirect discourse: subject of the infinitive (**Pompeium, Caesarem, consules**, etc. B 329-331; AG 580-81)
  c. "double" accusative (B 177-178; AG 391-96)
  d. extent of time and space (B 181)
  e. accusative of place to which (B 182; AG 426-27)
    (1) with preposition (**in Galliam, in Hispanias**, etc.)
    (2) without preposition (towns, small islands, and **domus**) (**Capuam, Arretium**)
  f. accusative after prepositions (**ad eum**, etc.)
2. Forms and use of the locative case (**Arimini**) (B 232: AG 427).
3. Exercise for this section.

---

[1]Pompey and the consuls have gone to Campania to raise and train troops. Other sources tell us that the meeting actually took place at Teandum Sidicium, near Capua (Cicero ad Att. 7.13B.3), but Caesar is using the well known, larger town for dramatic effect.
[2]**in Galliam**: i.e., back across the Rubicon, into his designated province.
[3]**Arimino**: on the "Italian" side of the Rubicon, so demanded here to emphasize that Caesar had to withdraw back across the Rubicon
[4]**exercitus dimitteret**: Caesar had officially been replaced as military governor of his provinces by Domitius Ahenobarbus; thus, Caesar had no right to maintain armies anymore.

11. [1] Erat iniqua condicio postulare, ut Caesar Arimino excederet atque in provinciam reverteretur, ipsum et provincias et legiones alienas tenere; exercitum Caesaris velle dimitti, delectus habere;[5] [2] polliceri, se in provinciam iturum, neque ante quem diem iturus sit definire, ut si peracto consulatu Caesaris non profectus esset, nulla tamen mendacii religione obstrictus videretur.[6] [3] Tempus vero colloquio non dare[7] neque accessurum polliceri magnam pacis desperationem afferebat. [4] Itaque ab Arimino Marcum Antonium cum cohortibus V Arretium mittit; ipse Arimini cum duabus [legionibus] subsistit ibique delectum habere instituit; Pisaurum, Fanum, Anconam singulis cohortibus occupat.[8]

Vocabulary

iniquus, -a, -um: unfair, unjust
perago, peragere, peregi, peractum (3): complete
mendacium, -i (n.): lie
religio, religionis (f.): religious scruple
obstringo, obstringere, obstrinxi, obstrictum (3): bind; put under obligation
desperatio, desperationis (f.): despair
affero, affere, attuli, allatum (irreg.): bring
subsisto, subsistere, substiti, — (3): take a stand
singuli, -ae, -a: one each

Caesar and Pompey in January, 49 BC

Pompey

---

[5]**velle...habere**: note how the the two opposite things, Caesar being required to give up his army and his enemies continuing to recruit theirs, is emphasized by asyndeton.

[6]**obstrictus**: i.e., he would not have violated any moral law.

[7]**dare...polliceri**: the infinitives are the subject of the verb **afferebat**.

[8]**occupat**: a nice propaganda coup: in fact Caesar had seized these towns the week immediately after crossing the Rubicon, as Pompey by now (January 25) knew. Cicero, who fled Rome on January 18 (ad Att. 9.10.4), knew already then that these towns had fallen. For the chronology of the Caesar/Roscius mission to mesh with the time required for the journeys up and down Italy, these men would have had to have left Rome about January 14th at latest. Thus, in sending Caesar/Roscius, Pompey was trying to negotiate, while Caesar was seizing towns. Not exactly the picture Caesar gives us here...

12. [1] Interea certior factus Iguvium[9] Thermum praetorem[10] cohortibus V tenere, oppidum munire, omniumque esse Iguvinorum optimam erga se voluntatem, Curionem[11] cum tribus cohortibus, quas Pisauri et Arimini habebat, mittit. [2] Cuius adventu cognito diffisus[12] municipii voluntati Thermus cohortes ex urbe reducit et profugit.[13] Milites in itinere ab eo discedunt ac domum revertuntur. [3] Curio summa omnium voluntate Iguvium recipit. Quibus rebus cognitis confisus municipiorum voluntatibus Caesar cohortes legionis XIII ex praesidiis deducit Auximumque[14] proficiscitur; quod oppidum Attius[15] cohortibus introductis tenebat delectumque toto Piceno circummissis senatoribus habebat.

Vocabulary

munio, munire, munivi, munitum (4): wall around, defend; make (a road)

optimus, -a, -um: best

tres, tria: three

diffido, diffidere, —, diffisum (3) (semi-deponent): lose confidence in (with dat.)

reduco, reducere, reduxi, reductum (3): lead back

domus, -us or -i (f.): house, home

recipio, recipere, recepi, receptum (3): receive; take duly

confido, -fidere, -fisum (3): be confident in

Mark Antony

---

[9]Also in Umbria, strategically located.

[10]This is Quintus Minucius Thermus, who served as propraetor for Asia from 52-50 BC, tribune of plebs in 62. Several letters of Cicero addressed to him remain, *ad fam.* XVI, 53-57.

[11]Gaius Scribonius Curio, quaestor in 54, tribune in 50 BC and elected as an opponent to Caesarian policies. He joined with Caesar after his tribunate was over (because he was bribed?) and after the failure of the senate to implement a disarmanent resolution for which he had won support. Much of Book II of the *Bellum Civile* is devoted to Curio's exploits and ultimate death in Africa fighting the forces of King Juba.

[12]This implication of lack of popular support is underscored by the contrast between **diffisus** (Thermus) and **confisus...Caesar**.

[13]As so often with the Pompeian forces. Here Caesar indicates to us, subtly and for the first time, that the position of Pompey, and therefore of the Senate, is not a strong one. This region of Italy had been believed to be strongly pro-Pompeian.

[14]Another strategic location, in Picenum, north and east of Rome.

[15]Publius Attius Varus, who held governorship of Africa sometime before 51 BC; he proved to be one of Pompey's strongest commanders.

Uses of the Accusative Case Reviewed in *FRP*

Name	Explanation	Environment	Examples	Grammar Reference
Direct object	The person or thing affected by the action of the verb.	transitive verbs may take an object	**Coronam Caesari donavit.** He gave the crown to Caesar.	B 172-176; AG 387
Double (1)	The person or thing affected + a predicate accusative (noun or adjective)	verbs of making, choosing, calling, showing	**Et id bonum vocavit.** And he called it good.	B 177; AG 392
Double (2)	The one person + one thing affected	verbs of requesting, demanding, teaching, inquiring, warning, concealing, etc.	**Eam panem orat.** He begs her for bread. **Coronam Caesarem postulat.** He demands a crown for Caesar.	B 178; AG 396
Duration of time or extent of space	Extent through space or over time	without preposition or with **per**	**Multos annos studebamus.** We studied over many years. **Iter viginti milia pasuum fecimus.** We made a journey of twenty miles.	B 181; AG 423-425
Place to which (limit of motion)	(1) most places (2) towns, small islands, and peninsulas	preposition **ad** (= goal or toward) without preposition	**Ad Californiam numquam ivimus.** We never went to California. **Cretam appropinquabamus.** We were approaching Crete.	B 182.1; AG 426 B 182.2-3; AG 427
Exclamation	Expresses an emotional outburst	without preposition	**O bonam filiam meam!** Oh my fine daughter!	B 183; AG 397d
Indirect discourse (accusative and infinitive)	Subject of the infinitive is in the accusative	verbs of speaking, etc. (see indirect discourse chart)	**Dico eum legatum esse.** I say that he is an envoy.	B 184; AG 397, 580
Object of a preposition	Many prepositions take the accusative	with preposition	**Mulieres in urbem adducit.** He leads the women into the town.	—

CAESAR: **The Civil War**
(*De bello civili*)
January ??, 49 BC

1.13 [1] Adventu Caesaris cognito decuriones[1] Auximi ad Attium Varum frequentes conveniunt; docent, sui iudicii[2] rem non esse; neque se neque reliquos municipes pati posse C(aium) Caesarem imperatorem, bene de republica meritum, tantis rebus gestis, oppido moenibusque[3] prohiberi; proinde habeat[4] rationem posteritatis et periculi sui.[5] [2] Quorum oratione permotus Varus praesidium, quod introducerat, ex oppido educit ac profugit. [3] Hunc[6] ex primo ordine[7] pauci Caesaris consecuti milites consistere coegerunt. [4] Commisso proelio deseritur a suis Varus; nonnulla pars militum domum[8] discedit; reliqui ad Caesarem perveniunt, atque una cum iis deprensus L(ucius) Pupius, primi pili centurio,[9] adducitur, qui hunc eundem ordinem in exercitum Cn(aei) Pompei antea duxerat. [5] At Caesar milites Attianos collaudat, Pupium dimittit, Auximatibus agit gratias seque eorum facti memorem fore[10] pollicetur.[11]

Vocabulary

neque...neque: neither...nor
municeps, municipis (m.): townsman, citizens of a municipium.
bene (adv.): well
mereor, mereri, —, meritum (dep.) (2): deserve; serve (in army)
oppidum, -i (n.): town
moenia, ium (n. pl.): town wall
prohibeo, prohibere, prohibui, prohibitum (2): hinder, prevent
proinde (adv.): accordingly
posteritas, posteritatis (f.): posterity, future generations
educo, educere, eduxi, eductum (3): lead out
consequor, consequi, —, consecutum (dep.) (3): pursue, over-take, get
consisto, consistere, constiti, constitum (3): take a stand
committo, committere, commisi, commissum (3): join; entrust
desero, deserere, deserui, desertum (3): desert
deprendo, deprendere, deprendi, deprensum (3): capture, seize
adduco, adducere, adduci, adductum (3): bring forward, lead up
antea (adv.): previously
memor, memoris: mindful

Grammar and Syntax

1. All pronouns (personal, reflexive, possessive, intensive, inter-rogative, demonstrative, and indefinite); see charts
   a. relative pronouns ("Who, whom, whose, which, what, that, as") (B 250-251; AG 147, 303-308). Review the basic usage and forms
      (1) relative pronouns relate subordinate clauses to a main clause
      (2) relative pronouns agree in gender and number with its antecedent, in case with its role in the subordinate clause
      (3) relative pronouns are often "resumptive;" that is, they begin a sentence, tying that sentence to the preceding one. These are best translated as "hic, haec, hoc"="this, that", not "which, what"

continued next page

---

[1] The members of the town councils of the Roman municipalities.
[2] Genitive of possession, used predicatively (B 198; AG 343.*b*).
[3] **oppido** and **moenibus** are ablatives expressing separation with **prohiberi** (B 214; AG 400).
[4] The subject is **Varus**; the subjunctive is jussive (B 275; AG 439).
[5] **posteritatis** ("future") and **periculi sui** are objective genitives with **rationem** (B 200; AG 348).
[6] I.e., **Varum.**
[7] The **primus ordo** is the "front ranks," implying the first century of the first cohort.
[8] accusative of place to which, without a preposition (B 182, AG 427.2).
[9] I.e., the highest ranking centurion in a legion.
[10] **fore = futurum esse** (B, p.57, n.3; AG 170.a).
[11] The famous Caesarian **clementia** is being illustrated here.

14. [1] Quibus rebus Romam nuntiatis[12] tantus repente terror invasit, ut, cum Lentulus consul[13] adaperiendum aerarium venisset ad pecuniam Pompeio ex senatus consulto proferendam, protinus aperto sanctiore aerario[14] ex urbe profugeret. Caesarem enim adventare iam iamque et adesse eius equites falso nuntiabantur. [2] Hunc Marcellus collega et plerique magistratus consecuti sunt.

Vocabulary

nuntio, nuntiare, nuntiavi, nuntiatum (1): report, announce
repente (adv.): suddenly
invado, invadere, invasi, invasum (3): rush upon; take possession
aperio, aperire, aperui, apertum (4): open; reveal
aerarium, -i (n.): state treasury
pecunia, -ae (f.): money
proferro, proferre, protuli, prolatus (irreg.): bring out
protinus (adv.): suddenly; immediately
iam (adv.): (by) now, already; iam iamque = immediately
eques, equitis (m.): rider; cavalryman, equestrian
falsus, -a, -um: false, incorrect, wrong

Grammar and Syntax

2. Reflexive pronoun **se** and adjective **suus, -a, -um** (B 244.1.II, II; AG 144, 145):
   a. direct reflexive pronouns (**in se commemorat; sese paratos esse imperatoris sui**): the reference is to the subject of the clause, whether main or subordinate
   b. direct reflexive pronouns (**obtrectatione laudis suae**): the reference is to the subject of the *main clause* even though the pronoun is in the subordinate clause (in this example, **suae** refers to Caesar, not to Pompey).
3. Exercises for this section.

temple of Saturn

---

[12]Not, as it would appear initially, the immediately preceding events, but the occupation of the cities by Caesarian troops.

[13]Lucius Cornelius Lentulus Crus, consul in 49 BC with Gaius Claudius Marcellus (14.2). Lentulus was a die-hard anti-Caesarian; after the Battle of Pharsalus he fled to Egypt where he met his end the day after Pompey. Caesar claimed that Lentulus was driven by desperation over his debt, and even among friends he seems to have been regarded as lazy, pretentious and indulgent.

[14]The **aerarium** was in the Temple of Saturn; the inner ("more sacred") treasury was a special reserve fund of gold to be used only in the most dire emergencies. Lentulus does not seem to have taken the money, or at least is not accused of such, but to have left this "inner sanctum" open, in which state it was discovered by Caesar.

Pronouns (B 84-B 92, AG 142-143)

PERSONAL PRONOUNS: the person speaking (first person); the person spoken to (second person); the person spoken about (third person) (B 84)

Number	Case	1st Person	2nd Person	3rd Person
		I, me	*you*	*he, she, it, him, her*
	nominative	ego	tu	is, ea, id
singular	genitive	mei	tui	eius, eius, eius
	dative	mihi	tibi	ei, ei, ei
	accusative	me	te	eum, eam, id
	ablative	me	te	eo, ea, eo
		we, us	*you*	*they, them*
	nominative	nos	vos	ei, eae, ea
plural	genitive	nostrum/nostri	vestrum/vestri	eorum, earum, eorum
	dative	nobis	vobis	eis, eis, eis
	accusative	nos	vos	eos, eas, ea
	ablative	nobis	vobis	eis, eis, eis

DIRECT REFLEXIVE PRONOUNS: (refers to the subject of the clause in which it stands; most common) (B 85, AG 144)

INDIRECT REFLEXIVE PRONOUNS: (refers to the subject of the main clause, rather unusual)

Number	Case	1st Person	2nd Person	3rd Person
		myself	*yourself*	*himself, herself, itself*
	nominative	—–	—–	—–
singular	genitive	mei	tui	sui
	dative	mihi	tibi	sibi
	accusative	me	te	se or sese
	ablative	me	te	se or sese
		ourselves	*yourselves*	*themselves*
	nominative	—–	—–	—–
plural	genitive	nostrum/nostri	vestrum/vestri	sui
	dative	nobis	vobis	sibi
	accusative	nos	vos	se or sese
	ablative	nobis	vobis	se or sese

POSSESSIVE PRONOUNS: shows possession; note that the forms are those of the first and second declension adjectives (1st & 2nd persons), and the genitive of **is, ea, id** (3rd person); these are actually adjectives and declined like them (B 86, AG 145)

	1st Person	2nd Person	3rd Person
	my, mine	*your, yours*	*his, her, hers, its*
singular	meus, -a, -um	tuus, -a, -um	eius: used non-reflexively
	our, ours	*your, yours*	*their, theirs*
plural	noster, -tra, -trum	vester, -tra, -trum	eorum, earum, eorum: used non-reflexively
singular & plural			suus, -a, -um: used only reflexively

Note: these can all be used as reflexive adjectives as well.

DEMONSTRATIVE PRONOUNS

For declensions of these, see B 87, AG 146:

hic, haec, hoc (*this*)

iste, ista, istud (*that, that of yours*)

is, ea, id (*this, that*)

idem, eadem, idem (*the same*)

ille, illa, illud (*that*)

INTENSIVE PRONOUN

For declensions of these, see B 88, AG 146:

ipse, ipsa, ipsum (*I myself, you yourself, she herself*, etc.)

RELATIVE PRONOUN
(B 89, AG147)

	Case	Masculine	Feminine	Neuter
singular	nominative	qui	quae	quod
	genitive	cuius	cuius	cuius
	dative	cui	cui	cui
	accusative	quem	quam	quod
	ablative	quo	qua	quo
plural	nominative	qui	quae	quae
	genitive	quorum	quarum	quorum
	dative	quibus	quibus	quibus
	accusative	quos	quas	quae
	ablative	quibus	quibus	quibus

INTERROGATIVE PRONOUN
(B 90, AG 148)

	Case	Masculine & Feminine	Feminine	Neuter
singular	nominative	quis		quid
	genitive	cuius		cuius
	dative	cui		cui
	accusative	quem		quid
	ablative	quo		quo
plural	nominative	qui	quae	quae
	genitive	quorum	quarum	quorum
	dative	quibus	quibus	quibus
	accusative	quos	quas	quae
	ablative	quibus	quibus	quibus

INDEFINITE PRONOUNS

Latin has many ways to express indefiniteness with pronouns.

Group 1:

quis, quid (*anyone, anything*)

aliquis, aliquid (*someone, something*)

quisquam, quidquam (*anyone, anything*)

quispiam, quidpiam (*anyone, anything*)

quisque, quidque (*each*)

These are all declined like quis, quid; any prefix or suffix remains unchanged:

	Case	Masculine & Feminine	Feminine	Neuter
	nominative	quis		quid
	genitive	cuius		cuius
singular	dative	cui		cui
	accusative	quem		quid
	ablative	quo		quo
	nominative	qui	quae	quae
	genitive	quorum	quarum	quorum
plural	dative	quibus	quibus	quibus
	accusative	quos	quas	quae
	ablative	quibus	quibus	quibus

Group 2:

quidam, quaedam, quiddam (a certain person or thing)
quivis, quaevis, quidvis (anyone, anything you wish)
quilibet, quaelibet, quidlibet (anyone, anything you wish)

These are all declined like qui, quae, quod except that quid is used instead of quod; any suffix remains unchanged:

	Case	Masculine	Feminine	Neuter
	nominative	quidam	quaedam	quiddam
	genitive	cuiusdam	cuiusdam	cuiusdam
singular	dative	cuidam	cuidam	cuidam
	accusative	quendam	quandam	quiddam (quoddam)
	ablative	quodam	quadam	quodam
	nominative	quidam	quaedam	quaedam
	genitive	quorundam	quarundam	quorundam
plural	dative	quibusdam	quibusdam	quibusdam
	accusative	quosdam	quasdam	quaedam
	ablative	quibusdam	quibusdam	quibusdam

CAESAR: **The Civil War** (*De bello civili*)
Late January-Early February, 49 BC

1.14 [3] Cn(aeus) Pompeius pridie eius diei ex urbe profectus iter ad legiones habebat, quas, a Caesare acceptas, in Apulia hibernorum causa disposuerat. [4] Delectus circa urbem intermittuntur: nihil citra Capuam tutum esse omnibus videtur. Capuae primum sese confirmant et colligunt delectumque colonorum, qui lege Iulia[1] Capuam deducti erant, habere instituunt; gladiatoresque,[2] quos ibi Caesar in ludo habebat,[3] ad forum productos Lentulus spe libertatis confirmat atque his equos attribuit et se sequi iussit; [5] quos, postea monitus ab suis quod ea res omnium iudicio reprehendebatur, circum familias[4] conventus Campaniae[5] custodiae causa distribuit.

15. [1] Auximo[6] Caesar progressus omnem agrum Picenum percurrit. Cunctae earum regionum praefecturae[7] libentissimis animis eum recipiunt exercitumque eius omnibus rebus iuvant.

Vocabulary

pridie (adv.): the day before (+ gen.)
accipio, accipere, accepi, acceptum (3): receive
citra: with acc.: this side of, the near side of
colligo, colligere, collegi, collectum (3): bring together, collect
deduco, deducere, deduxi, deductum (3): lead to
ludus, -i (m.): training center for gladiators
attribuo, attribuere, attribui, attributum (3): give, assign, allot
moneo, monere, monui, monitum (2): warn, advise
iudicium, -i (n.): judgement, opinion
circum: with acc.: around, about
conventus, -us (m.): gathering, assembly
custodia, -ae (f.): guard, surveillance
progredior, progredi, —, progressum (dep.) (3): advance
ager, agri (m.): land or territory of a community; farm
percurro, percurrere, percucurri, percursum (3): speed through
cunctus, -a, -um: the entire, altogether, all
libens, -entis: free, willing
iuvo, iuvare, iuvi, iutum (1): help, benefit; delight

Grammar and Syntax

1. Demonstrative adjectives (**hic, haec hoc; is, ea, id**, etc.). These have the same endings as the demonstrative pronouns. See the pronoun charts on pages 65-67.
2. Continue the review of all pronouns.
3. Exercises for this section.

gladiators (from a painting at Pompeii)

---

[1] When Caesar was consul in 59 BC he sponsored a law (**lex Iulia**) which offered land to veterans, among them Pompey's veterans from his Eastern campaigns, to settle in the Campanian region.

[2] Another indication of the desperation or foolishness of Lentulus; arming slaves, and gladiators at that, was viewed as inappropriate for many reasons, not least of which was the memory of the revolt of Spartacus only 23 years before. The reaction to Lentulus' plan is expressed in section 5, **reprehendebatur.**

[3] Many members of the upper classes maintained private gladiatorial schools, to make available "entertainers" for the games which Roman office holders were expected to stage.

[4] **familias**: these are establishments of slave-gladiators; the **ludus** is the place where gladiators are trained while the **familia** is the group of gladiators themselves. These **familiae** would be secure places to send these particular gladiators, as they would have the necessary security measures already in place.

[5] "The Campanian Citizen Cooperative," a group consisting of Roman citizens banded together to promote the interests of the area and its inhabitants.

[6] **Auximo**, ablative showing place from which, with **progressus** (B 229; AG 427); cf. **Cingulo** below, with **veniunt**.

[7] This refers to Italian towns with the rights of Roman citizenship, but whose governance is handled by **praefecti**, annually appointed by Rome. **Municipia**, on the other hand, have their own governing bodies (**decuriones**) and chief magistrates.

[2] Etiam Cingulo, quod oppidum Labienus[8] constituerat suaque pecunia exaedificaverat, ad eum legati veniunt, quaeque imperaverit, se cupidissime facturos[9] pollicentur. [3] Milites imperat: mittunt.[10] Interea legio XIII Caesarem consequitur. Cum his duabus[11] Asculum Picenum proficiscitur. Id oppidum Lentulus Spinther[12] X cohortibus tenebat; qui Caesaris adventu cognito profugit ex oppido cohortesque secum abducere conatus magna parte militum deseritur.

Vocabulary

cupidus, -a, -um: eager, enthusiastic

Roman gladiator and his patron

---

[8]Titus Labienus, chief legate of Caesar in Gaul. He deserted to Pompey in early January 49 BC, and there is speculation that he was always a partisan of Pompey (both were from Picenum). Labienus fought at Pharsalus and in the African campaign; he died at Munda in 45 BC. With the desertion of his chief legate still fresh in his mind (and rankling deeply), Caesar must have been satisfied at this turn of events.

[9] **facturos**: supply **esse.**

[10]Caesar is underscoring, again, the weakness of the Pompeian position and the unreliability of the Pompeians' support. However, in a letter to Atticus in December of 50 BC (ad Atticum 7.5) Cicero refers to his own meetings with senators and **equites** outside of Rome and their desire for peace, even if it meant complying with Caesar's demands. Perhaps this desire to avoid war, rather than a commitment to either side, better explains the actions of the communities.

[11] I.e., legions XII and XIII.

[12]Not to be confused with the previous Lentulus Crus. This Lentulus Spinther was consul in 57 BC when he worked for Cicero's recall from exile. Spinther was executed after Pharsalus.

CICERO: **Letters to Atticus**
(*Epistulae ad Atticum*)

Written in Campania, January 20, 49 BC
Cicero Attico salutem (dicit):

7.11. [1] Quaeso, quid est hoc? aut quid agitur? mihi enim tenebrae sunt. "Cingulum," inquit, "nos tenemus, Anconam amisimus; Labienus discessit a Caesare." Utrum de imperatore populi Romani an de Hannibale[1] loquimur? O hominem amentem et miserum, qui ne umbram quidem umquam τοῦ καλοῦ[2] viderit! Atque haec ait omnia facere se dignitatis causa. Ubi est autem dignitas nisi ubi honestas? Honestum igitur habere exercitum nullo publico consilio, occupare urbis[3] civium quo[4] facilior sit aditus ad patriam, χρεῶν ἀποκοπάς, φυγάδων καθόδους[5], sescenta[6] alia scelera moliri, τὴν θεῶν μεγίστην, ὥστ' ἔχειν τυραννίδα?[7] Sibi habeat suam fortunam! Unam me hercule[8] tecum apricationem in illo Lucretilino[9] tuo sole malim quam omnia istius modi regna, vel potius mori miliens quam semel istius modi quicquam cogitare....

Hannibal

Vocabulary

quaeso, quaesere, —, — (3): ask; beg
tenebra, -ae (f.): darkness, obscurity
utrum...an: whether...or; of... or...?
amens, -ntis: mad, stupid
miser, -era, -erum: wretched, poor
umbra, -ae (f.): shadow
umquam (unquam) (adv.): ever, at any time
aio, ait: I say, he says
ubi (adv.): where; when
aditus, -us (m.): approach, access
scelus, sceleris (n.): wickedness, evil
molior, moliri, —, molitum (dep.) (4): undertake, attempt
apricatio, -onis (f.): place in the sun
tuus, -a, -um: your
sol, solis (m.): sun
malo, malle, malui, — (irreg.): want more, prefer; often constructed, as here, with quam (than...)
regnum, -i (n.): kingship; kingdom, realm
miliens (adv.): a thousand times
semel (adv.): once

Grammar and Syntax

1. Accusative of exclamation (**hominem amentem et miserum**). The accusative may be used for an interjection (B 183; AG 397.*d*).
2. Independent Subjunctives. Two types appear in this passage:
   a. jussive (**habeat**) (B 275; AG 439-440): used to express a command, usually in the third person, sometimes in the second person, never in the first person (which is called the "hortatory" subjunctive).
   b. potential (**malim**) (B 280, especially 280.2.a; AG 446-447): used to express a possibility. Translate as a more or less vague possibility ("may"), or as a conditional ("should," "would"), whether or not a formal "should-would" condition is fully laid out with a protasis and apodosis.
3. Exercises for this section.

---

[1] The Carthaginian commander from the 3rd century BC who laid waste much of Italy and nearly defeated Rome. To compare Caesar to one of Rome's most notorious enemies shows the depth of Cicero's feeling at this time. He uses the same comparison later in his career, comparing Mark Antony to Hannibal, thus marking Antony — as Caesar, here — as a terrible threat to the Roman state.

[2] "of what is good," "of what is right."

[3] **urbis**: an i-stem.

[4] **quo**, introducing a purpose clause, as is common when the purpose clause contains a comparative (B 282; AG 531.2*a*).

[5] "the abolition of debts, the repatriation of exiles."

[6] sescenta: literally, "six hundred", but the meaning is "myriad," "a huge number."

[7] "to obtain the greatest of the gods, a tyranny." Cicero is quoting from a play by Euripides (Athens, 5th Century BC), the *Phoenician Women*.

[8] **me hercule**: " by Hercules!" = "by God!", a very common exclamation.

[9] Referring to a locale in the Sabine region where Atticus had a villa.

Independent Uses of the Subjunctive

Used independently (i.e., as the main verb of a clause) the subjunctive can express exhortation or command, potential or conditional ideas, deliberative or rhetorical questions, and wishes.

Hortatory/Jussive
- expresses command or exhortation
- shows the speaker trying to enforce his/her will
- uses the present subjunctive
- usually translated by the English "let"
- second person jussive is roughly equivalent to an imperative in tone and intent
- negative is **ne**

Potential
- expresses a conditional idea
- shows the speaker expressing his/her opinion
- uses the present or perfect subjunctive when referring to potential action in the future; the imperfect subjunctive when referring to potential action in the past
- usually translated by the English "would" (present/perfect subjunctive) or "would have" (imperfect subjunctive)
- negative is **non**

Deliberative
- expresses a rhetorical question
- shows the speaker's doubt or frustration
- always uses an interrogative
- uses the present subjunctive for present time, the imperfect for past time
- usually translated by the English "should" or "am" in the present as in "**quid faciam?**": what am I to do? what should I do?; by the English "would have" or "was" in the imperfect as in "**quid faceret?**": what would he have done? what was he to do?
- negative is **non**

Optative
- expresses a wish
- shows what the speaker hopes will happen, was happening, or would have happened
- frequently introduced by **utinam (uti, ut)**
- uses present/perfect subjunctive for wishes which may yet be fulfilled; the imperfect for wishes not being fulfilled at the present; the pluperfect for wishes not fulfilled in the past
- usually translated by English "may"(present/perfect); "were" (imperfect); "should have" or "had" (pluperfect): **utinam ille veniat** (may he come); **utinam ille veniret** (I wish he were coming); **utinam ille venisset** (I wish he had come).
- negative is **ne**

CAESAR: **The Civil War**

(*De bello civili*)

Late January-Early February, 49 BC

1.15 [4] Relictus [Spinther] in itinere cum paucis incidit in Vibullium Rufum,[1] missum a Pompeio in agrum Picenum confirmandorum hominum causa. A quo factus Vibullius certior, quae res in Piceno gererentur, milites ab eo accipit, ipsum dimittit. [5] Item ex finitimis regionibus, quas potest, contrahit cohortes ex delectibus Pompeianis; in his Camerino fugientem Lucilium Hirrum[2] cum sex cohortibus, quas ibi in praesidio habuerat, excipit; quibus coactis XIII efficit. [6] Cum his ad Domitium Ahenobarbum[3] Corfinium magnis itineribus[4] pervenit Caesaremque adesse cum legionibus duabus nuntiat. [7] Domitius per se circiter XX cohortes Alba, ex Marsis et Paelignis, finitimis ab regionibus coegerat.

Vocabulary

incido, incidere, incidi, incasum (3): (with prep. in + acc.) fall in with, come upon unexpectedly

cohors, cohortis, cohortium (f.): cohort (a sub-unit of a legion; about 450-500 men)

fugio, fugere, fugi, fugitum (3): flee (from), run away (from)

excipio, excipere, excepi, exceptum (3): intercept

efficio, efficere, effeci, effectum (3): produce; bring about

circiter: about (with acc.; also adv.)

finitimus, -a, -um: neighboring

Grammar and Syntax

1. Indirect questions (**quae res in Piceno gererentur**) (B 90, 300; AG 330, 573-576). (See explanation this section)
2. Relative pronouns continued (B 250-251; AG 147, 303-307). Continue to practice recognizing relative pronouns and their antecedents
3. Exercise for this section

---

[1]**Lucius Vibullius Rufus**, a loyal Pompeian and Pompey's chief engineer; as Caesar records, Rufus twice fell into his hands, at Corfinium (*BC* 1.36.1) and in Spain and was twice released. In view of this he was used by Caesar as an envoy to Pompey (*BC* 3.10.1).

[2]**Caius Lucilius Hirrus**, one of the tribunes of 53 BC.

[3]**Lucilius Domitius Ahenobarbus** ("bronze-beard"), consul 54 BC. He had been virulently opposed to both Caesar and Pompey, until the latter broke from Caesar. He was married to Porcia, the sister of Marcus Porcius Cato Uticensis.

[4] **magnis itineribus**—i.e., by marching at top speed, "by forced marches"

CICERO: **Letters to Atticus**
(*Epistulae ad Atticum*)

Copy of a letter from Pompey to Cicero written at Luceria on February 11, 49 BC

8.11A. Cn(aeus) Magnus Proco(n)s(ul) s(alutem) d(icit) M(arco) Ciceroni Imp(eratori):

Q(uintus) Fabius ad me venit a(nte) d(iem) IIII Id(us) Febr(uarias).[5] Is nuntiat L(ucium) Domitium cum suis cohortibus XII et cum cohortibus XIIII quas Vibullius adduxit ad me iter habere; habuisse in animo proficisci Corfinio a(nte) d(iem) V Id(us) Febr(uarias)[6]; C(aeum) Hirrum cum V cohortibus subsequi. Censeo ad nos Luceriam venias[7]; nam te hic tutissime puto fore.

Vocabulary

subsequor, subsequi, —, subsecutum (dep.) (3): follow closely after

puto, putare, putavi, putatum (1): think, consider

young Pompey

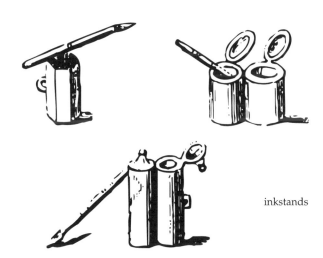

inkstands

---

[5] **a(nte) d(iem) IIII Id(us) Febr(uarias)**—February 10.
[6] **a(nte) d(iem) V Id(us) Febr(uarias)**—February 9
[7] Supply **ut**: censeo [ut] ad nos Luceriam venias.

Indirect Questions

When a substantive clause expresses a question tied to a verb of asking, telling, etc., it is called an Indirect Question; it uses the subjunctive mood in Latin. Such subordinated, dependent clauses are introduced by interrogative pronouns, adjectives, adverbs, and other phrases (**cum, quare, quo modo**, etc.). The forms of the interrogative pronouns are virtually the same as those of the relative pronouns (see paradigm B 90; AG 148); note, however, that in the singular the interrogative has **quis** (m. & f.) **quid** (n.), whereas the relative has **qui, quae, quod**. Interrogative pronouns must carefully be distinguished from relative clauses. Note especially that

a. an interrogative has no antecedent

b. indirect questions are always in the subjunctive.

Logically, one can ask questions about the present, past or future; but Latin has no future subjunctive and must, therefore, rely on a periphrasis using the future active participle and an appropriate form of **esse.**

As with other subordinate subjunctive clauses, the tense of subjunctive employed in the indirect question is determined by the phenomenon of "sequence of tenses;" see section 3. Consider the following examples, divided according to primary and secondary tenses:

Primary

Rogat *	quid facias.
	quid feceris.
	quid factura sis.

She asks	what you are doing.
	what you have done (did).
	what you are going to do (will do).

*or **rogabit** (will ask); **rogaverit** (will have asked); **roget** (let her ask); **roga** (ask!); on occasion **rogavit** (has asked, present perfect only)

Secondary

Rogabat **	quid faceres.
	quid fecisses.
	quid factura esses.

She was asking	what you were doing (did).
	what you had done.
	what you were going to do (would do).

or **rogavit (asked); **rogaverat** (had asked); **rogaret** (would have asked)

CICERO: **Letters to Atticus**
(*Epistulae ad Atticum*)
Copy of a letter from Pompey to Domitius Ahenobarbus written at Luceria on February 11, 49 BC

8.12B. Cn(aeus) Magnus Proco(n)s(ul) s(alutem) d(icit) L(ucio) Domitio Proco(n)s(uli):

[1] Valde miror te ad me nihil scribere et potius ab aliis quam a te de re publica me certiorem fieri. Nos disiecta manu[1] pares adversariis esse non possumus; contractis nostris copiis spero nos et rei publicae et communi saluti prodesse posse. Quam ob rem cum constituisses,[2] ut Vibullius mihi scripserat, a(nte) d(iem) V Id(us) Febr(uaras)[3] Corfinio proficisci cum exercitu et ad me venire, miror[4] quid causae fuerit qua re[5] consilium mutaris[6]....[2] Quam ob rem etiam atque etiam te rogo et hortor, id quod non destiti superioribus litteris a te petere, ut primo quoque die[7] Luceriam ad me venires,[8] antequam copiae quas instituit Caesar contrahere in unum locum coactae vos a nobis distrahant....

Vocabulary
miror, mirari, —, miratum (dep.) (1): wonder at; be amazed at
disicio, disicere, disieci, disiectum (3): break up; scatter
manus, -us (f.): hand; handful, band of people
par, paris, parium: equal (to, with dat.)
contraho, contrahere, contraxi, contractum (3): draw together, assemble
prosum, prodesse, profui (irreg.): be of advantage to (with dat.)
ob: with acc.: because of, on account of; quam ob rem, for which reason
muto, mutare, mutavi, mutatum (1): change, alter
rogo, rogare, rogavi, rogatum (1): ask
desisto, desistere, destiti, destitum (3): stop, leave off
peto, petere, petivi (petii), petitum (3): ask for; attack
instituo, instituere, institui, institutum (3): organize; equip
distraho, distrahere, distraxi, distractum (3): separate

Grammar and Syntax
1. Uses of the dependent subjunctive (See chart p. 77).
2. Exercise for this section.

Lucius Domitius Ahenobarbus

---

[1]**manu**: The "other" meaning of **manus**: band, or force; translate "with our forces separated."
[2]**constituisses...proficisci...venire**: the latter two verbs are complementary infinitives with **constituisses**.
[3]**a(nte) d(iem) V Id(us) Febr(uaris)**—February 9.
[4]**miror** is followed by a dependent indirect question: **quid causae fuerit** ("what has been the reason"); which in turn is followed by another: **qua re consilium muta(ve)ris** ("why you have changed your plan").
[5]**quid causae fuerit qua re**, "why"; literally, "what (of) reason there was why. " **causae** is a genitive of the whole (partitive genitive) with **quid** (B 201.2; AG 346); **qua** is a relative pronoun with the literal antecedent **causa**--but this antecedent is repeated within the relative clause by another word, the generalizing **re**.
[6]**mutaris=mutaveris**; syncopated (contracted) perfect subjunctive (B 116.1; AG 181).
[7]**primo quoque die**: "on the earliest day possible."
[8]**venires**: note the secondary sequence dependent on **destiti** —not on **rogo** and **hortor**, which would produce primary sequence.

CAESAR: **The Civil War**
(*De bello civili*)
Early February, 49 BC

1.16 [1] Recepto Firmo[9] expulsoque Lentulo Caesar conquiri milites, qui ab eo discesserant, delectumque institui iubet; ipse unum diem ibi rei frumentariae[10] causa moratus Corfinium contendit.

Vocabulary
recipio, recipiere, recepi, receptum (3): retake, reover
expello, expellere, expulsi, expulsum (3): drive out
conquiro, conquirere, conquisivi, conquistum (3): seek out

coin minted at Corfinium during the Social War (91-89 BC)

ad Corfinium contendunt…

---

[9]**Recepto Firmo** —This happened in early February, Firmum Picenum would be on Caesar's route to Asculum.
[10]**rei frumentarie**: grain supply.

Uses of the Subjunctive in Dependent Clauses

Concessive expresses the idea of "granted that" (NOTE: concession   B 278, 308;
can also be expressed by other clauses, such as with   AG 535.e
cum, licet, and quamquam—the latter taking the indicative.)
- introduced by a relative pronoun
- translated by *although...*
- subjunctive
- acts as an adverb in relation to the main clause
- answers the question, "how?" or "why?"

Purpose expresses the end to which an action is directed   B 282;
- introduced by **ut (uti)**, a relative pronoun, an adverb   AG 529-533
(ubi, unde, quo); ne (negative)
- translated by *that (not), in order that (not), lest*
- subjunctive
- acts as an adverb in relation to the main clause
- answers the question, "why?"

Characteristic expresses a quality or characteristic of an antecedent, especially   B 283;
when an antecedent is general or otherwise undefined—   AG 534-535
NOT of a particular person/thing.
- introduced by a relative pronoun
- translated by *a person/thing of the sort to...*
- subjunctive
- answers the question, "what sort of person (thing)?"

Result expresses the end toward which an action is headed   B 284;
(sometimes called "final" clauses)   AG 536-538
- introduced by **ut**, a relative pronoun, an adverb;
ut non, quin (negative)
- indicators in main clause are **tantus, talis, tot, tam, ita, sic, adeo**
- translated by *that (not), so that (not), with the result that (not)*
- subjunctive
- acts as an adverb in relation to the main clause
- answers the question, "how?" "in what way?"

Causal expresses the reason for an action   B 285;
- introduced by **quod, quia, quoniam, cum, quando**   AG 539-540
- translated by *because, since*
- indicative (reason of the author)
- subjunctive (reason of another)
- acts as an adverb in relation to the rest of the sentence
- answers the question, "why?"

Temporal   expresses time
                • introduced by **antequam, postquam, ut/uti** (=when),   B 287-293;
                  cum, simul   AG 541, 543, 545-548
                • translated by *after, when, as soon as, while, until*
                • indicative (present or future single point of time; certainty)
                • subjunctive (general situation or circumstances of past event;
                   anticipation)
                • acts as an adverb in relation to the main clause
                • answers the question, "when?"

Substantive   a clause which, as a whole, functions as a noun/pronoun;   B 294-299;
                  this is usually as the subject or the object of a verb   AG 560-562
                • introduced by **ut, ne** (negative), or **ut non** with verbs expressing such
                  ideas as commanding, permitting, preventing, deciding, striving, wish-
                  ing, and fearing; with impersonals such as "it is necessary..."; with
                  interrogative words; and with **quod**
                • translated by *that*
                • subjunctive or indicative (see B or AG)
                • acts as a noun, usually a subject or object, in relation to the main clause
                • *includes the following sub-categories:*

        Jussive/Indirect Command
                expresses a command   B 295.1;
                • introduced by **ut; ne** (negative)   AG 563
                • subjunctive

        Fear
                expresses a fear
                • introduced by **ne, ut,** and **ne non**   B 296.2;
                • subjunctive   AG 564

        Indirect question
                expresses a question
                • introduced by an interrogative word (pronoun, adverb, etc.) B 300;
                • subjunctive   AG 573-576

CICERO: **Letters to Atticus**
(*Epistulae ad Atticum*)
Copy of a letter from Pompey to Domitius
Ahenobarbus written at Luceria on
February 16, 49 BC

8.12C [1] Litteras abs[1] te M. Calenius[2] ad
me attulit a(nte) d(iem) XIIII Kal(endas)
Mart(ias)[3]; in quibus litteris scribis tibi
in animo esse observare Caesarem
et, si secundum mare ad me ire
coepisset, confestim in Samnium ad me
venturum, sin autem ille circum istaec[4]
loca commoraretur, te ei[5], si propius
accessisset, resistere velle. Te animo
magno et forti istam rem agere existimo,
sed diligentius nobis est videndum ne
distracti pares esse adversario non[6]
possimus, cum ille magnas copias habeat
et maiores brevi[7] habiturus sit.... [2] Quam
ob rem te magno opere hortor ut quam
primum cum omnibus copiis huc venias;
consules constituerunt idem facere....[3]...
nobis providendum est ut summam rei
publicae rationem habeamus.[8] Etiam atque
etiam[9] te hortor ut cum omni copia quam
primum ad me venias. Possumus etiam
nunc rem publicam erigere, si communi
consilio negotium administrabimus; si
distrahemur, infirmi erimus. Mihi hoc
constitutum est. [4] His litteris scriptis
Sicca[10] abs te mihi litteras et mandata
attulit. Quod me hortare[11] ut istuc veniam,
id me facere non arbitror posse, quod non
magno opere his legionibus confido.[12]

---

[1]**abs**: alternate form of **ab**.
[2]**M. Calenius**—an unknown.
[3]**a(nte) d(iem) XIIII Kal(endas) Mart(ias)**—February 16.
[4]**istaec**: the "c" acts as an intensifier; the form **istae** is alternate form of the neuter plural; **locus** in the plural can be either masculine
or (as here) neuter).
[5]**ei**: dative object of **resistere**.
[6]**non** is an adverb intensifying the **ne**: "at all," by any means."
[7]**brevi** —supply **tempore**.
[8]**rationem habeamus:** an expression meaning "have regard for;" "be concerned about."
[9]One may well question Domitius' wisdom in ignoring the advice of a seasoned commander like Pompey; Domitius seems determined to fulfill Cicero's opinion of him (*ad Att*.8.1.3), "**nemo nec stultior est quam L. Domitius**."
[10]**Sicca**—Unknown in this context; Cicero mentions a friend of the same name (*ad Att*.3.2), but it is not clear what connection that
Sicca would have either to Pompey or Domitius.
[11]**hortare = hortaris.**
[12]Lending weight to Caesar's estimation of the reliability of Pompey's troops.

Vocabulary

observo , observare, observavi, observatum (1): observe, deduce
secundum: with acc.: by (next to); alongside (of)
propius (adv.) near
fortis, -e: brave, resolute, strong
brevis, -e: short
magno opere (magnopere) (adv.): greatly
quam primum (adv.): as soon as possible
huc (adv.): to this place, hither
provideo, providere, providi, provisum (2): foresee
erigo, erigere, erexi, erectum (3): arouse, inspire
communis, -e: common, shared
consilium, -i (n.): plan
negotium, -i (n.): business
administro, administrare, administravi, administratum (1):
    conduct,manage
istuc (adv.): there
confido, confidere, confisum (semi-dep.) (3): trust (with dat.)

Grammar and Syntax

1. Continue reviewing the dependent subjunctives. See the
chart in section 28.
2. Semi-deponant verbs (B 114; AG 192): these verbs, like **confido** here, are normal in the present tenses, but deponent in the
perfect tenses.
3. Infinitives (see section 10).
4. Conditions (see section 12).
5. Exercises for this section.

The following material is a series of longer reading comprehension sections. In preparing the section, try the following procedure: Read through the passage aloud, looking for the general sense; read through the passage silently, identifying the main clause (subject and verb) and subordinate clauses; read through the passage word by word, noting the endings and keeping in mind the possibilities of various words and groups of words (subject, object, adverbial uses, ablative absolutes, gerundive for gerunds, and so on); look up in the accompanying vocabulary list and dictionary words that elude you—make vocabulary cards and learn as many as you can; fit together the elements of the sentence into an English translation. Finally, read through the sentence once more aloud, with the emphasis that its Latin meaning requires.

CAESAR: **The Civil War**
(*De bello civili*)
February, 49 BC

1.16 [2] Eo[1] cum venisset,[2] cohortes praemissae a Domitio ex oppido pontem fluminis[3] interrumpebant,[4] qui erat ab oppido milia passuum[5] circiter III. [3] Ibi cum antecursoribus Caesaris proelio commisso celeriter Domitiani[6] a ponte repulsi se in oppidum receperunt. [4] Caesar legionibus traductis ad oppidum constitit iuxtaque murum castra posuit.

17 [1] Re cognita Domitius ad Pompeium in Apuliam peritos[7] regionum magno proposito praemio cum litteris mittit, qui[8] petant atque orent, ut sibi subveniat[9]: Caesarem duobus exercitibus et locorum angustiis facile intercludi posse frumentoque prohiberi.

Vocabulary

praemitto, praemittere, praemisi, praemissum (3): send ahead
pons, pontis, pontium (m.): bridge
flumen, fluminis (n.): river
interrumpo, interrumpere, interrupi, interruptum (3): break apart
milia, milium, milibus: thousands (with genitive)
milia passuum: mile
antecursor, -cursoris (m.): advance guard
celer, celeris: quick; celeriter (adv.) = quickly
repello, repellere, repulli, repulsum (3): drive back, repel
traduco, traducere, traduxi, traductum (3): lead...across
iuxta (with acc.): next to, near to
murus, -i (m.): (town) wall
castra, -orum (n. pl.): (military) camp
pono, ponere, posui, positum (3): put, place
peritus, -a, -um: experienced, skilled
oro, orare, oravi, oratum (1): beg, beseech
subvenio, subvenire, subveni, subventum (4): aid, relieve
angustiae, -arum (f.): narrow place, defile
intercludo, intercludere, interclusi, interclusum (3): cut off, blockade
frumentum, -i (n.): wheat, grain; plur. crops

---

[1] **eo**: adverbial.

[2] On February 15. The siege at Corfinium lasted February 15-21.

[3] **fluminis**: the river Aternus (see map).

[4] **interrumpebant**: here, emphasizing the "conative" use of the imperfect indicative which expresses the idea of "attempting to do" something (B 260.3; AG 471c).

[5] **milia passuum**: in the plural, **milia** is generally a substantive and therefore declined; it is followed by the genitive.

[6] I.e., **milites**.

[7] **peritus** commonly uses the objective genitive to express the thing in which one is skilled.

[8] **qui = ut ei**, a relative clause of purpose (B 282.2; AG 531.2).

[9] **subveniat**: The subject implied is **Pompeius**.

[2] Quod nisi fecerit,[10] se cohortesque amplius[11] XXX[12] magnumque numerum senatorum atque equitum Romanorum in periculum esse venturum.

[3] Interim suos cohortatus tormenta in muris disponit certasque cuique partes[13] ad custodiam urbis attribuit; [4] militibus in contione agros ex suis possessionibus pollicetur, quaterna in singulos iugera,[14] et pro rata parte[15] centurionibus evocatisque.[16]

18 [1] Interim Caesari nuntiatur[17] Sulmonenses,[18] quod oppidum a Corfinio VII milium[19] (passuum) intervallo abest, cupere ea facere, quae vellet, sed a Q(uinto) Lucretio senatore et Attio Paeligno prohiberi, qui id oppidum VII cohortium praesido tenebant. [2] Mittit eo M(arcum) Antonium cum legionis XIII cohortibus V. Sulmonenses, simulatque signa nostra viderunt, portas aperuerunt, universique, et oppidani et milites, obviam gratulantes Antonio exierunt. [3] Lucretius et Attius de muro se deiecerunt.[20] Attius ad Antonium deductus petit, ut ad Caesarem mitteretur. Antonius cum cohortibus et Attio eodem die, quo profectus erat, revertitur.

Vocabulary

amplius (adv.): more, more than
numerus, -i (m.): number, quantity
interim (adv.): meanwhile
cohortor, cohortari, —, cohortatum (dep.) (1): urge on, encourage
tormentum, -i (n.): artillery
attribuo, attribuere, attribui, attributum (3): assign, allot
contio, contionis (f.): public meeting, rally
quaterni, -ae, -a: four each (distributive adj.)
ratus, -a, -um: established, approved
intervallum, -i (n.): distance, interval
absum, abesse, afui, — (irreg.): be away, not to be there
signum, -i (n.): standard (military); sign, signal;
porta, -ae (1): (city) gate
gratulor, gratulari, gratulatum (dep. 1): give thanks to
exeo, exire, exivi, exitum (irreg.): go out, go forth

Corfinium and Sulmo

---

[10] **fecerit**: the perfect subjunctive in the protasis of a condition in indirect statement, standing for an original future perfect indicative; the apodosis is expressed by **esse venturum** (B 319; AG 589).

[11]**amplius**: = **amplius quam**; (See B 217.2; AG 407c). Omission of **quam** is usual with numerals.

[12]**XXX**: in 15.6 (section 30) Caesar says that Domitius had raised XX **per se**; this figure of XXX would include cohorts from both Vibullius and Hirrus, and would seem rather low if the original estimate of XX were correct. Letters of Cicero (ad Att. 8.11a and 12a) indicate that Domitius had XII with him; the XX is perhaps a copyist's error (not at all unusual with numerals), not Caesar's. In any event, it is perhaps the size of his force which encouraged Domitius' over-confidence in his position.

[13]**certasque cuique partes**: "fixed duties for everyone."

[14]**iugera**: four **iugera** would be about 3 acres of land, the amount Romans thought of as the minimum "family farm."

[15]**pro rata parte**: according to the agreed upon proportions. Booty, rewards, etc., were distributed on a sliding scale with higher officers(here the centurions) and recalled veterans (**evocati**) getting proportionately more than the common soldiers (**milites**).

[16]It was normal for centurions to receive pay double that of the common soldier, and veterans who were recalled for duty would likewise be paid more. Domitius appears to be offering "proportionately more" in keeping with these expectations.

[17]**nuntiatur**: to be read as an historical present, and here treated as a secondary tense, making **quae vellet** consonant with the usual sequence of tenses. The historical present is sometimes treated as a primary and sometimes as a secondary tense.

[18]**Sulmonenses**: The inhabitants of Sulmo, southeast of Corfinium, and the subject of **cupere.** Cicero has word by February 22 that Sulmo has been handed over (ad Att. 8.4), and feels it is all over: "**confecta res est,**" he writes.

[19]**milium**: genitive plural form of **mille**.

[20]**deiecerunt**: It seems clear that Caesar did not mean that they committed suicide, given Attius' appearance in the next sentence. **Deiecerunt** must, therefore, refer to their haste in moving down from the wall; the verb is often used to refer to violent displacement, which here seems appropriate.

18. [4] Caesar eas cohortis cum exercitu suo coniunxit Attiumque incolumem dimisit. Caesar primis diebus castra magnis operibus munire et ex finitimis municipiis frumentum comportare reliquasque copias expectare instituit. [5] Eo triduo[21] legio VIII ad eum venit cohortesque ex novis Galliae delectibus XXII equitesque ab rege Norico[22] circiter CCC.[23] Quorum adventu altera castra ad alteram oppidi partem ponit; his castris Curionem praefecit.[24] [6] Reliquis diebus oppidum vallo castellisque circumvenire instituit. Cuius operis maxima parte effecta eodem fere tempore missi a Pompeio revertuntur.

Vocabulary

incolumis, -e: unharmed
comporto, comportare, comportavi, comportatum (1): collect, gather
triduum, -i: (n.): three-day period
vallum, -i (n.): rampart
castellum, -i (n.): fortress
circumvenio, circumvenire, circumveni, circumventum (4): surround.

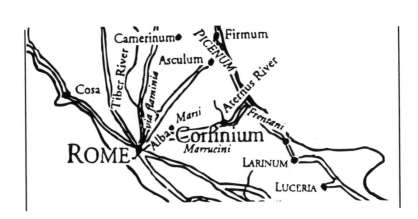

area about Corfinium

---

[21]**Eo triduo**: That is, on the third day of the siege at Corfinium.
[22]**ab rege Norico**: "from the king of Noricum"; Noricum is the region in the south of Germany and Austria, between the Danube and Alps (see map). This obligation may extend from Caesar's defeat of the Boii and Helvetii (*BG* 1.5) in 58 BC, who were enemies of the Norici.
[23]Caesar had left Ravenna a month earlier with one legion; his strength is now over five legions.
[24]Increased responsibilities for Curio, a young and inexperienced officer, suggest two circumstances: his increased favor with Caesar and the lack of more seasoned leadership at the higher levels of Caesar's army.

CICERO: **Letters to Atticus**
(*Epistulae ad Atticum*)
Copy of Letter from Pompey to Domitius
Ahenobarbus, at Corfinium written at
Luceria (southern Italy) on
February 17, 49 BC

Cn(aeus) Magnus Proco(n)s(ul) s(alutem)
d(icit) L(ucio) Domitio Proco(n)s(uli):

8.12D [1] Litterae mihi a te redditae sunt
a(nte) d(iem) XIII Kal(endas) Mart(ias)[1], in
quibus scribis Caesarem apud Corfinium
castra posuisse. Quod putavi et praemonui
fit, ut nec in praesentia comittere
tecum proelium velit et omnibus copiis
conductis penitus te implicet, ne ad me
iter tibi expeditum sit[2] atque istas copias
coniungere optimorum civium possis[3]
cum his legionibus de quarum voluntate
dubitamus[4]. Quo etiam magis tuis litteris
sum commotus; neque enim eorum
militum quos mecum habeo voluntate[5]
satis confido ut de omnibus fortunis rei
publicae dimicem neque etiam qui[6] ex
dilectibus conscripti sunt consulibus[7]
convenerunt.

[2] Qua re da operam[8], si ulla ratione
etiam nunc efficere potes, ut te explices,
hoc quam primum venias, ante quam
omnes copiae ad adversarium conveniant.

Vocabulary
praemoneo, praemonere, praemonui, praemonitum (2):
  foretell, forewarn
praesentia, -ae (f.): present
conduco, conducere, conduxi, conductum (3): bring together,
  assemble
penitus (adv.): completely
implico, implicare, implicavi, implicatum (1): envelope
*civis, civis, civium (m.): citizen
*dubito, dubitare, dubitavi, dubitatum (1): hesitate; doubt
  quo...magis (adv.): all the more
commoveo, commovere, commovi, commotum (2): upset
*fortuna, -ae (f.): luck, fortune
dimico, dimicare, dimicavi, dimicatum (1): struggle, fight
explico, explicare, explicavi, explicatum (1): set free, release
adversarius, -i (m.): enemy

Roman soldiers

---

[1]February 17.

[2]**te implicet ne ad me iter tibi expeditum sit**: "hems you in so that a way is not open for you to (come to) me."

[3] **possis**: also governed by the preceding **ne.**

[4]Again the lack of confidence, as Pompey himself has expressed before.

[5]Pompey, like Caesar, seems to employ the ablative with **confido** (and related words) when the object is not personal, the dative with persons.

[6]**qui**: the antecedent (understood) is "**ei.**"

[7]**consulibus**: dative of agent; to be understood with **conscripti.**

[8]**qua re da operam**: "so, do your best...."

Neque enim celeriter ex dilectibus hoc homines convenire possunt et, si convenirent, quantum iis committendum sit[9] qui inter se ne noti quidem sunt contra veteranas legiones non te praeterit.

CAESAR: **The Civil War 1**
(*De bello civili*)
February, 49 BC

1.19 [1] Litteris perlectis, Domitius dissimulans in consilio pronuntiat, Pompeium celeriter subsidio[10] venturum, hortaturque eos, ne animo deficiant, quaeque usui ad defendendum oppidum sint, parent.[11] [2] Ipse arcano cum paucis familiaribus suis colloquitur consiliumque fugae capere constituit.[12] Cum[13] vultus Domitii cum oratione[14] non consentiret, atque omnia trepidantius timidiusque ageret, quam superioribus diebus consuesset,[15] multum[16] que cum suis consiliandi causa secreto praeter consuetudinem colloqueretur, concilia conventusque hominum fugeret, res diutius tegi dissimularique non potuit. [3] Pompeius enim rescripserat, sese rem[17] in summum periculum deducturum non esse, neque suo[18] consilio aut voluntate Domitium se[19] in oppidum Corfinium contulisse: proinde, si qua[20] fuisset facultas, ad se cum omnibus copiis veniret.

Vocabulary

quantum (adv.): how much

notus, nota, notum: well known

veteranus, -a, -um: veteran

perlego, perlegere, perlegi, perlectum: read through carefully

dissimulo, dissimulare, dissimulavi, dissimulatum (1): disguise, dissemble, keep a secret

pronuntio, pronuntiare, pronuntiavi, pronuntiatum (1): relate, announce

subsidium, -i (n.): reserve, support, help

deficio, deficere, defeci, defectum (3): fail in, run out of

usus, -us (m.): use; experience

arcano (adv.): in secret, privately

colloquor, —, colloqui, collocutum (dep. 1): discuss

fuga, fugae (f.): flight, running away

vultus, -us (m.): visage

trepido, trepidare, trepidavi, trepidatum (1): be jumpy, nervous

timidus, -a, -um : fearful

consilior, consiliari, —, consiliatum (dep. 1): take counsel

secreto (adv.): in secret, in private

praeter: with acc.: past; besides; contrary to

diu (adv.): long, for a long time; diutius (adv.) = still longer, for a very long time

tego, tegere, texi, tectum (3): cover, hide

dissimulo, dissimulare, dissimulavi, dissimulatum (1): conceal, dissimulate

rescribo, rescribere, rescripsi, rescriptum (3): write back

secret conversations

---

[9]**quantum iis committendum sit**...: to be understood as the subject of **praeterit** or its predicate (if **praeterit** is translated impersonally); "it does not escape your notice **(te)** how much trust should be placed in those who..."

[10]**subsidio**: dative of purpose or tendency (B 191; AG 382), as also **usui** and **fugae** just below.

[11]**parent**: supply **ut**; this and **ne...deficiant** are substantive clauses, sometimes called jussive noun clauses (B 295), dependent on **hortatur.**

[12]**consilium fugae capere**: "to make arrangements for flight."

[13]The following verbs are taken with **cum: consentiret, ageret, colloqueretur, fugeret.**

[14]I.e., his manner of speech.

[15]=**consuevisset**; subjunctive by attraction (B324; AG 593); translate like a pluperfect indicative.

[16]**multum**: adverbial; note how Domitius is spending a lot of time in secret consultations with personal advisors and avoiding public appearances.

[17]**rem**: i.e., their cause

[18]**suo** =Pompeius; confirmed by Cicero (*ad Atticum* 8.12.6), "omnino culpem omnem Pompeius in Domitium confert."

[19]**se**: Domitius.

[20]**qua**: indefinite adverb: "if in any way."

[4] Id ne fieri posset, obsidione atque oppidi circummunitione fiebat.[21]

20 [1] Divulgato Domitii consilio milites qui erant Corfinii primo vesperi secessionem faciunt atque ita inter se per tribunos militum centurionesque atque honestissimos sui generis[22] colloquuntur: [2] obsideri se a Caesare, opera munitionesque prope esse perfectas; ducem suum Domitium, cuius[23] spe atque fiducia permanserint, proiectis omnibus fugae consilium capere: debere se suae salutis rationem habere. [3] Ab his primo Marsi[24] dissentire incipiunt eamque oppidi partem, quae munitissima videretur,[25] occupant, tantaque inter eos dissensio exsistit, ut manum conserere[26] atque armis dimicare conentur; [4] post paulo tamen internuntiis ultro citroque missis, quae[27] ignorabant, de L(ucii) Domitii fuga, cognoscunt. [5] Itaque omnes uno consilio Domitium productum in publicum circumsistunt et custodiunt legatosque ex suo numero ad Caesarem mittunt: sese paratos esse portas aperire, quaeque imperaverit, facere et L(ucium) Domitium vivum eius potestati tradere.

Vocabulary

obsidio, obsidionis (f.): siege, blockade

circummunitio, circummunitionis (f.): encirclement, circumvallation

divulgo, divulgare, divulgavi, divulgatum (1): reveal, divulge, publicize

secessio, secessionis (f.): withdrawal

opus, operis (n.): structure, building; product of work

munitio, munitionis (f.): fortification

prope: with acc.: near (also adv. = nearly)

permaneo, permanere, permansi, permansum (2): remain, endure

proicio, proicere, proieci, proiectum (3): betray, abandon

dissentio, dissentire, dissensi, dissensum (4): disagree, be in conflict

dissensio, dissensionis (f.): conflict, dissention

incipio, incipere, incepi, inceptum (3): take on, begin

exsisto, exsistere, exstiti, exstitum (3): emerge, arise

consero, conserere, conservi, consertum (3): join, tie; manum conserere: fight hand to hand

conor, conari, —, conatum (dep. 1): try, attempt

internuntius, -i: (m.): intermediary, messenger

ultro citroque (adv.): back-and-forth

ignoro, ignorare, ignoravi, ignoratum (1): fail to recognize, be ignorant of

publicus, -a, -um: official, public

circumsisto, circumsistere, circumsteti, — (3): surround

officers discuss the situation…

---

[21]This final sentence is Caesar's own comment on the situation.

[22]**sui generis**: that is, of the rank and file, the common soldiers.

[23]**cuius**: an objective genitive; because of their hope and trust in him (**cuius**) they stayed.

[24]**Marsi**: best known, perhaps, for the lead which they took in the Social Wars of 91-87 BC, demanding their Roman citizenship; they inhabit the mountains and passes near Lake Fucinus, east of Rome.

[25]**quae munitissima videretur**: a clause of characteristic, focusing our attention on the quality of the area (B 283; 534-535).

[26]**manum conserere**: "to join in hand-to-hand combat."

[27]**quae = ea quae.**

CAESAR: **The Civil War**
(*De bello civili*)
Late February, 49 BC

1.21[1] Quibus rebus cognitis Caesar, etsi magni interesse[1] arbitrabatur quam primum oppido potiri cohortesque ad se in castra traducere, ne qua[2] aut largitionibus aut animi confirmatione aut falsis nuntiis commutatio fieret voluntatis, quod saepe in bello parvis momentis magni casus intercederent, [2] tamen veritus ne militum introitu et nocturni temporis licentia oppidum diriperetur,[3] eos, qui venerant,[4] collaudat atque in oppidum admittit, portas murosque asservari iubet. [3] Ipse in iis operibus, quae facere instituerat, milites disponit, non certis spatiis intermissis, ut erat superiorum dierum consuetudo, sed perpetuis vigiliis,[5] stationibusque, ut contingant inter se atque omnem munitionem expleant; [4] tribunos militum et praefectos circummittit atque hortatur, non solum ab eruptionibus caveant,[6] sed etiam singulorum hominum occultos exitus asservent. [5] Neque vero tam remisso ac languido animo quisquam omnium fuit, qui ea nocte conquieverit.[7] [6] Tanta erat summae rerum expectatio, ut alius in aliam partem[8] mente atque animo traheretur, quid[9] ipsis Corfiniensibus, quid Domitio, quid Lentulo, quid reliquis accideret, qui quosque eventus exciperent.

Vocabulary

potior, potiri, —, potitum (with abl. or gen.) (3): get control of
confirmatio, confirmationis (f.): encouragement
nuntius, -i (m.): messenger; news, message
commutatio, commutationis (f.): change
momentum, -i (n.): importance
intercedo, intercedere, intercessi, intercessum (3): occur
vereor, vereri, —, veritum (dep.) (2): fear, be apprehensive
introitus, -us (m.): entrance
nocturnus, -a, -um: nocturnal
licentia, -ae (f.): license, lack of restraint
diripio, diripere, diripui, direptum (3): plunder
asservo, asservare, asservavi, asservatum (1): guard, watch over
dispono, disponere, disposui, dispositum (3): station, assign
perpetuus, -a, -um: continuous, uninterrupted
vigilia, -ae (f.): guard, sentinal; watch of the night
statio, stationis (f.): guard station; pl. = sentries
contingo, contingere, contigi, contactum (3): be in contact
expleo, explere, explevi, expletum (2): fill out, fill up
praefectus, -i (m.): prefect (commander of allied troops)
circummitto, circummittere, circummisi, circummisum (3): send around to
solum (adv.): only; non solum...sed etiam = "not only...but also"
eruptio, eruptionis (f.): sortie, sally
caveo, cavere, cavi, cautum (2): beware (ab = beware of)
occultus, -a, -um: hidden
tam (adv.): so (with adjs. and advs.)
languidus, -a, -um: weak, sluggish
quisquam, cuiusquam: anyone
conquiesco, conquiescere, conquievi, conquietum (3): rest, take a nap
expectatio, expectationis (f.): anticipation
mens, mentis (f.): mind; heart
traho, trahere, traxi, tractum (3): draw, pull
quis, quis, quid: who? what? (interrogative pron.)
eventus, -us (m.): fortune; outcome

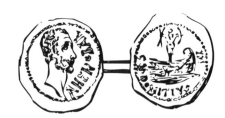

coin of Ahenobarbus (the son)

---

[1]**magni interesse**: "that it was of great importance"; **magni** is the genitive expressing the degree of concern (B 211.3; AG 417).

[2]**qua = aliqua** and modifies **commutatio.**

[3]Subjunctive in a clause of fearing, introduced by **veritus** (B 296.2; AG 564); **ne** indicates what the person fears may happen, but hopes it will not!

[4]That is, the soldiers who had come from Domitius, offering to turn him over to Caesar.

[5]**perpetuis vigiliis**: this contrasts with **certis spatiis intermissis**, above, and refers to an unbroken line (**perpetuis**) of watchmen.

[6]Supply **ut** with both **caveant** and **asservent.**

[7]A relative clause expressing result (B 284.2 AG 537).

[8]"one drawn in one direction, another in another direction"; Latin employs this shorthand method with various combinations of **alius** (B 253.2; AG 315c).

[9]**quid...accideret**: the series of indirect questions explains the thoughts running through everyone's hearts and minds (**mente atque animo**); supply "as they asked what..."

22[1] Quarta vigilia[10] circiter Lentulus Spinther de muro cum vigiliis custodibusque nostris colloquitur: velle, si sibi fiat potestas, Caesarem convenire. [2] Facta potestate ex oppido mittitur, neque ab eo prius[11] Domitiani milites discedunt, quam in conspectum Caesaris deducatur. [3] Cum eo[12] de salute sua agit, orat atque obsecrat, ut sibi[13] parcat, veteremque amicitiam commemorat Caesarisque in se beneficia exponit, [4] quae[14] erant maxima: quod per eum in collegium pontificum venerat, quod provinciam Hispaniam ex praetura habuerat, quod in petitione consulatus[15] erat sublevatus. [5] Cuius[16] orationem Caesar interpellat: se non maleficii causa ex provincia egressum, sed uti se a contumeliis inimicorum defenderet, ut tribunos plebis [in ea re] ex civitate expulsos in suam dignitatem restitueret, ut se et populum Romanum[17] factione paucorum oppressum in libertatem vindicaret. [6] Cuius oratione confirmatus Lentulus, ut in oppidum reverti liceat, petit: quod[18] de sua salute impetraverit fore etiam reliquis ad suam spem solacio;[19] adeo esse perterritos nonnullos, ut suae vitae durius consulere[20] cogantur. Facta potestate discedit.

23 [1] Caesar, ubi luxit, omnes senatores senatorumque liberos, tribunos militum equitesque Romanos ad se produci iubet.

[2] Erant quinque ordinis senatorii, L(ucius) Domitius, P(ublius) Lentulus, (Lucius) Caecilius Rufus, Sex(tus) Quintilius Varus quaestor, L(ucius) Rubrius; praeterea filius Domiti aliique complures adulescentes et magnus numerus equitum Romanorum et decurionum, quos ex municipiis Domitius evocaverat.

Vocabulary

quartus, -a, -um: fourth
vigilius, -i (m.): watchman, picket
conspectus, -us (m.): sight, view
obsecro, obsecrare, obsecravi, obsecratum (1): beseech, implore
parco, parcere, peperci, parsurum (3): spare
expono, exponere, exposui, expositum (3): declare, lay out
collegium, -i (n.): college, association
pontificus, -a, -um: pontifical, priestly
praetura, -ae (f.): praetorship
sublevo, sublevare, sublevavi, sublevatum (1): aid, support
interpello, interpellare, interpellavi, interpellatum (1): interrupt
maleficium , -i (n.): offense, harm, injury
egredior, egredi, —, egressum (dep.) (3): go out; disembark
expello, expellere, expulsi, expulsum (3): drive out
dignitas, dignitatis (f.): dignity, reputation
factio, factionis (f.): party, faction
opprimo, opprimere, oppressi, oppressum (3): oppress, crush
libertas, libertatis (f.): freedom
vindico, vindicare, vindicavi, vindicatum (1): set (in libertatem: set free)
licet, licuit (2): it is allowed
solacium, -i (n.): comfort (+ad = "for...")
durus, -a, -um: severe, harsh
luceo, lucere, luxi, —, (2): to dawn
liberus, -i (m.): child
quinque (indecl.): five
filius, -i (m.): son
complures, complura (-ium): a considerable number of

---

[10]**vigilia**: nightwatch. The Romans divided the evening into four watches from sunset to sunrise, 3 to 4 hours in length, depending on the time of year. The time would probably be around 4:00 a.m.

[11]**prius**: to be taken with **quam** and the clause which follows it; the subjunctive **deducatur** denotes an anticipated act (B 292; AG 551).

[12]I.e., "Caesare."

[13]I.e., "Lentulo."

[14]This seems to be Caesar's voice. Lentulus is not reminding Caesar of his benefactions; Caesar, rather, is reminding his reader of the kindnesses already conferred on Lentulus and therefore of Lentulus' betrayal of Caesar's friendship.

[15]In the campaign of 58 BC for the consulship of 57 BC.

[16]I.e., Lentulus.

[17]This linkage of self and public interest is something Caesar had already established in his narrative of the *Bellum Gallicum*; nor is it unique to Caesar. We find in numerous letters of Cicero, for example, that his own well-being and **dignitas** is, certainly in his own mind, consonant with the well-being of the **res publica.**

[18]**quod...impetraverit**: the subject of **fore.**

[19]**solacio**: dative of purpose or tendency, to be read with **reliquis**, the dative of reference.

CAESAR: **The Civil War**
(*De bello civili*)
Late February–Early March, 49 BC

1.23 [3] Hos omnes productos a contumeliis militum conviciisque prohibet;[1] pauca apud eos loquitur, quod[2] sibi a parte eorum gratia relata non sit pro[3] suis in eos maximis beneficiis; dimittit omnes incolumes.[4] [4] HS [sestertium] LX,[5] quod advexerat Domitius atque in publico deposuerat, allatum ad se ab duumviris Corfiniensibus Domitio reddit,[6] ne continentior in vita hominum quam in pecunia fuisse videatur, etsi eam pecuniam publicam esse constabat datamque a Pompeio in stipendium.[7] [5] Milites Domitianos sacramentum[8] apud se dicere iubet atque eo die castra movet[9] iustumque iter[10] conficit, VII omnino dies ad Corfinium commoratus, [11] et per fines Marrucinorum, Frentanorum, Larinatium, in Apuliam pervenit.

24 [1] Pompeius his rebus cognitis, [12] quae erant ad Corfinium gestae, Luceria proficiscitur Canusium atque inde Brundisium. Copias undique omnes ex novis delectibus[13] ad se cogi iubet; servos, pastores armat atque iis equos attribuit[14]: ex his circiter CCC equites conficit.

Vocabulary

sestertia, -ium (n. pl.): 100,000 sesterces

adveho, advehere, advexi, advectum (3): carry, transport

depono, deponere, deposui, depositum (3): deposit

duumvir, -i (m.): a local magistrate

continens, continentis (adj.): self-controlled

consto, constare, constiti, constatum (1): (of facts): be well known

stipendium, -i (n.): pay for soldiers

sacramentum, -i (n.): military oath of allegiance

iustus, -a, -um: just, fair, proper (+ iter = normal day's march)

commoror, commorari, —, commoratum (dep. 1): delay

inde: from that place, thence

servus, -i (m.): slave

pastor, pastoris (m.): shepherd

armo, armare, armavi, armatum (1): arm

procul (adv.): at a distance

equitatus, -us (m.): cavalry

conspicor, conspicari, —, conspicatum (dep. 1): catch sight of

praesum, praeesse, praefui, — (irreg.): be in charge of (with dat.)

transfero, transferre, transtuli, translatum (irreg.): transfer; go over (to)

[3] L(ucius) Manlius praetor Alba cum cohortibus sex profugit, Rutilius Lupus praetor Tarracina tribus; quae procul equitatum Caesaris conspicatae, cui praeerat Vibius Curius, relicto praetore signa ad Curium transferunt atque ad eum transeunt.

---

[1]**prohibet**: "protects."

[2]**quod**: "namely that..."

[3]**pro**: "in proportion to."

[4]Against all expectation; Caesar himself must have been aware of the dire predictions, for as he states in a letter of March 5, 49 BC, he had already decided to demonstrate his clemency and try to win back the good will of all, and he did not intend to follow in Sulla's footsteps ("...L. Sullam quem imitaturus non sum...") (Cicero, *ad Atticum* 9.7C.1)."

[5]**HS LX** = 6,000,000 (**sexagies centena millia sestertium**); the symbol HS is really a crossed Roman numeral II; the two symbols together stand for "duo et semis," or 2-1/2 asses, which equals one sestertius.

[6]Although Cicero claims, in a letter to Atticus, that the money was not returned (*ad Atticum* 8.14.3).

[7]The 6,000,000 could have covered the expenses for an entire legion (6,000 men) for a whole year (Ruebel).

[8]**sacramentum**: an oath of loyalty.

[9]**castra movet**: "breaks camp," a military idiom.

[10]**iustum iter**: a regular day's march (16-20 miles), as opposed to a forced march (**magnum iter**).

[11]That is, from February 15-21, inclusive.

[12]Caesar again misleads regarding the sequence of events. Pompey was already at Canusium on the 20th of February, and Brundisium on the 25th (Cicero, *ad Atticum* 8.11; 9.10); so Pompey actually began his move to leave Italy during the siege of Corfinium, not after. Thus, Caesar (probably accidentally?) makes him look better than his actual actions warrant.

[13]Pompey's regular force consisted of the two legions which he had from Caesar, so he had a need to recruit more soldiers.

[14]The arming of slaves and peasants is meant to be interpreted as a sign of Pompey's desperation and lack of judgment; it is also a typical charge laid against an enemy to undermine his image.

[4] Item reliquis itineribus nonnullae cohortes in agmen Caesaris, aliae in equites incidunt. Reducitur ad eum deprensus ex itinere N(umerius) Magius Cremona,[15] praefectus fabrum[16] Cn(aei) Pompei.[17] [5] Quem Caesar ad eum remittit cum mandatis: quoniam ad id tempus facultas colloquendi non fuerit, atque ipse Brundisium sit venturus, interesse reipublicae et communis salutis,[18] se cum Pompeio colloqui, [6] neque vero idem profici longo itineris spatio, cum per alios condiciones ferantur, ac si[19] coram de omnibus condicionibus disceptetur.

25 [1] His datis mandatis Brundisium[20] cum legionibus VI pervenit, veteranis III et reliquis, quas ex novo delectu confecerat atque in itinere compleverat;[21] Domitianas enim cohortes protinus a Corfinio in Siciliam[22] miserat. [2] Repperit, consules Dyrrhachium[23] profectos cum magna parte exercitus, Pompeium remanere Brundisii cohortibus viginti; [3] neque certum inveniri poterat, obtinendine[24] Brundisii causa ibi remansisset, quo[25] facilius omne Hadriaticum mare extremis Italiae partibus regionibusque Graeciae in potestate haberet atque ex utraque parte[26] bellum administrare posset, an inopia navium ibi restitisset, [4] veritusque, ne ille[27] Italiam dimittendam non[28]

Vocabulary

agmen, agminis (n.): column, army (on march)
proficio, proficere, profeci, profectum (3): accomplish
longus, -a, -um: long; far
discepto, disceptare, disceptavi, disceptatum (1): discuss, debate
reperio, reperire, repperi, repertum (4): find (by looking for)
viginti (indecl.): twenty
mare, maris (abl. -i) (n.): sea
bellum, -i (n.): war
administro, adminstrare, adminstravi, administratum (1): manage, govern
inopia, -ae (f.): shortage, lack
navis, navis, navium (f.): ship
administratio, administrationis (f.): management
portus, us (m.): port, harbor

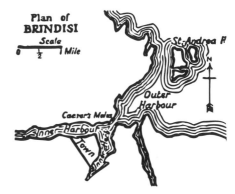

plan of the area of Brundisium

coin of Brundisium

existimaret, exitus administrationesque Brundisini portus impedire instituit.

---

[15]Cremona = Cremonensis, an unusual usage.

[16]**praefectus fabrum**: chief engineer.

[17]Caesar himself makes reference to this incident in a letter (Cicero, *ad Atticum* 9.7C) of March 5, 49 BC: he says he quite naturally followed his customary practice and let Magius go free; that this is the second prefect of engineers to fall into his grasp and be released; that they should show their gratitude by encouraging Pompey to prefer his (Caesar's) friendship to that of those who are really his enemies and working against the interests of the state.

[18]**interesse**...: with the genitive of the person or thing affected (B 211; AG 355).

[19]**ac si**: "as if"; this responds to the previous **idem.**

[20]March 9.

[21]**compleverat**: "had raised to their full capacity."

[22]Where Cato was stationed.

[23]In Epidamnus, on the eastern shore of the Adriatic; the point of embarkation from the East, as Brundisium is from the West.

[24]**obtinendine**: the -ne introduces the first of two indirect questions, the second beginning with **an inopia.**

[25]**quo = ut eo**, usual with a comparative (B 282.1a; AG 531.a).

[26]That is, from both sides of the Adriatic.

[27]Pompeius.

[28]**ne...non:** used instead of the more common **ut** to express what one fears may <u>not</u> happen (B 296.2a; AG 564).

Caesar's narration of events in Brundisium continues, in English translation:

(25.5) This was how Caesar did it: at the place where the harbor's entrance was most narrow, he constructed a breakwater of earth and rubble from either side of the shore, since there the sea was shallow. As he moved further out from shore, since the earthen breakwater could not be held together in the deeper water, he positioned just off the breakwater two rafts, thirty feet square, and he anchored them at each corner so they would not be tossed about in the waves. After these rafts were finished and in place, he joined other rafts of like size, one after the other, and covered them with earth and rubble so as to remove any impediment to approaching and manning them for defensive purposes. Also, in the front and on either side he provided protective cover with wickerwork screens and mantlets, and on every fourth raft he raised towers two storeys high, so as to defend more easily against naval attacks and assault by fire.

(26) In opposition to these preparations, Pompey was equipping large merchant ships which he had seized in the harbor of Brundisium. On them he was erecting towers three storeys high, loaded with many missiles and every type of weapon, and he was moving them up to Caesar's fortifications with the intent of breaking up the rafts and throwing the siegeworks into disarray. Consequently, there was on either side daily fighting at a distance, with slings and arrows and other sorts of missiles. Yet Caesar continued to conduct his actions so as not to preclude conditions for peace, although he was greatly surprised that Magius, whom he had sent to Pompey with proposals, was not sent back to him. And still, even though his frequent attempts at negotiation slowed the pace of his advance and overall strategy, Caesar thought he should persevere in his attempts using every possible means. So, he sent his legate Caninius Rebilus, an intimate friend and kinsman of Scribonius Libo, to confer with Libo. Caesar instructed Rebilius to urge Libo to work for peace, and in particular he asked that Libo himself confer with Pompey. Caesar indicated that he was very confident that, if an opportunity should be afforded for such a conference, there would be an end to hostilities with fair and equal terms. He also indicated that a large measure of praise and credit for this outcome would come to Libo, if the cessation of hostilities occurred through his initiative and agency. Libo left his meeting with Caninius and went to Pompey. A little while later he reported back Pompey's decision that, in the absence of the consuls, there could be no action taken about any agreement. At this point Caesar decided that he should now bring to an end

the often tried, but pointless, process of negotiation and should instead take action to plan for war.

(27) After Caesar had used up nine days in completing nearly half the siegeworks, the ships which had been sent back from Dyrracchium by the consuls, after transporting there the first part of the army, returned to Brundisium. At the fleet's arrival Pompey, either because he was disconcerted by Caesar's preparations or because he had determined from the outset to leave Italy, began his preparations for departure. First, in order better to slow down Caesar's attack and keep the soldiers from breaking into the town during the departure process, Pompey blocked the gates, barricaded the side streets and main thoroughfares, dug trenches across the roads and fixed in them pointed stakes and logs. These trenches he leveled out with light wickerworks and earth on top. With huge sharpened logs he fenced in the two roads which went outside the town wall to the port. Once these things had been prepared, Pompey ordered his soldiers to board the ships in silence, while he placed, scattered along the wall and on the towers, light-armed troops from among his veterans, along with archers and slingers. He arranged for these troops to be summoned back at a fixed signal after all the soldiers had embarked, and he left for them some swift ships in a convenient spot.

(28) The people of Brundisium, resentful because of their abuse at the hands of Pompey's soldiers and the insults from Pompey himself, supported Caesar's cause. Therefore, when Pompey's departure became known, the townspeople signaled the news from the rooftops, while Pompey's men were roaming about busy with the work at hand. Caesar, as soon as the news reached him, ordered scaling ladders to be readied and his troops to be armed, so as not to miss any opportunity for action. Pompey weighed anchor late at night. Those who had been stationed on the wall were recalled at the agreed-upon signal and ran down to the ships along marked routes. Caesar's men, after positioning their scaling ladders, climbed the walls; but once warned by the Brundisians to beware of the hidden trench and stakes, they halted. Guided by the townspeople, Caesar's men arrived at the port after a long detour, and making use of skiffs and rowboats, they caught and took charge of two ships, with the soldiers on board, which had run aground on Caesar's breakwaters.

(Translation by P. Vaughn)

29 [1] Caesar, etsi ad spem conficiendi negotii maxime probabat coactis navibus mare transire et Pompeium sequi,[29] priusquam ille sese transmarinis auxiliis confirmaret, tamen eius rei moram temporisque longinquitatem timebat, quod omnibus coactis navibus Pompeius praesentem facultatem insequendi sui ademerat. [2] Relinquebatur[30] ut ex longinquioribus regionibus Galliae Picenique et a freto[31] naves essent expectandae. Id propter anni tempus longum atque impeditum videbatur. [3] Interea veterem exercitum, duas Hispanias confirmari,[32] quarum erat altera maximis beneficiis Pompei devincta, auxilia, equitatum parari, Galliam Italiamque temptari se absente nolebat.

30 [1] Itaque in praesentia Pompei sequendi rationem omittit, in Hispaniam proficisci constituit...

Vocabulary

auxilia, -orum (n.): auxiliaries (foreign troops)
mora, -ae (f.): delay
longinquitas, longinquitatis (f.): length, duration
insequor, insequi, —, insecutum (dep. 3): follow, pursue; attack
longinquus, -a, -um: distant
fretum, -i (m): strait
annus, -i (m.): year
impeditus, -a, -um: difficult
devinctus, -a, -um: strongly attached (to)
absens, absentis: absent, away
nolo, nolle, nolui, — (irreg.): be unwilling, not to want
omitto, omittere, omisi, omissum (3): abandon

(30.2) Caesar ordered the magistrates of all the Roman towns to gather ships and to ensure that they were sent to Brundisium. He sent his legate Valerius to Sardinia with one legion and Curio as propraetor to Sicily with two legions. The latter he ordered to take his legions on to Africa, once he had secured Sicily. At that time M. Cotta was in charge of Sardinia, M. Cato of Sicily; Tubero was waiting to take control of his allotted province Africa. Now the Caralitani, as soon as they heard that Valerius was being sent to them, voluntarily ejected Cotta from the town, though Valerius had yet to leave Italy. Cotta, thoroughly alarmed once he realized that the entire province shared the same opinion of him, fled from Sardinia to Africa. In Sicily, Cato was in the process of refitting old warships and ordering new ones from the towns, all with great zeal. In addition, he was conducting, through his legates, troop levies of Roman citizens in the region of the Lucani and the Bruttii, and exacting a certain number of cavalry and infantry from the towns of Sicily. When these preparations were almost completed and

---

[29] In the preceding section, Pompey had escaped Caesar's blockade.
[30] **Relinquebatur ut**: "the option remaining was to..."
[31] That is, the Sicilian strait.
[32] **confirmari...parari...temptari**: all are complementary infinitives with **nolebat**.

Curio's approach was known, Cato convened a public assembly and complained that he had been abandoned and betrayed by Pompey; that Pompey had in fact undertaken an unnecessary war completely unprepared, when he had, upon questioning, assured both Cato and others in the senate that everything was in readiness and prepared for war. Now Cato, once he had made his complaint in public, fled from his province.

(31) Valerius and Curio thus arrived at their provinces with their armies and gained control of their respective provinces, Sardinia and Sicily, when the provinces were without leadership. When Tubero had arrived in Africa, he found Attius Varus in command there. Attius, as shown previously, went right on to Africa in his flight after losing his troops at Auximum; he, on his own initiative, took command of Africa, since it had no governor at the time, and he had put together two legions, after holding a troop levy. Attius relied on his familiarity with the people and region and his experience in the province to do this, since a few years previously he had been governor of the province after his praetorship. As Tubero approached Utica with his ships, Attius prevented him from entering either the harbor or the town and did not even permit him to disembark his son who was ill at the time; rather, Attius forced him to weigh anchor and depart from the area.

(Translation by P. Vaughn)

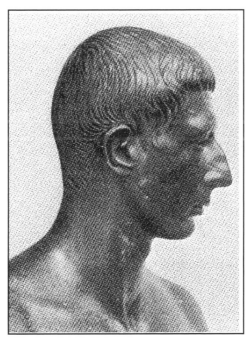

Marcus Porcius Cato

CAESAR: **The Civil War** (*De bello civili*)
Late March-April, 49 BC

1.32 [1] His rebus confectis Caesar, ut reliquum tempus a labore intermitteretur,[1] milites in proxima municipia deducit; ipse ad urbem[2] proficiscitur. [2] Coacto senatu[3] iniurias inimicorum commemorat. Docet[4] se nullum extraordinarium honorem appetisse, sed expectato legitimo tempore[5] consulatus eo fuisse contentum, quod omnibus civibus pateret. [3] Latum ab X tribunis plebis contradicentibus inimicis, Catone vero acerrime repugnante et pristina consuetudine dicendi mora dies extrahente,[6] ut sui ratio absentis haberetur, ipso consule Pompeio;[7] qui si improbasset,[8] cur ferri passus esset? si probasset,[9] cur se uti populi beneficio prohibuisset? [4] Patientiam proponit suam cum de exercitibus dimittendis ultro postulavisset in quo iacturam dignitatis atque honoris ipse facturus esset. [5] Acerbitatem inimicorum docet, qui, quod ab altero postularent, in se recusarent[10] atque omnia permisceri mallent quam imperium exercitusque dimittere. [6] Iniuriam in eripiendis legionibus praedicat, crudelitatem et insolentiam in circumscribendis tribunis plebis; condiciones a se latas,[11] expetita colloquia et denegata commemorat. [7] Pro quibus rebus hortatur ac postulat, ut rem publicam suscipiant atque una secum administrent;

Vocabulary

extraordinarius, -a, -um: extraordinary, special
appeto, appetere, appetivi, appetitum (3): strive after; claim for oneself; seek
legitimus, -a, -um: lawful, proper
pateo, patere, patui (2): lie open, be open
contradico, contradicere, contradixi, contradictum (3): oppose, speak against
repugno, repugnare, repugnavi, repugnatum (1): oppose
pristinus, -a, -um: earlier
extraho, extrahere, extraxi, extractum (3): waste (of time); draw, drag out
improbo, improbare, improbavi, improbatum (1): disapprove, reject
cur (adv.): why
probo, probare, probavi, probatum (1): approve
patientia, -ae (f.): patience, long-suffering
ultro (adv.): of one's own accord; beyond
acerbitas, acerbitatis (f.): harshness, bitterness
recuso, recusare, recusavi, recusatum (1): refuse
praedico, praedicare, praedicavi, praedicatum (1): proclaim, assert
crudelitas, crudelitatis (f.): cruelty
insolentia, -ae (f.): arrogance, insolence
circumscribo, circumscribere, circumscripsi, circumscriptum (3): restrict; thwart the purpose of
expeto, expetire, expetivi, expetitum (4)): demand; long for
denego, denegare, denegavi, denegatum (1): deny

voting on a bill ("A" = "[ut] antiquo," i.e., "no")

---

[1]**ut reliquum...intermitteretur**: "so that the remaining time might pass by free from toil."
[2]That is, **Romam.**
[3]On April 1. The narrative gives the impression that Caesar convened the Senate, when, according to Dio (41.15) it was Antony and Longinus who actually gathered the remains of the senate, outside the city limits (**pomerium**) so that Caesar could attend legally.
[4]Caesar, throughout, is consistent in the grievances which he has.
[5]The normal 10 years between offices.
[6]**Catone...extrahente**: an ablative absolute construction.
[7]In 52 BC.
[8]**improbasset=improbavisset.**
[9]**probasset=probavisset.**
[10]**qui quod...recusarent**: "who refuse in their own case what they demand of another."
[11]**latas**: "proposed."

sin timore defugiant, illis se oneri[12] non futurum[13] et per se rem publicam administraturum. [8] Legatos ad Pompeium de compositione mitti oportere, neque se reformidare, quod in senatu Pompeius paulo ante dixisset, ad quos[14] legati mitterentur, his auctoritatem attribui timoremque eorum, qui mitterent, significari. [15] Tenuis atque infirmi haec animi[16] videri. [9] Se vero, ut operibus anteire studuerit, sic iustitia et aequitate velle superare.

33 [1] Probat rem senatus de mittendis legatis;[17] sed, qui mitterentur,[18] non reperiebantur, maximeque timoris causa pro se quisque id munus legationis recusabat. [2] Pompeius enim discedens ab urbe[19] in senatu dixerat, eodem se habiturum loco, qui Romae remansissent et qui in castris Caesaris fuissent. [20] [3] Sic triduum[21] disputationibus excusationibusque extrahitur. Subicitur etiam L(ucius) Metellus[22] tribunus plebis ab inimicis Caesaris, qui hanc rem distrahat reliquasque res, quascumque agere instituerit, impediat. [4] Cuius cognito consilio Caesar frustra diebus aliquot consumptis,[23] ne reliquum tempus amittat, infectis iis, quae agere

Vocabulary

defugio, defugere, defugi, defugitum (3): avoid, evade, shy away from
onus, oneris (n.): burden
compositio, compositionis (f.): reconciliation (of friends)
reformido, reformidare, reformidavi, reformidatum (1): dread, shrink from
significo, significare, significavi, significatum (1): signify, indicate
tenuis, -e: puny, insignificant
anteeo, anteire, anteii, anteitum (irreg.): excel, surpass
aequitas, aequitatis (f.): fairness
supero, superare, superavi, superatum (1): overcome
probo, probare, probavi, probatum (1): approve
munus, muneris (n.): duty, public task
disputatio, disputationis (f.): argument, debate
subicio, subicere, subieci, subiectum (3): suborn
quicumque, quaecumque, quodcumque: whoever, whatever
frustra (adv.): in vain
aliquot (adv.): several
consumo, consumere, consumpsi, consumptum (3): waste
infectus, -a, -um: undone, unachieved
destino, destinare, destinavi, destinatum (1): determine, resolve
ulterior, -ius : further

on the road…

destinaverat, ab urbe proficiscitur atque in ulteriorem Galliam[24] pervenit.

---

[12]**oneri**: dative of purpose.

[13]Supply **esse** with both **futurum** and **administraturum.**

[14]**ad quos**: the antecedent is actually **his**, which follows.

[15]That is, Pompey is concerned with appearances; he will not send legates because that could be perceived as a sign of weakness and would confer an unintended measure of respect on Caesar.

[16]**tenuis atque infirmi...animi**: genitive of characteristic; "these seem to be the mark of a weak and cowardly spirit."

[17]**rem...de mittendis legatis**: the proposal concerning the dispatch of legates.

[18]**qui mitterentur**: a relative clause of characteristic (B 283; AG 534-535).

[19]This departure did not sit well with Cicero and others of the senatorial class; at the time of its occurrence Cicero was outraged, but on reflection, he thought it may have solidified public opinion against Caesar (*ad Atticum* 7.11). Unfortunately, Cicero underestimated the strength of Caesar's popular support outside the elite classes.

[20]An illustration of the fear which Pompey can inspire through such ruthless statements, which we are no doubt intended to juxtapose with Caesar's **clementia.**

[21]April 1-3.

[22]Best known for his stand blocking Caesar's access to the treasury in the Temple of Saturn; Metellus was forcibly removed and Caesar looted the gold as well, though there is no mention of it here. Cicero seemed to feel that Caesar lost something of his appearance of clemency and largess in his maltreatment of Metellus and his plundering of the public treasury (*ad Atticum* 10.8.6): **"in odium acerbissimum venerit."**

[23]I.e., the three days, April 1-3.

[24]That region of Gaul beyond the Alps.

CAESAR: **The Civil War**
(*De bello civili*)
March, 49 to July, 48 BC

Caesar returns to Rome and tries to establish a "legitimate" government. He fails, and leaves to pursue his next military goal, the annihilation of Pompey's troops in Spain. This expedition takes until early August, 49 BC, but he is entirely successful not only in destroying Pompey's army and base in Spain, but in taking the important Pompeian city of Massalia (Marseille) at the mouth of the Rhone river. Returning to Rome once again, Caesar manipulates the Roman constitution in order to get himself elected consul for 48 BC. In January, 48 BC, Caesar is ready to go after Pompey who has taken up a position on the western coast of Greece, at Dyrrachium. In a daring move, Caesar attempts to lay seige to Pompey's much larger army with his relatively small force (April, 48 BC). Ultimately, this proves impossible, as Pompey breaks out of the encirclement and leads his army east, into Thessaly (July, 48 BC).

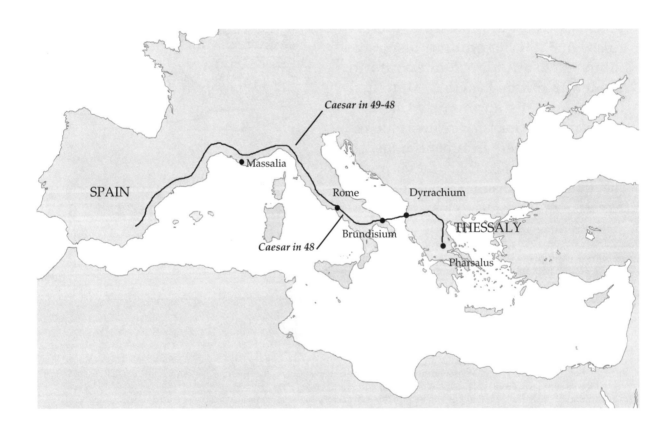

CAESAR: **The Civil War**
(*De bello civili*)
Ca. August 1, 48 BC

3.82 [1] Pompeius paucis post[1] diebus in Thessaliam[2] pervenit contionatusque apud cunctum exercitum suis agit gratias, Scipionis milites[3] cohortatur, ut parta iam victoria praedae ac praemiorum velint esse participes,[4] receptisque omnibus in una castra legionibus suum cum Scipione honorem partitur classicumque apud eum cani et alterum illi iubet praetorium tendi.[5]

[2] Auctis copiis Pompei duobusque magnis exercitibus coniunctis pristina omnium confirmatur opinio, et spes victoriae augetur, adeo ut, quicquid intercederet temporis, id morari reditum in Italiam videretur,*

Cicero writes well after the fact (May, 46 BC) of this tendency earlier, while the army was still at Dyrrachium (ad Fam. 7.3.2):

Quae [i.e., the selfish behavior of the Pompeians] cum vidissem, desperans victoriam, primum coepi suadere pacem, cuius fueram semper auctor; deinde, cum ab ea sententia Pompeius valde abhorreret, suadere institui, ut bellum duceret. Hoc interdum probabat et in ea sententia videbatur fore, et fuisset fortasse, nisi quadem ex pugna [i.e, that victory at Dyrrachium] coepisset suis militibus confidere. Ex eo tempore vir ille summus nullus imperator fuit. Signa, tirone et collectitio exercitu, cum legionibus robustissimis contulit.

Vocabulary

contionor, -ari, —, -atum (dep.) (1): speak before a crowd
pario, parere, peperi, partum (3): win, get; give birth to
praeda, -ae (f.): booty
classicum, -i (n.): battle horn, bugle
cano, canere, cecini, cantum (3): sound [a horn]
augeo, augere, auxi, auctum (2): increase
collectitius, -a, -um: hastily gathered

tabernacula—common soldiers' tents

---

[1]**post**: "after"—but an adverb, not a preposition.
[2]**Thessaliam**: In central Greece. Pompey hoped to raise a larger army from his allies, friends, and clients in the eastern part of the Romans' empire. Thessaly was, presumably, to be a rallying place for that army.
[3]**Scipionis milites**: Scipio had brought the troops he had raised in Asia Minor to Pompey's aid. So now Pompey had a double army.
[4]**particeps**: "sharers" (takes the genitive).
[5]**praetorium tendi**: an official military commander's tent (**praetorium**) was set up for Scipio's use to emphasize the fact that Pompey was not assuming overall command; Pompey did this to avoid bruising the egos of the senators who were with him.

82 [3] et si quando quid Pompeius tardius aut consideratius faceret, unius[6] esse negotium diei, sed illum[7] delectari imperio et consulares praetoriosque servorum habere numero[8] dicerent. [4] Iamque inter se palam de praemiis ac de sacerdotiis contendebant in annosque[9] consulatum definiebant, alii domos bonaque eorum, qui in castris erant Caesaris, petebant;** [5] magnaque inter eos in consilio fuit controversia, oporteretne[10] Lucili Hirri, quod is a Pompeio ad Parthos missus esset, proximis comitiis praetoriis absentis rationem haberi,[11] cum eius necessarii fidem implorarent Pompei, praestaret, quod proficiscenti recepisset,[12] ne per eius auctoritatem deceptus videretur, reliqui, in labore pari ac periculo ne unus omnes antecederet, recusarent.

**Cicero remarks a specific example of this (ad Att. 11.6 [November 27, 48 BC, after the battle of Pharsalus]):*

Lucius vero Lentulus [the consul of 49 BC] Hortensi domum sibi et Caesaris hortos et Baias desponderat.[13]

Vocabulary

quando (adv.) (indefinite after "si"): ever, at any time
tardus, -a, -um: slow
delector, delectare, delectatum (dep.) (1): love, delight in (+ abl.)
palam (adv.): openly
-ne (enclitic): whether (introduces a question)
comitia, -orum (n.): electoral assembly
necessarius, -i (m.): friend, kinsmen
praesto, praestare, praestiti, praestitum (1): perform
antecedo, antecedere, antecessi, antecessum (3): take precedence over, surpass

a wealthy man's villa

QVINTVS HORTENSIVS

---

[6]**unius**: after the **si quid**-clause, the rest of the sentence is governed by **dicerent**, which introduces indirect discourse.
[7]**illum**: Pompey.
[8]**numero**: = "in loco."
[9]**in annos**: for the years to come.
[10]**oporteretne**: introduces indirect discourse with the subject **rationem** and verb **haberi**.
[11]**rationem haberi**: an idiom which means, "conduct a candidacy." This is, of course, exactly what Caesar wanted to do in running for the consulship for 48 BC without giving up his army and returning to the city to campaign.
[12]**recepisset**: "undertaken," "promised."
[13]Hortensius has stayed in Rome and so was counted an enemy by the Pompeians. He had died in 99 B.C.

CAESAR: **The Civil War**
(*De bello civili*)
Ca. August 1, 48 BC

3.83 [1] Iam de sacerdotio Caesaris[1] Domitius, Scipio Spintherque Lentulus cotidianis contentionibus ad gravissimas verborum contumelias palam descenderunt, cum Lentulus aetatis honorem[2] ostentaret, Domitius urbanam gratiam[3] dignitatemque iactaret, Scipio affinitate Pompei confideret. [2] Postulavit[4] etiam Lucium Afranium proditionis exercitus[5] Acutius Rufus apud Pompeium, quod gestum in Hispania diceret.[6] [3] Et Lucius Domitius in consilio dixit placere sibi bello confecto ternas tabellas dari ad iudicandum eis, qui ordinis essent senatorii belloque una cum ipsis[7] interfuissent, sententiasque de singulis ferrent,[8] qui Romae remansissent quique intra praesidia Pompei[9] fuissent neque operam in re militari praestitissent: [4] unam fore tabellam, qui[10] liberandos omni periculo censerent; alteram, qui capitis[11] damnarent; tertiam, qui pecunia multarent. [5] Postremo omnes aut de honoribus suis aut de praemiis pecuniae aut de persequendis inimicitiis agebant nec, quibus rationibus superare possent, sed, quemadmodum uti victoria deberent, cogitabant.

Vocabulary

sacerdotium, -i (n.): priesthood
cotidianus, -a, -um: daily
contentio, contentionis (f.): dispute
verbum, -i (n.): word
urbanus, -a, -um: of the city
iacto, iactare, iactavi, iactatum (1): boast, brag about
confido, confidere, —, confisum (semi-dep.) (3): trust (with abl. or dat.)
proditio, proditionis (f.): betrayal
placeo, placere, placui, placitum (2): please; seem right, proper
terni, -ae, -a: three (each)
una (adv.): together
intersum, interesse, interfui (irreg.): take part
remaneo, remanere, remansi, remansum (2): remain
opera, -ae (f.) : assistance
censeo, censere, censui, censum (2): propose; believe
damno, damnare, damnavi, damnatum (1): condemn
multo, multare, multavi, multatum (1): fine
postremo (adv.): at last, finally
persequor, persequi, —, persecutum (dep.) (3): take vengeance on
quemadmodum (adv.): how, in what way

another voting scene ("v" = "uti [rogas]," i.e., "yes")

---

[1]**sacerdotio Caesaris**: Caesar had been elected as pontifex maximus in 63 BC; this coveted post was now being fought over by the Pompeians, as if Caesar were already dead and buried.

[2]**aetatis honorem**: "the esteem his age had brought him; " he had been consul in 57 BC, while Domitius had been consul in 54 and Scipio in 52 BC.

[3]**urbanam gratiam**: his influence with the city crowd.

[4]**postulavit**: a technical usage meaning arraign someone on some charge—demand that they be persecuted on some charge.

[5]**proditionis exercitus**: an interesting combination of genitives: **proditionis** is a genitive of the charge (B 208); **exercitus** is an objective genitive.

[6]**gestum in Hispania**: events told in the second half of book 1 of the *BC*. Afranius hardly betrayed the army; the accusation is noted to show the rifts among the Pompeians.

[7]**ipsis**: that is, **Pompeianis**.

[8]**ferrent**: "give," "record."

[9]**intra praesidia Pompei**: had been with the forces of Pompey.

[10]**qui**: understand "eis" as the antecedent for this and the next two "qui."

[11]**capitis**: another genitive of charge. **caput** = "capital charge," which could mean either exile or death.

CICERO: **Letters to Atticus**
(Epistulae ad Atticum)
November 27, 48 BC [i.e., after Pharsalus]

Cicero had determined to stay at Dyrrachium on the coast of the Ionian Sea and did not participate in the battle of Pharsalus. After Pompey's defeat, he pondered his next move, and recalled the sort of actions that Caesar has just described on the part of the hard-core Pompeians.

11.6 [2] Me discessisse ab armis numquam paenituit[12]. Tanta erat in illis crudelitas, tanta cum barbaris gentibus coniunctio,[13] ut non nominatim, sed generatim proscriptio esset informata,[14] ut iam omnium iudicio constitutum esset omnium vestrum bona[15] praedam esse illius victoriae.

Vocabulary

paeniteo, paenitere, paenitui (2): to cause to regret
tantus, -a, -um: so much, so great
crudelitas, crudelitatis (f.): cruelty
barbarus, -a, -um: foreign, barbarian
informo, informare, informavi, informatum (1): form, shape
iudicium, -i (n.): judgement, opinion
vester, -tra, -trum: your

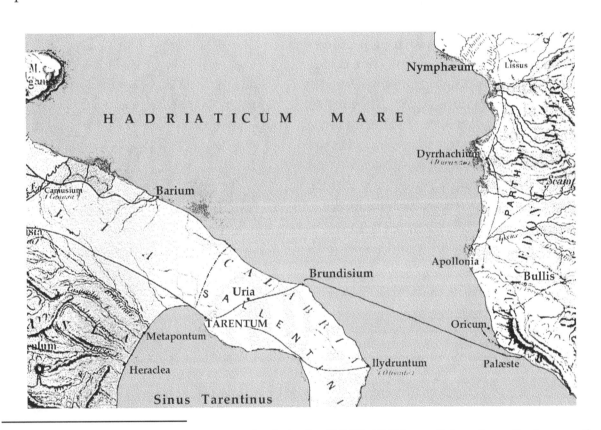

---

[12]**paenituit**: cf. the genitive used with certain impersonal verbs (section 17; B 209; AG 354). **paenitet** uses the genitive to express the person or thing toward which the feeling of regret is directed; it uses the accusative to express the person who does the regretting. Translate: "I never regretted my deed."

[13]**barbaris gentibus coniunctio**: Cicero hates Pompey's strategy of using foreign allies to destroy fellow Romans in a civil war. Caesar in his propaganda picks up this negative aspect of Pompey's strategy and exploits it (see section below).

[14]**ut non...**: "that proscription had been planned not against individuals, but generally..."

[15]**bona**: "goods," "property."

CICERO: **Letter to his friend Marius**

(Epistulae ad familiares)

May, 46 BC

Now well after the fact, and in a Rome controlled by Caesar, Cicero again looks back on those fateful days in 49-48 BC. He wonders about the wisdom of his decision to cast his lot with Pompey because, as he describes it now, Pompey's army was made up of unworthy men; it was only their cause, the salvation of the res publica, that made them attractive. Again, Cicero concurs in Caesar's own description of the Pompeians.

7.3 [2] Cuius me mei facti paenituit, non tam[16] propter periculum meum, quam propter vitia multa, quae ibi offendi, quo veneram.[17] Primum neque magnas copias neque bellicosas;[18] deinde extra ducem paucosque praeterea (de principibus loquor), reliqui primum in ipso bello rapaces deinde in oratione ita crudeles, ut ipsam victoriam horrerem[19]; maximum autem aes alienum amplissimorum virorum.[20] Quid quaeris? nihil boni praeter causam.[21]

Vocabulary

vitium, -i (n.): fault; offense
offendo, offendere, offendi, offensum (3): run up against; come upon
rapax, rapacis (adj.): grasping, insatiable
crudelis, -e: cruel
horreo, horrere, horrui, — (2): dread; shudder at

Caesar and Pompey very much alike, especially Pompey.

Roma and Victoria on a coin of Marcus Cato (47-46 B.C.)

---

[16] **tam...quam**: so much...as.

[17] **quo veneram**: Cicero had finally left Italy in the spring of 49 BC after much vacillation and had joined Pompey in Greece, at Dyrrachium.

[18] **bellicosas**: "ready for war." Understand a verb such as **vidi.**

[19] Understand the verb **fuerunt** with **reliqui.**

[20] Understand **fuit** with **maximum...aes alienum.**

[21] **nihil boni praeter causam**: an encapsulation of Caesar's entire propaganda: he attempts to co-opt the cause (the defense of the **res publica**), and to show how evil the **factio paucorum** was as individuals. The efficacy of the approach is exemplified in this confession by Cicero.

CICERO: **Letter to his friend Cn. Plancius**

(*Epistulae ad familiares*)
January, 45 BC

Again, Cicero broods upon the foul character of his fellow Pompeians.

Vocabulary

recordor, recordari, —, recordatum (dep.) (1): recall, recollect
modo: only
pertimesco, pertimescere, pertimescui, — (3): become afraid, alarmed
discepto, disceptare, disceptavi, disceptatum (1): dispute; decide
vinco, vincere, vici, victum (3): conquer
cupiditas, cupiditatis (f.): desire

4.14 [2] Quo in periculo[22] non nihil[23] me consolatur cum recordor haec me tum vidisse, cum secundas etiam res nostras, non modo adversas: pertimescebam videbamque quanto periculo[24] de iure publico disceptaretur armis. Quibus si vicissent ii[25] ad quos ego pacis spe non belli cupiditate adductus accesseram,[26] tamen[27] intelligebam, et iratorum hominum et cupidorum et insolentium[28] quam crudelis esset futura victoria...

Pax (from a coin of Augustus)

---

[22]**Quo in periculo**: read as **in quo periculo**.
[23]**non nihil**: "not a little;" used adverbially.
[24]**quanto periculo**: with how much danger.
[25]**ii = ei =** the Pompeians; the antecedent of **quibus** is **armis**.
[26]**ad quos**...: "to whom I...drawn by...had gone (literally, "approached").
[27]**si...tamen**: these words correlate two verbs, **vicissent** and **intelligebam.**
[28]**iratorum**...: "of angry, grasping, and immoderate men," these genitives modify **victoria**, which is also modified by **crudelis.**

The Civil War
(De bello civili)
August 19, 48 BC

Caesar has engaged Pompey's forces in skirmishes, especially honing his greatly outnumbered cavalry's tactics. But Pompey has refused to fight a pitched battle. Just as Caesar is breaking camp, ready to take up a strategy of constant movement in order to tire out Pompey's army in pursuit,

3.86 [1] Pompeius quoque, ut postea cognitum est, suorum omnium hortatu statuerat proelio decertare.

Pompey outlines his plan for success in battle, which is built around utilizing his numerical superiority in cavalry to turn Caesar's right flank and rout his army. Then...

3.86 [5]Simul denuntiavit, ut essent animo parati in posterum et, quoniam fieret dimicandi potestas, ut saepe rogitavissent, ne usu manuque[1] reliquorum opinionem fallerent.

Vocabulary

hortatus, -us (m.): urging, exhortation
decerto, decertare, decertavi, decertatum (1): fight it out; come to a decision
opinio, opinionis (f.): expectation; opinion; reputation
fallo, fallere, fefelli, falsum (3): deceive; let down, fail to live up to

Roman cavalryman

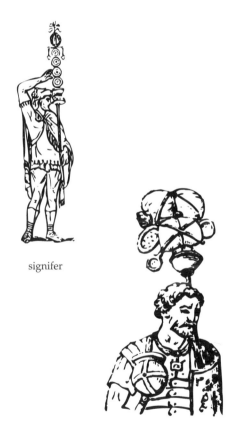

signifer

soldier on the march

Roman hastatus

---

[1]**usu manuque**: "in the battle itself;" literally, "in skill and combat," with **hendiadys** = "skillful combat."

Caesar describes other preparations by the Pompeians and then, in 88 and 89, describes how each army is arranged for battle. He makes allowance for Pompey's flanking strategy.

Vocabulary

mos, moris (m.): custom, manner
pugna, -ae (f.): fight, battle
imprimis (adv.): first and foremost, especially
testis, -is (m. or f.): witness
abutor, abuti, —, abusum (dep.) (3): misuse (with abl.)
sanguis, sanguinis (m.) or sanguen, sanguinis (n.): blood
alteruter, -utra, -utrum: either
privo, privare, privavi, privatum (1): deprive
exposco, exposcere, expoposci, — (3): demand
ardeo, ardere, arsi, arsum (2): burn

3.90 [1] Exercitum cum militari more ad pugnam cohortaretur suaque in eum perpetui temporis officia praedicaret, imprimis commemoravit, testibus se militibus uti posse, quanto studio pacem petisset, quae per Vatinium in colloquiis, quae per Aulum Clodium cum Scipione egisset, quibus modis ad Oricum cum Libone de mittendis legatis contendisset.² [2] Neque se umquam abuti militum sanguine neque rem publicam alterutro exercitu privare voluisse. [3] Hac habita oratione exposcentibus militibus et studio pugnae ardentibus tuba³ signum dedit.

a general addresses his troops

civilian tubicines

tuba

military tubicen

---

²**Vatinium...Aulum Clodium...cum Libone**: these were three failed attempts at negotiations which Caesar had initiated at Oricum and at Dyrrachium. Vatinius is at *BC* III.19; Clodius at III.57, and Libo at III.16.
³**tuba**: the long, straight battle horn of the Romans.

91 [1] Erat Crastinus evocatus in exercitu Caesaris, qui superiore anno apud eum primum pilum[4] in legione X[5] duxerat,[6] vir singulari virtute. [2] Hic signo dato, "Sequimini me, " inquit, "manipulares mei[7] qui fuistis, et vestro imperatori, quam constituistis, operam date. Unum hoc proelium superest; quo confecto et ille suam dignitatem et nos nostram libertatem recuperabimus."[8] [3] Simul respiciens Caesarem, "Faciam," inquit, "hodie, imperator, ut aut vivo mihi aut mortuo gratias agas." [4] Haec cum dixisset, primus ex dextro cornu procucurrit, atque eum electi milites circiter CXX voluntarii eiusdem centuriae[9] sunt prosecuti.

Vocabulary

respicio, respicere, respexi, respectum (3): look at
mortuus, -a, -um: dead
cornu, cornus (n.): horn; wing (of army)
procurro, procurrere, procucurri, procursum (3): rush forward
prosequor, prosequi, —, prosecutum (3) (dep.): follow

plan of the Battle of Pharsalus (Kelsey)

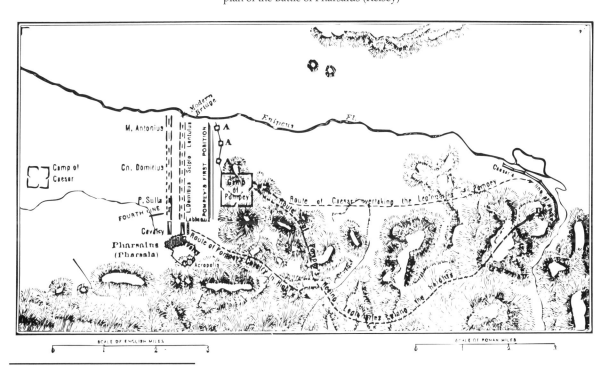

[4]**primum pilum**: the chief centurion in the legion; there were 60 in all. He was the most important non-commissioned officer, and crucial to the discipline and success of the legion.
[5]**legione X**: the Tenth was always Caesar's favorite legion during the Gallic wars.
[6]**duxerat**: "had held the office of...."
[7]**manipulares mei**: literally, "my fellows of the same maniple." There were 30 maniples in a legion and so, theoretically, 200 men in each. But this 120 men is not a maniple, but rather a picked force from the entire cohort (in theory, 600 men).
[8]**dignitatem...libertatem**: a summary of what Caesar has contended all along he was fighting for.
[9]**centuriae:** so the manuscripts. But something is wrong, as there cannot be more than 100 men in a century and there were probably at this time many fewer. Some editors have suggested "cohortis" instead. Or, the number CXX is in error.

CAESAR: **The Civil War**
(*De bello civili*)
August 19, 48 BC

The battle begins. Pompey sets in motion his flanking tactic, which at first succeeds, driving Caesar's cavalry back on the right. But Caesar's superior generalship saves the day: having anticipated Pompey's flanking action, he moves a line of fresh troops up on his right flank. These troops rout Pompey's cavalry; Caesar's cavalry, having regrouped, now pursues, turns Pompey's own left flank, and attacks his army from the rear. With that, the battle is lost for Pompey.

94 [5] Sed Pompeius, ut equitatum suum pulsum vidit atque eam partem, cui maxime confidebat perterritam animadvertit, aliis quoque diffisus acie excessit [6] protinusque se in castra equo contulit et eis centurionibus, quos in statione ad praetoriam portam posuerat, clare, ut milites exaudirent "Tuemini," inquit, "castra et defendite diligenter, si quid durius acciderit. Ego reliquas portas circumeo et castrorum praesidia confirmo." [7] Haec cum dixisset, se in praetorium contulit, summae rei diffidens et tamen eventum expectans.

Vocabulary

pello, pellere, pepuli, pulsum (3): drive back
animadverto, animadvertere, animadverti, animadversum (3): notice; realize
equus, -i (m.): horse
clarus, -a, -um: clear, evident
exaudio, exaudire, exaudivi, exauditum (4): hear clearly
confero, conferre, contuli, collatum (irreg.): with se = go to, head for

a fortified camp (from the Vatican Vergil)

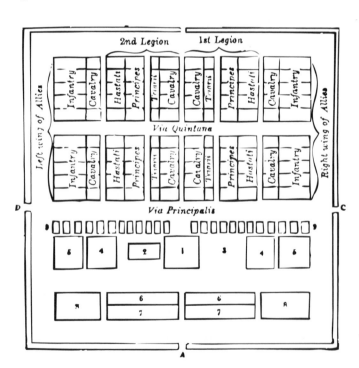

castra legionum II

95 [1] Caesar Pompeianis ex fuga intra vallum[1] compulsis nullum spatium perterritis dari oportere existimans milites cohortatus est, ut beneficio fortunae uterentur castraque oppugnarent. [2] Qui, etsi magno aestu fatigati (nam ad meridiem[2] res erat perducta), tamen ad omnem laborem animo parati imperio paruerunt. [3] Castra a cohortibus, quae ibi praesidio erant relictae, industrie defendebantur, multo etiam acrius a Thracibus barbarisque auxiliis.[3] [4] Nam, qui [ex] acie refugerant milites, et animo perterriti et lassitudine confecti, missis plerique armis signisque militaribus, magis de reliqua fuga quam de castrorum defensione cogitabant. [5] Neque vero diutius, qui in vallo constiterant, multitudinem telorum sustinere potuerunt, sed confecti[4] vulneribus locum reliquerunt, protinusque omnes ducibus usi centurionibus tribunisque militum in altissimos montes, qui ad castra pertinebant, confugerunt.

signa legionis

aquilifer

Vocabulary

oppugno, oppugnare, oppugnavi, oppugnatum (1): attack, storm
aestus, us (m.): heat
perduco, perducere, perduxi, perductum (3): prolong, drag out
industrius, -a, -um: diligent, industrious
refugio, refugere, refugi, — (3): flee from
lassitudo, lassitudinis (f.): exhaustion
magis (adv.): more
telum, -i (n.): weapon, spear, javelin (a weapon effective from afar)
sustineo, sustinere, sustinui, sustentum (2): withstand
vulnus, vulneris (n.): wound
altus, -a, -um: high; deep
mons, montis, montium (m.): mountain, hill
confugio, confugere, confugi (3): flee; take refuge

tribuni militum

centuriones

---

[1]**vallum**: the ditch-and-rampart fortifications of the legionary camp.
[2]**ad meridiem**: until the middle of the day.
[3]**auxilii**: note that the despised barbarian troops actually perform the most bravely!
[4]**confecti**: note how Caesar juxtaposes his own troops' quality (**ad omnem laborem animo parati**) to the Pompeians (**perterriti... lassitudine confecti...confecti**.)

CAESAR: **The Civil War**
(*De bello civili*)
August 19, 48 BC

3.96 [1] In castris Pompei videre licuit trichilas structas,[1] magnum argenti pondus expositum, recentibus caespitibus tabernacula constrata,[2] Lucii etiam Lentuli et nonnullorum tabernacula protecta[3] hedera, multaque praeterea, quae nimiam luxuriam et victoriae fiduciam designarent, ut facile existimari posset nihil eos de eventu eius diei timuisse, qui non necessarias[4] conquirerent voluptates.

Vocabulary
argentum, -i (n.): silver; money
pondus, ponderis (n.): weight; mass
caespes, caespitis (m.): sod
hedera, -ae (f.): ivy
nimius, -a, -um: very much; excessive
voluptas, voluptatis (f.): sensual pleasure, indulgence

trichila

---

[1]**trichilas structas**: "trichilae" are bowers, a sort of gazebo for leisurely, bucolic entertaining.
[2]**recentibus caespitibus tabernacula constrata**: tents paved with freshly cut sod to, again, enhance the bucolic atmosphere.
[3]**protecta**: "covered with."
[4]**non**: the "non" goes with **necessarias**, not with **conquirerent**.

96 [2] At hi miserrimo ac patientissimo exercitui Caesaris luxuriem obiciebant,* cui semper omnia ad necessarium usum defuissent. [3] Pompeius, iam cum intra vallum nostri versarentur, equum nactus, detractis insignibus imperatoris,[5] decumana porta[6] se ex castris eiecit protinusque equo citato Larissam contendit. [4] Neque ibi constitit, sed eadem celeritate, paucos suos ex fuga nactus, nocturno itinere non intermisso, comitatu equitum XXX ad mare pervenit navemque frumentariam[7] conscendit, saepe, ut dicebatur, querens tantum se opinionem fefellisse, ut, a quo genere hominum victoriam sperasset, ab eo initio fugae facto paene proditus videretur.

*Suetonius, Vita Divi Iuli *67.1 also makes note of the propensity of Caesar's troops for luxuries:* Ac nonumquam post magnam pugnam atque victoriam remisso officiorum munere licentiam omnem passim lasciviendi permittebat, iactare, solitus milites suos etiam unguentatos bene pugnare posse. *Clearly, the taunt here is related to the perception that Caesar's troops were effeminate luxuriators.*

Vocabulary

obicio, obicere, obieci, obiectum (3): throw up, taunt
intra: with acc.: within
detraho, detrahere, detraxi, detractum (3): remove
eicio, eicere, eieci, eiectum (3): throw out
citatus, -a, -um: swift
isdem, eadem, idem: the same
celeritas, celeritatis (f.): speed, swiftness
comitatus, -us (m.): troop (of cavalry)
conscendo, conscendere, conscendi, conscensum (3): board (a ship), get on
tantum (adv.): so much
fallo, fallere, fefelli, falsum (3): deceive, trick
prodo, prodere, prodidi, proditum (3): betray

navis frumentaria

---

[5]**insignibus imperatoris**: most especially, the blood-red commander's cloak (**paludamentum**).
[6]**decumana porta:** the "back door" of the camp.
[7]**navem frumentariam**: a vessel for shipping grain; Thessaly was a grain-exporting area.

CAESAR: **The Civil War**
(*De bello civili*)
August 48 BC

After seizing Pompey's camp, Caesar traps the remnants of Pompey's army on a nearby mountain. The army surrenders, and Caesar spares them all.

3.99 [1] In eo proelio non amplius[8] CC milites desideravit, sed centuriones, fortes viros, circiter XXX amisit. Interfectus est etiam fortissime pugnans Crastinus, cuius mentionem supra[9] fecimus, gladio in os adversum coniecto. [2] Neque id fuit falsum, quod ille in pugnam proficiscens dixerat. Sic enim Caesar existimabat, eo proelio excellentissimam virtutem Crastini fuisse, optimeque eum de se meritum iudicabat. [3] Ex Pompeiano exercitu circiter milia xv cecidisse videbantur, sed in deditionem venerunt amplius milia XXIII (namque etiam cohortes, quae praesidio in castellis[10] fuerant, sese Sullae[11] dediderunt), multi praeterea in finitimas civitates refugerunt; signaque militaria ex proelio ad Caesarem sunt relata CLXXX[12] et aquilae VIII...[13]*

*Asinius Pollio, a contemporary of events, tells us (Suetonius Vita Divi Iuli 30.4) that Caesar, gazing out over the battlefield dense with fallen citizens, said, "Hoc voluerunt; tantis rebus gestis condemnatus essem, nisi ab exercitu auxilium petissem."

Vocabulary

desidero, desiderare, desideravi, desideratum (1): lose (men as casualties)
interficio, interficere, interfeci, interfectum (3): kill
supra: above, previously (adv. & prep. usually with acc., sometimes with abl.)
gladium, -i (n.) or gladius, -i (m.): sword
adversum (adv.): facing
conicio, conicere, conieci, coniectum (3): hurl, throw
dedo, dedere, dedidi, deditum (3): surrender
finitimus, -a -um: nearby, neighboring
aquila, -ae (f.): eagle (standard of a legion)

supplicatio

aquila legionis

C. Marius

---

[8]**amplius**: note that the expected **quam** after a comparative is omitted, as often with **amplius, plus,** and **minus.**
[9]**supra**: BC 3.91.1-4, not quoted in this text.
[10]**castellis**: outlying fortlets, away from the primary military camp, the **castra.**
[11]**Sulla**: yet another Sulla, P. Cornelius, and not a very appealing fellow. He first worked with his uncle during the proscriptions of the late 80's BC and made himself a rich man. Consul in 65 BC, he then allegedly got involved in the Catilinarian Conspiracy of 63 BC, but was gotten off in a trial when defended by Cicero and Hortensius. Now, during the Civil War, he has joined Caesar. He will again make money off the property of his dead enemies, this time the Pompeians, and will die in 45 BC.
[12] These would be standards of maniples, of which there were 30 in each legion, and of centuries, of which there were 60 in each legion.
[13]**aquilae**: each legion since the time of Marius had had one standard, an eagle. These, then, represent the standards of eight Pompeian legions.

Lucius Domitius, Caesar's old nemesis from Corfinium and Massalia, is killed by Caesar's cavalry, completing the confrontation begun at the beginning of Caesar's invasion of Italy in book 1. Then, in a brief interlude, Caesar catches up his readers on some military action in Sicily and Italy. There Pompeians enjoy minor successes, but when news of Pharsalus reaches them, they break off action. Following this digression, Caesar returns to his main narrative.

Vocabulary

rursus (adv.): again
comparo, comparare, comparavi, comparatum (1): gather together
renovo, renovare, renovavi, renovatum (1): renew
quantumcumque: as much as

102 [1] Caesar omnibus rebus relictis persequendum sibi Pompeium existimavit, quascumque in partes se ex fuga recepisset, ne rursus copias comparare alias et bellum renovare posset, et, quantumcumque itineris equitatu efficere poterat, cotidie progrediebatur legionemque unam minoribus itineribus subsequi iussit. [2] Erat edictum Pompei nomine Amphipoli[14] propositum, uti omnes eius provinciae iuniores,[15] Graeci civesque Romani, iurandi causa[16] convenirent.

edictum legens...

Flight of Pompey

---

[14]**Amphipoli**: the form is locative. Amphipolis was a major port on the coast of Thrace, north of Thessaly.
[15]**iuniores**: men of military age, i.e., between 18 and 46.
[16]**iurandi causa**: that is, for the purpose of swearing a military oath to continue the struggle, presumably under new leadership.

CAESAR: **The Civil War**
(*De bello civili*)
Autumn, 48 BC

anchorae

3.102 [3] Sed utrum avertendae suspicionis causa Pompeius proposuisset, ut quam diutissime longioris fugae consilium occultaret, an novis delectibus, si nemo premeret, Macedoniam tenere conaretur, existimari non poterat. [4] Ipse ad ancoram[1] una nocte constitit et vocatis ad se Amphipoli hospitibus et pecunia ad necessarios sumptus corrogata cognito Caesaris adventu ex eo loco discessit et Mytilenas[2] paucis diebus venit. [5] Biduum tempestate retentus navibusque aliis additis actuariis[3] in Ciliciam atque inde Cyprum pervenit. [6] Ibi cognoscit, consensu omnium Antiochensium[4] civiumque Romanorum, qui illic negotiarentur,[5] arcem captam esse excludendi sui causa nuntiosque dimissos ad eos, qui se ex fuga in finitimas civitates recepisse dicerentur, ne Antiochiam adirent: id si fecissent, magno eorum capitis[6] periculo futurum...

Vocabulary

suspicio, suspicionis (f.): suspicion
premo, premere, pressi, pressum (3): pursue
existimo, existimare, existimavi, existimatum (1): evaluate
hospes, hospitis (m.): friend; guest
sumptus, -us (m.): expense, cost
biduum, -i (n.): a period of two days
tempestas, tempestatis (f.): storm; season, weather
illic (adv.): there
negotior, negotiari, —, negotiatum (dep. 1): do business
arx, arcis (f.): citadel, fortress, stronghold
adeo, adire, adii or adivi, aditum (irreg.): approach
caput, capitis (n.): head; capital

navis actuaria

Fortuna, symbol of Antioch

---

[1]**ad ancoram**: at anchor, that is, his ship stays only one night in the harbor.

[2]**Mytilenas:** Mytilene was a town on the island of Lesbos, off the coast of Asia Minor. It looks like the reception at Amphipolis was so lukewarm that Pompey gave up hope of holding Macedonia and fled east. He had left his wife Cornelia and younger son, Sextus, at Mytilene, awaiting news of the outcome of the military confrontation.

[3]**navibus...actuariis:** swift ships. Isidore of Seville (*Origines* 19.1.24) defines as follows: "actuariae naves sunt, quae velis simul et remis aguntur."

[4]**Antiochensium**: Antioch was the main city of Syria, and the most important city of the Roman East; only Alexandria, in a still-independent Egypt, was larger. News that the Antiochenes had turned against him was a serious blow.

[5]**negotiarentur**: probably these men mostly engaged in moneylending.

[6]**capitis**: the danger affects their heads; that is, they would be in danger of their lives.

News of Caesar's victory spreads, and Pompeian survivors, as well as Pompey himself, are refused entrance to towns.

103 [1] Quibus cognitis rebus Pompeius deposito adeundae Syriae consilio pecunia societatis[7] sublata[8] et a quibusdam privatis sumpta et aeris magno pondere ad militarem usum[9] in naves imposito duobusque milibus hominum armatis, partim quos ex familiis[10] societatum delegerat, partim a negotiatoribus coegerat, quosque ex suis quisque ad hanc rem idoneos existimabat, Pelusium[11] pervenit.

Vocabulary

societas, societatis (f.): business association, corporation
partim (adv.): partly
deligo, deligere, delegi, delectum (3): choose, select
negotiator, negotioris (m.): businessman

Flight of Pompey

---

[7]**societatis**: Roman corporations operated in the provinces as tax collectors; Pompey is seizing currently collected taxes.
[8]**sublata**: note that Pompey continues here to pillage his "allies;" he had done the same of his "friends" at Amphipolis (**pecunia...corrogata**).
[9]**usum**: apparently, to pay the troops in bronze coin.
[10]**familiis**: the familia is the household, including the slaves; here means slaves which the **societas** maintained. Besides once again confiscating property of his "friends," Pompey is reduced to using a sorry lot to form a military force.
[11]**Pelusium**: the only port along the Suez peninsula; the last stop before Alexandria.

113

CAESAR: **The Civil War**
(De bello civili)
Autumn, 48 BC

Vocabulary

puer, pueri (m.): boy, child; slave
soror, sororis (f.): sister
disto, distare, distavi, distatum (1): locate at a distance; stand apart
hospitium, -i (n.): hospitality; friendship
despicio, despicere, despexi, despectum (3): despise; express comtempt for

3.103 [2] Ibi casu rex erat Ptolomaeus,[12] puer aetate, magnis copiis cum sorore Cleopatra[13] bellum gerens, quam paucis ante mensibus per suos propinquos atque amicos regno expulerat; castraque Cleopatrae non longo spatio ab eius castris distabant. [3] Ad eum Pompeius misit, ut pro hospitio atque amicitia patris[14] Alexandria reciperetur atque illius opibus in calamitate tegeretur. [4] Sed qui ab eo missi erant, confecto legationis officio liberius cum militibus regis colloqui coeperunt eosque hortari, ut suum officium Pompeio praestarent neve eius fortunam despicerent. [5] In hoc erant numero complures Pompei milites, quos ex eius exercitu acceptos in Syria Gabinius Alexandriam traduxerat belloque confecto apud Ptolomaeum, patrem pueri, reliquerat.[15]

Ptolemy II and wife, Arsinoe, ancestors of Cleopatra VII

Cleopatra VII

---

[12]**Ptolomaeus:** This would be the thirteenth Ptolemy, born in 63 BC and the husband-brother of Cleopatra.
[13]**Cleopatra:** the seventh Cleo, and by far the most famous. She was born in 69 BC and was at this time co-ruler with and wife of her younger brother, Ptolemy XIII. However, Ptolemy had initiated a coup, and had ejected her shortly before this time.
[14]**hospitio...amiticia patris:** Pompey had been instrumental in getting Ptolemy & Cleo's father, Ptolemy XII "The Flute Player," re-installed as King of Egypt in 55 BC.
[15]Gabinius had been the person in charge of actually installing Ptolemy XII in 55 BC; he had used Pompeian troops left in Syria when Pompey had returned to Rome after his successful eastern wars (66-63 BC). Gabinius was a long-time ally of Pompey who ultimately ended up fighting for Caesar in the Civil War; he was killed in 48/47 BC fighting in Illyricum.

104 [1] His tunc cognitis rebus amici regis, qui propter aetatem eius in procuratione erant regni,[16] sive timore adducti, ut postea praedicabant, sollicitato exercitu regio ne Pompeius Alexandriam Aegyptumque occuparet, sive despecta eius fortuna, ut plerumque in calamitate ex amicis inimici exsistunt, his, qui erant ab eo missi, palam liberaliter responderunt eumque ad regem venire iusserunt; [2] ipsi clam consilio inito Achillam, praefectum regium,[17] singulari hominem audacia, et Lucium Septimium[18] tribunum militum ad interficiendum Pompeium miserunt.

Vocabulary

sollicito, sollicitare, sollicitavi, sollicitatum (1): stir up, incite
plerumque (adv.): often
liberaliter (adv.): generously
ineo, inire, inii or inivi, initum (irreg.): begin; undertake
singularis, -e: outstanding, unparalleled

ancient Roman navy (from a fresco in Pompeii)

---

[16]**procuratione ... regni**: these men were the regents for the young monarchs.

[17]**Achillam, praefectum regium**: Achillas was the military commander in the Egyptian forces and became the main minister of the king.

[18]**Lucium Septimium**: this fellow, whose name shall live in infamy, is practically unknown except for the details given here by Caesar and repeated by later sources. He had been a chief centurion (**primipilus**) under Pompey during his war against the pirates (67 BC).

CAESAR: **The Civil War**
(De bello civili)
September 28, 48 BC

3.104 [3] Ab his liberaliter ipse appellatus et quadam notitia[19] Septimii productus, quod bello praedonum apud eum ordinem duxerat,[20] naviculam parvulam conscendit cum paucis suis: ibi ab Achilla et Septimio interficitur. Item Lucius Lentulus comprehenditur ab rege et in custodia necatur.[21]

Caesar describes divine prodigies which had appeared to predict the victory over his enemies at Pharsalus.

106 [1] Caesar paucos dies in Asia moratus,[22] cum audisset[23] Pompeium Cypri[24] visum, coniectans eum in Aegyptum iter habere propter necessitudines regni reliquasque eius loci opportunitates, cum legione una, quam se ex Thessalia sequi iusserat, et altera, quam ex Achaia[25] a Quinto Fufio[26] legato evocaverat, equitibusque DCCC et navibus longis[27] Rhodiis[28] X et Asiaticis paucis Alexandriam pervenit.

Vocabulary

praedo, praedonis (m.): pirate
comprehendo, comprehendere, comprehendi, comprehendsum (3): seize, arrest
neco, necare, necavi, necatum (1): kill
coniecto, coniectare, coniectavi, coniectatum (1): guess, conjecture
opportunitas, opportunitatis (f.): suitability; advantage

navis parvula (scapha)

war galley

navis longa

---

[19]**quadam notitia**: "a certain familiarity."

[20]**ordinem duxerat**: "had been a centurion."

[21]**necatur**: in general, **neco** means to put to death without a weapon (starving, poisoning, etc.), whereas **interficio** means to slay with a weapon. But such distinctions must not be pressed too far.

[22]**Asia moratus**: Caesar is following Pompey's trail.

[23]**audisset**: a syncopated form.

[24]**Cypri**: aha! A small island. A locative case.

[25]**Achaia**: southern Greece, the Peloponnese.

[26]**Quinto Fufio**: Q. Fufius Calenus was a steady supporter of Caesar throughout the fifties and the civil war period.

[27]**navibus longis**: war ships.

[28]**Rhodiis**: the Cicero of islands, Rhodes was always vacillating, trying to guess which side would be the winner. Early favorable toward Caesar, she had offered support for Pompey (*BC* 3.26) when he looked like a winner, then had refused entrance to fleeing Pompeians after Pharsalus (*BC* 3.102.7). Now they supply ships to Caesar, who looks like a winner.

[2] In his erant legionibus hominum milia tria CC; reliqui vulneribus ex proeliis et labore ac magnitudine itineris confecti consequi non potuerant.[29] [3] Sed Caesar confisus fama rerum gestarum infirmis auxiliis proficisci non dubitaverat, aeque omnem sibi locum tutum fore existimans. [4] Alexandriae de Pompei morte cognoscit...

The Bellum Civile *goes on to detail Caesar's trials at Alexandria, then breaks off unexpectedly as he is being beseiged by Ptolemy XIII's troops led by Achillas. His work of self-justification no longer needed, Caesar simply stopped writing. Or did he not care to continue with an episode which included his liaison with Cleopatra...?*

Vocabulary

mors, mortis (f.): death
morbus, -i: illness
imbecillitas, imbecilitatis (f.): weakness
exanimo, exanimare, exanimavi, exanimatum (1): dishearten, scare a lot
gratus, -a, -um: pleasing, welcome
quocumque (adv.): wherever
integer, -ra, -rum: whole; honest
castus, -a, -um: pure; virtuous

CICERO: **Letter to Atticus**
(*Epistulae ad Atticum* 11.6.5)
November 27, 48 BC

Tulliae meae[30] morbus et imbecillitas corporis me exanimat. Quam tibi intellego magnae curae esse, quod est mihi gratissimum. De Pompei exitu mihi dubium numquam fuit. Tanta enim desperatio rerum eius omnium regum et populorum animos occuparat,[31] ut, quocumque venisset, hoc putarem futurum. Non possum eius casum non dolere; hominem enim integrum et castum et gravem cognovi.

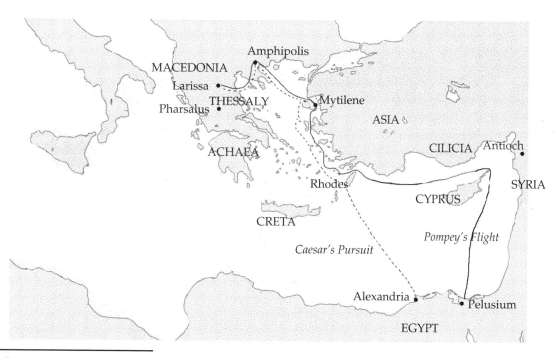

---

[29]Normally, two legions would number about 9,000 men (with a notional strength of 12,000).
[30]**Tulliae meae**: Cicero's daughter.
[31]**occuparat**: syncopated form.

Plutarch gives a dramatic account of the death of Pompey, which affected so many so much:

Potheinus the eunuch, Theodotus of Chios and Achillas the Egyptian, advisers to young king Ptolemy, meet and decide that Pompey the Great must be killed upon his arrival in Egypt.

78.   After deciding upon this plan, the advisers entrusted the execution of it to Achillas. Achillas took with him a man called Septimius, who had once been one of Pompey's officers, a centurion named Salvius, and three of four attendants. With these he put to sea and sailed towards Pompey's ship. Those on board, when they saw that instead of anything regal or splendid about their reception or anything to justify Theophanes' hopeful expectations, there were just a few men sailing toward them in a single fishing boat, grew suspicious at this apparent lack of respect and advised Pompey to have his ship rowed back out to open sea while they were still out of range of missiles. By this time, however, the boat had drawn near. First Septimius rose stood up and in Latin saluted Pompey as "Imperator;" then Achillas greeted him in Greek and invited him to come aboard the boat, noting that in this region there was shallow water for a long distance from shore, and that because of the sand shoals the sea was not deep enough for the trireme. At the same time it could be seen that some of the King's ships were being manned and that armed soldiers occupied the whole shore, so that there seemed to be no way of escape, even if they changed their minds. Besides, such a lack of confidence might merely provide the murderers with an excuse for their crime. So Pompey embraced Cornelia, who was already lamenting in anticipation of his death, and he ordered two centurions to go on board before him, as well as a freedman of his called Philip and a servant named Scythes. Then, as Achillas was already stretching out his hand to him from the boat, Pompey turned to his wife and son and recited the verses of Sophocles:

*Whoever makes his way into a tyrant's presence
In essence is his slave, though he went unto him a free man.*

79.   After these last words to his friends, Pompey went into the boat. It was some distance from the trireme to the land and since none of those on board addressed a single friendly word to him, Pompey let his eyes fall on Septimius and said, "Surely I am not mistaken. You and I were fellow-soldiers together." Septimius only nodded his head, saying nothing and showing no friendliness. Again there was utter silence, and Pompey took out a small scroll in which he

had written in Greek the speech which he was prepared to use in addressing Ptolemy, and he began to go over it. Then, as they drew near to the shore, Cornelia and his friends watched from the trireme to see what would happen. Cornelia was very distressed, but she began to take heart when she saw many of the King's people gathering at the landing place, as if to give Pompey an honorable welcome. Just then, however, while Pompey grasped Philip's hand so as to rise to his feet more easily, Septimius from behind ran him through the body with his sword; then Salvius and Achillas drew their daggers and stabbed him. Pompey, drawing his toga over his face with both hands, endured their blows; he neither said nor did anything unworthy of himself, but only groaned a little and so ended his life just one day after his birthday, having lived fifty-nine years.

80.   When the people on the ships saw the murder, they sent up such a wail that it could be heard from the shore. Then Pompey's companions quickly weighed anchor and fled. A strong wind helped them as they ran out to sea, and as a result the Egyptians turned back, although they wished to pursue them. Then they cut off Pompey's head and threw his naked body out of the boat, leaving it there for those who desired such a spectacle. Philip, however, stayed by the body until the others had enough of gazing at it; he then washed it in sea water and wrapped it in one of his own tunics. Then, since he had nothing else, he searched all along the coast until he found some broken planks from a small fishing boat, old to be sure, but enough to make a funeral pyre for a naked and decapitated body. As Philip was gathering the wood and building the pyre, a Roman man, aged now but one who in his youth had done his first military service with Pompey, said, "Who are you, sir, who intend to offer burial rites for Pompey the Great?" When Philip said that he was Pompey's freedman, the old man said, "But you will not have this honor all to yourself. Let me share in this act of reverence, a godsend offered to me. In this way, I shall not completely regret my life in a foreign land if, in return for many hardships, I find this happiness at least — to touch with my own hands and to prepare for burial the greatest Roman Imperator." Thus were performed the burial rites for Pompey.

(Translation by P. Vaughn)

Appendix One
Some Useful Terminology

amicitia "friendship" as a political term; either as an element of foreign diplomacy, establishing ties between Rome and another state or individual or as an element of internal political allegiance; the *amici* of a powerful public figure could serve as his public and personal advisors and as his political base in Rome

auctoritas the leadership authority granted to another by virtue of his reputation, popularity and personal influence

contio a public meeting, civic or military, at which the politician or general presented his views, addressing the assembled group from an elevated platform

cupiditas in the context of *FRP* an immoderate desire to achieve power and authority beyond what one is due; unbridled and unseemly ambition

dignitas rank, position, reputation, and honor; the means, if you will, by which one achieves *auctoritas*; loss of *dignitas*, therefore, means loss of position and rank within the community

dominatio as a neutral term within the Roman tradition, the absolute authority as, for example, that of the *paterfamilias* over his family; but in *FRP* it is no better than *regnum*—tyranny, absolute rule and a subversion of the traditional republican system

factio as a neutral term, no more than a gathering of *amici* or *socii*; but in its negative implication (as so often here) a partisan group which engages in unfair and subversive practices

imperium the supreme exercise of power, granted to certain magistrates of the Roman state, conferring command in war and the interpretation and execution of law; it is the authority granted to the *imperator* to give orders and exact obedience at all costs

inimicitia basically the opposite of *amiticia*, this personal enmity involves direct action to diminish the *dignitas* and *auctoritas* of another

intercessio the process of veto; in particular, the right of the tribunes to veto the actions of magistrates

s.c.u. the *senatus consultum ultimum*; specifically a declaration of a state of emergency, authorizing the magistrates to take whatever measures necessary to protect the state and to ensure it came to no harm; the *s.c.u.* was often interpreted as granting the suspension of legal procedure, which naturally led to controversy about its imposition and application

virtus the essential characteristic of a "manly" Roman, embodying military valor, loyalty, strength of character, mental acumen, moral excellence and adherence to Roman traditional values

Cursus Honorum

The cursus honorum ("career path") consists of the elective posts through which a politician had to pass to reach the top of the political world. The Censor, at the head of the list, was elected normally once every five years for an eighteen-month term of office. The remaining posts were elected annually for a twelve-month term. If, as consul or praetor, one was sent to a province as a governor, one could have one's powers extended (*prorogatio*) for an additional year; these officials are customarily called proconsuls and propraetors. While most politicians ran for every office in its turn, the only required posts in the late Republic were the quaestorship, the praetorship, and the consulship. In addition, only plebeians could run for the Tribunate of the Plebs. The order of offices and the number in each office during the late Republic are as follows:

Censor (2)
Consul (2)
Praetor (8)
Aedile (Plebeian Aedile and Curule Aedile) (2-2)
Tribune of the Plebs (10)
Quaestor (20)

Censor	in charge of census, letting public contracts, and supervision of public morality
Consul	chief military and civic magistrate
Praetor	chief magistrate in Rome in absence of consuls; administrator of law and legal process; could be military commander/governor of a province
Aedilis	superintendent of public works
Tribunus plebis	the tribunes of the people were charged with the defense of the persons and property of the plebeians and were originally established to protect the plebs from oppression by the patrician class; among their numerous powers is the right of veto against acts of magistrates and each other
Quaestor	financial officer, frequently attached to the office of provincial governors

[Students are urged to consult, as an initial reference, the *Oxford Classical Dictionary*, for a full definition of each office, the changes made to it over time, and its overall responsibilities.]

Let's follow one of the stalwarts of Roman political fame, Marcus Porcius Cato (Cato Maior) through his career path:

217	Contubernalis (orderly) of Fabius Maximus; Cato is only 17, and here is where his political career really began
214	Military Tribune (served in Sicily)
204	Quaestor (his election to this post made him eligible to become a permanent member of the Senate; he served under Scipio in Africa)
199	Plebeian Aedile
198	Praetor (sent as governor to Sardinia)
195	Consul (sent to Spain; in 194 the Senate extended his powers for another year)
191	Military Tribune (served in Greece under Acilius Glabrio; he was elected to this post by the Populus Romanus)
189	Legatus (sent to Fulvius Nobilior in Aetolia)
189	Censor
171	Commissioner to Investigate Spanish Governors
153	Ambassador (member of a commission to Carthage to mediate a dispute between Masinissa and Carthage)

[at some point prior to 149 he was probably elected to the College of Augurs]

The Roman Name

A Roman man regularly had three names: (1) the **praenomen** (or personal name); (2) the **nomen** (or name of the family, house or tribe); (3) the **cognomen** (often a nickname, or mark of distinction).

Thus, for example, in the name **Marcus Tullius Cicero** we have:

MARCUS (M.)	praenomen
TULLIUS	**nomen**, properly an adjective denoting "of the gens [family] Tullius"
CICERO	**cognomen**; in this case, a nickname attached (probably) to an early ancestor, from **cicer** ("chickpea")—perhaps in reference to a blemish

Often a fourth or fifth cognomen was given as a mark of honor, or to show adoption (a frequent Roman practice) from another gens. Examples:

Lucius Cornelius Sulla **Felix**	**Felix** ("Lucky") was a nickname taken from Fortune's favoring Sulla's actions
Publius Cornelius Scipio **Aemilianus Africanus**	**Aemilianus**. Cognomina in -ianus often indicate adoption from another family; Scipio was adopted from the Aemilian family.
	Africanus. An honorific cognomen from both his grandfather's accomplishments against Hannibal and his own against Carthage in Africa.

Women in classical times commonly had no personal names, but were known only by the name of the gens [family] (in feminine form): Cicero's wife, for example, was called "Terentia" (she was born into the **gens Terentia**), and his daughter, who was born into the Tullian gens, was called "Tullia," A family could have more than one daughter, each with the same name, designated only by "prima," "secunda," "tertia" and so on, in chronological order of birth. A woman was frequently referred to by her name and her husband's or father's name in the genitive (indicating possession): e.g., Caecilia Metelli, "Caecilia, [daughter of] Metellus."

Common Roman male personal names (**praenomina**), and their abbreviations:

A.=Aulus	App.(Ap.) = Appius	C.(G.) = Gaius
Cn.(Gn.) = Gnaeus	D. = Decimus	K. = Kaeso (Caeso)
L. = Lucius	M. = Marcus	M'. = Manius
Mam. = Mamercus	N.(Num.) = Numerius	P. = Publius
Q. = Quintus	Ser. = Servius	Sex.(S.) = Sextus
Sp. = Spurius	T. = Titus	Ti.(Tib.) = Tiberius

Glossary of Persons

Bold names appear in the Latin text of FRP. Other names appear in the notes.

Achillas	regent of Ptolemy XIII; murderer of Pompey in Egypt, 48
Aulus **Acutius** Rufus	partisan of Pompey; otherwise unknown
Lucius **Afranius**	long-time partisan of Pompey; cos. 60; defeated by Caesar in Spain, 49; fled after Pharsalus; killed after Thapsus, 46
Cnaeus Domitius **Ahenobarbus, son of Lucius**	see Domitius
Lucius Domitius **Ahenobarbus**	see Domitius
Marcus **Antonius**	strong partisan of Caesar; dissolute fellow; brave and capable officer; with Caesar in Gaul, 54; augur, 50; tribune of the people, 49; in command in Italy while Caesar is in Spain, 49; commanded left wing at Pharsalus, 48; cos. with Caesar, 44; suicide after Actium defeat, 30
Caius **Appuleius** Saturninus	turbulent tribune whose second tribunate, in 100 BC, provoked grievous opposition among the oligarchs, much civil disorder, and, ultimately, his death by tiling.
Atia	niece of Caesar; married Caius Octavius; mother of Octavius (later Augustus)
Titus Pomponius **Atticus**	see Pomponius
Publius **Attius** Varus	partisan of Pompey; praetor by 53; failed to hold northern Italy against Caesar's advance, 49; Pompeian commander in Africa, defeated Caesarian Curio; fled to Spain after Thapsus, 46; killed at Munda, 45 and head delivered to Caesar
Caius **Attius** Paelignus	partisan of Pompey; otherwise unknown
Augustus	see Octavius

	Aurelia	of Aurelii Cottae family; mother of Caesar; died, 54
Lucius	**Aurelius** Cotta	partisan of Caesar in civil wars; cos. 65; censor 64; related to Caesar's mother
Cornelius	**Balbus**	see Cornelius
Cornelius	**Bibulus**	see Cornelius
	Bocchus	son of betrayer of Jugurtha to Sulla, 106; joint king of Mauretania with brother Bogud; served Caesar in Africa in civil wars
	Bogud	joint king of Mauretania with brother Bocchus; served Caesar in Africa in civil wars
Marcus Iunius	**Brutus**	see Iunius
Lucius	**Caecilius** Metellus	partisan of Pompey; tribune of the people, 49, in which office he fruitlessly tried to keep Caesar from the treasury; final fate unknown
Quintus	**Caecilius** Metellus Pius Scipio	strong partisan of Pompey; born Publius Cornelius Scipio, adopted by Caecilius Metellus; aided Pompey in disorders of 53; married daughter, Cornelia, to Pompey, 52, in which year he also was consul; led attempts to remove Caesar from Gallic command, 51-49; held Syria as province, 49, which he plundered; joined Pompey at Pharsalus, 48, in which battle he commanded the center of the line; led Pompeians in Africa, 48-46; defeated at Thapsus, 46; committed suicide soon thereafter
Marcus	**Caelius** Rufus	opportunist partisan of Caesar; spectacular combination of talent and profligacy; involved with Catiline in 63, with Clodius and, especially, his sister Clodia in the early fifties; supporter of Caesar from expediency, 49; praetor, 48; desperately in debt, supported measures to cancel same; stripped of his office, joined Milo in rebellion in southern

		Italy; killed there by men loyal to Caesar, 48
Caius Iulius **Caesar**		see Iulius
Lucius Iulius **Caesar adulescens**		see Iulius
Lucius Iulius **Caesar pater**		see Iulius
Marcus **Calenius**		details of life unknown
Quintus Fufius **Calenus**		see Fufius
Marcus **Calidius**		partisan of Caesar; famous orator; praetor, 57
Lucius **Calpurnius** Piso Caesoninus		uninspired and uninspiring scion of a most famous plebian family, daughter married to Caesar, 59; consul, 58; plundered Macedonia as governor, 57-56; deadly enemy of Cicero; censor, 50; followed Pompey from Rome, but not to Greece, 49; remained neutral in civil wars
Quintus **Cassius** Longinus		partisan of Caesar; quaestor in Spain, 54, where his rapacity almost cost him his life; tribune of the people, strong supporter of Caesar in Rome, 49; governor of Further Spain, 49; barely escaped assassination at Corduba, 48; center of further civil strife in Further Spain; drowned at sea, 47
Quintus Sergius **Catilina**		see Sergius
Marcus Porcius **Cato**		see Porcius
Marcus Porcius **Cato the Elder**		see Porcius
Marcus Tullius **Cicero**		see Tullius
Marcus **Claudius** Marcellus		successful orator; consul 51; friend of Cicero; brother of Caius Marcellus; half-hearted partisan of Pompey, 51-48; fled Rome and Italy, but offered little active help; retired to Mytilene after Pharsalus; recalled from exile by Caesar, 44; assassinated in Greece on return voyage to Rome
Caius **Claudius** Marcellus		partisan of Pompey; consul 50; cousin of Marcus Marcellus noted above and Caius Marcellus below; married to Octavia, Caesar's niece and sister to the later Augustus Caesar; sponsored bill to take the two

		"Parthian" legions from Caesar, 50; strongly urged military opposition to Caesar, 50, but provided lackluster, even timid aid to the Pompeians subsequently—remained in Italy throughout the civil war; died 41, in good time for Octavia's political marriage to Marcus Antonius
Caius	**Claudius**	Marcellus	strong partisan of Pompey; brother of Marcus Marcellus noted above; consul, 49; attacked Caesar strongly in early 49; minor commander in the civil war, in which he apparently was killed
	Cleopatra	joint ruler of Egypt with brother Ptolemy XIII, 51-48; driven from throne; restored by Caesar, 48; suicide after Actium defeat, 30
	Clodia	sister of Publius Clodius; husband of Lucullus; friend of Catullus and? his Lesbia; (?) incestuous lover of brother; famously profligate
Aulus	**Clodius**	partisan of Caesar; details of life unknown
Publius	**Clodius**	Pulcher	brother of Clodia; engineered Cicero's exile from Rome, 58; instrumental in civil discord of the 50s; killed by Milo, 52
	Cornelia	daughter of Quintus Caecilius Metellus Pius Scipio, born Publius Cornelius Scipio and adopted by Metellus; married to Crassus' son until his death in 53, then married to Pompey, 52, who adored her beauty, learning, and sophistication
	Cornelia	Fausta	daughter of Sulla; profligate; married to Milo
Lucius	**Cornelius**	Bibulus	bitter enemy of Caesar; advanced in tandem with him (aedile 65, praetor 62, consul 59); married Porcia, daughter of Cato; partisan of Pompey in civil wars; died 48
	Cornelius	Balbus	friend of both Caesar and Pompey; native of Gades (Hispania); worked for Caesar's interests in civil war

Lucius	**Cornelius**	Lentulus Crus	partisan of Pompey; origins obscure; consul 49; led actions against Caesar in Rome early that year; half-heartedly followed Pompey from Rome and Italy, 49; subsequently played no important role; followed Pompey to Egypt; killed there, 48
Lucius	**Cornelius**	Sulla	captured Iugurtha, 106; successful general; cos. 88; marched on Rome, 87; seized Rome again, 82, and murders his enemies; dictator until 79; died, 78
Publius	**Cornelius**	Sulla	partisan of Caesar; nephew of the dictator Sulla; elected cos. 65, but deposed for bribery; probably a conspirator with Catiline, 63; commanded Caesar's right wing at Pharsalus
Faustus	**Cornelius**	Sulla	partisan of Pompey; son of the dictator Sulla, twin of Fausta; married daughter of Pompey; resembled his father only in his extravagance
Publius	**Cornelius**	Lentulus Spinther	favored by Caesar in early 50s, turned to opposition of First Triumvirate as consul, 57; commanded forces in northern Italy at outbreak of civil war; captured at Corfinium and released by Caesar; joined Pompey in Greece, 49; fled after Pharsalus to Rhodes; fate unknown
Aurelius	**Cotta**		see Aurelius
Marcus Licinius	**Crassus**		see Licinius
	Crastinus		*primus pilus, evocatus* in Caesar's 10th Legion, 48
Caius Scribonius	**Curio**		see Scribonius
Caius Scribonius	**Curio**		see Scribonius
Vibius	**Curius**		see Vibius
Cnaeus	**Domitius**	Ahenobarbus,	the son of Lucius; partisan of Pompey; present at Pharsalus; pardoned by Caesar; one of his assassins, 44
Lucius	**Domitius**	Ahenobarbus	strong supporter of conservative *factio*; married to Porcia, sister of Cato; cos. 54; appointed to succeed

	Caesar in Gaul, 49; defeated by Caesar at Corfinium and at Massalia, 49; killed (by Marcus Antonius?) at Pharsalus, 48
Caius **Fabius**	partisan of Caesar; tribune of the people, 55?; lieutenant commander under Caesar, 54-49
Quintus **Fabius**	details of life unknown
Quintus **Fufius** Calenus	strong supporter of Caesar; praetor, 59; effective emissary for Caesar, 51-47
Aulus **Gabinius**	dissipated follower of, first, Pompey and then, Caesar; consul, 58; installed Ptolemy XII as King of Egypt, 55; exiled for illegal acts as general, 54; recalled by Caesar, 49
Servius Sulpicius **Galba**	see Sulpicius
Tiberius Sempronius **Gracchus**	see Sempronius
Caius Sempronius **Gracchus**	see Sempronius
Hannibal	scourge of Rome during Second Punic War; fought in Italy 218-204; defeated by Scipio at Zama, 202
Caius Lucilius **Hirrus**	see Lucilius
Aulus **Hirtius**	strong supporter of Caesar; lieutenant commander in Gaul 58-50; continuator of Caesar's literary works; activity during the civil wars uncertain
Quintus **Hortensius**	leading orator in Rome, 114-50; cos. 69; rival of Cicero, staunch conservative; died 49
Iuba	king of Numidia; partisan of Pompey; defeated Curio in Africa, 49; committed suicide after defeat at Thapsus, 46
Caius **Iulius** Caesar	cos. I, 59; ruler of the Roman world, 44
Lucius **Iulius** Caesar pater	cos. 64; legate of Caesar, 52; remained in Rome during civil war; uncle of Marcus Antonius
Lucius **Iulius** Caesar filius	Pompeian partisan; ineffectual: Cicero calls him "a bundle of loose broomsticks" (*scopae solutae*)
Marcus **Iunius** Brutus	a leader of the conservative *factio*; served with Pompey; pardoned by

			Caesar after Pharsalus, 48; an assassin of Caesar, 44
Titus		**Labienus**	partisan of Caesar, 63-50; served with Caesar in Gaul with distinction; defected to Pompey, 49; fought Caesar at Pharsalus, 48, Thapsus, 46, Munda, 45 where he was killed and his head brought to Caesar
Publius	Cornelius	**Lentulus** Spinther	see Cornelius
Lucius	Cornelius	**Lentulus Crus**	see Cornelius
Lucius	Scribonius	**Libo**	see Scribonius
	Marcus	**Licinius** Crassus	partisan of Sulla, made a fortune in the Sullan proscriptions; early rival of Pompey; consul with him, 70; censor, 65; financially supported Caesar, 62; reconciled to Pompey in First Triumvirate with Caesar, 60-53; killed in war against the Parthians, 53
Quintus	Cassius	**Longinus**	see Cassius
	Caius	**Lucilius** Hirrus	partisan of Pompey; tribune of the people, 53; commander and emissary for Pompey in civil wars; pardoned by Caesar, joined Sextus Pompey after Caesar's murder; end unknown
	Quintus	**Lucretius** Vespillo	partisan of Pompey; prefect in northern Italy at the outbreak of civil war, 49; commanded part of Pompey's fleet, 49
	Numerius	**Magius**	partisan of Pompey; chief engineer *(praefectus fabrum)* and emissary between Caesar and Pompey, 49
	Lucius	**Manlius** Torquatus	partisan of Pompey; scion of distinguished family and a learned man; praetor, 49; lost Alba to Caesar, 49, and Oricum, 48; fled to Africa after Pharsalus; killed there, 46
Marcus	Claudius	**Marcellus**	see Claudius
Caius	Claudius	**Marcellus**	see Claudius
	Lucius	**Marcius** Philippus	consul, 56; closely connected with Caesar's family: married Atia, Caesar's niece, at the death of her first husband, Octavius—Atia was the mother of the future Augustus

		Caesar; married his daughter to Cato; neutral in the civil wars, irresolute afterwards, lived long enough to see his step-son rule the Roman world
Lucius	**Marcius** Philippus the son	partisan of Caesar; son of the foregoing; tribune of the people, 49; praetor, 44, suffect consul, 38; "vir patre, avo, maioribus suis dignissimus" (*Cic. Phil.* 3.10)
Caius	**Marius**	seven times consul between 105 and 86 although a *novus homo*; reformer of army and greatest general of his generation; opponent of Sulla, murderer of hundreds in his proscriptions, 86; died sick and bitter, 86
Lucius Caecilius	**Metellus**	see Caecilius
Quintus Caecilius	**Metellus Pius** Scipio	see Caecilius
Quintus	**Minucius** Thermus	partisan of Pompey; propraetor in northern Italy, but fled at Caesar's advance, 49; followed Sextus Pompey after Caesar's murder, but deserted him, 35; end unknown
	Octavia	daughter of Octavius and Atia, brother of the later Augustus Caesar, niece of Caesar; veteran of political marriages, Caesar unsuccessfully offered to get her to divorce her current husband, C. Marcellus, to marry Pompey at death of Julia, 54; subsequently married to Marcus Antonius to cement his alliance with the young Octavian, 41, who divorced her, 32; universally admired for humanity, intelligence, and beauty; grandmother of Claudius, great-grandmother of Caligula and Nero; died, 11
	Octavius	son of C. Octavius and Atia, grand-nephew of Caesar; adopted by him in his will as Caius Iulius Caesar Octavianus; received honorific "Augustus" from senate, 27; ruled

	Roman world until his death, AD 14
Quintus Caecilius Metellus **Pius** Scipio	see Caecilius
Attius **Paelignus**	see Attius
Lucius Calpurnius **Piso**	see Calpurnius
Cnaeus **Plancius**	correspondent of Cicero's; partisan of Pompey, his role in the civil war unknown, but still in exile, 46-45
Cnaeus **Pompeius** Magnus	a man of great abilities and ego; arrogated to himself the cognomen Magnus, in imitation of Alexander the Great, 81; accomplished opportunist, supported Sulla, 83-79, but later sponsored the repeal of his political legislation, 70; greatest warlord of 60s, joined old enemy Crassus and Caesar in First Triumvirate to secure political aims, 60; emerged as leader of the conservative, anti-Caesarian group by late 50s; in command of anti-Caesarian forces, 50-48; defeated at Pharsalus, fled to Egypt and murdered there, 48
Sextus **Pompeius**	son of Pompeius Magnus; participated in anti-Caesarian action in defeats at Thapsus, 46, and Munda, 45; declared an outlaw after death of Caesar, seized Sicily and opposed the Second Triumvirate until defeat by Agrippa; after fleeing to Asia, killed, 35
Titus **Pomponius** Atticus	close friend of Cicero and recipient of many letters; a wealthy, highly educated, savvy and brilliant bystander in the political struggles of the late Republic; died 32, having survived almost all the major players in the *finis rei publicae*
Porcia	sister of Cato (Uticensis); married to Domitius Ahenobarbus (consul, 54); died 46, with Cicero giving her funeral oration

Marcus **Porcius** Cato the Elder	outstanding literary figure, orator, politician, and general of the late third and early second centuries; a *novus homo*, and curmudgeon in the best Roman tradition of *gravitas* and *severitas*; died 149
Marcus **Porcius** Cato	great-grandson of the preceding; orphaned at early age, raised in household of uncle, Livius Drusus; center of support for "old-fashioned" Roman ways; idealism made him politically ineffective, if not dangerous, in the 50s; abandoned principles, supported Pompey, 52; ineffectual war leader in civil war, 49-48, moral leadership considerable then and afterwards, in Africa, 46; committed suicide at Utica rather than accept the clemency of Caesar, 46—hence "Uticensis" as a posthumous cognomen
Ptolemeus XIII	younger brother of Cleopatra VII; co-ruler of Egypt with her, 51-48; opposed Caesar, 48; drowned in Nile, weighed down by his golden armor, 48
Lucius **Pupius**	head centurion of a legion (*centurio primi pili*) handed over to Caesar upon the surrender of Attius Varus' forces in northern Italy; not otherwise known
Sextus **Quintilius** Varus	partisan of Pompey; quaestor, 49, when he surrendered at Corfinium to Caesar; fought Curio in Africa, 49; pardoned by Caesar; fought for tyrannicides at Philippi, 42, after which defeat he had a freedman kill him
Lucius **Roscius** Fabatus	lieutenant commander for Caesar in Gaul, 54; praetor, 49, when he carried a message from the Senate to Caesar at Ariminum, and Caesar's response back to Pompey; other activity in the civil war unknown; killed at Mutina, 43

Lucius **Rubrius**	partisan of Pompey; a senator captured and released at Corfinium; otherwise unknown
Acutius **Rufus**	see Acutius
Lucius Caelius **Rufus**	see Caelius
Marcus Caelius **Rufus**	see Caelius
Publius **Rutilius** Lupus	partisan of Pompey; praetor, 49; deserted by his men at Tarricina upon Caesar's advance; returned briefly to Rome, then joined Pompey in Greece, where he was put in command in Achaia; end unknown
Caius Appuleius **Saturninus**	see Appuleius
Quintus Caecilius Metellus Pius **Scipio**	see Caecilius
Caius **Scribonius** Curio	talented but profligate; tribune of the people, 50, when he disingenuously maneuvered in Caesar's favor while pretending to offer compromises in the developing crisis; openly declared for Caesar, 49; sent to Sicily and Africa, where he perished in battle against Pompeians and King Juba of Numidia
Lucius **Scribonius** Libo	partisan of Pompey; commanded Pompeian fleet
Caius **Sempronius** Gracchus	tribune of the people, 123-122; attempted more extensive reforms than his brother, Tiberius; murdered under *SCU* by the consul Opimius, 121
Tiberius **Sempronius** Gracchus	tribune of the people, 133; attempted land reform to strengthen army recruitment base; alienated senate; murdered, 133
Lucius **Septimius**	centurion under Pompey against the pirates, 67; tribune of the soldiers left in Egypt with Roman troops who protected the newly installed Egyptian dependent kings, 55-48; in collusion with the Egyptian Achillas, the murderer

	of Pompey, 48; a despicable fellow
Quintus **Sergius** Catilina	renegade patrician senator; Sullan agent in civil war and proscriptions, 82; political successes failed to match ambitions; plotted a coup to replace the ruling clique, 63; betrayed, fled Rome, 63; killed in battle, 62
Servius **Sulpicius** Galba	partisan of Caesar; successful lieutenant commander under Caesar in Gaul, 58-56; praetor, 54; failed of election as Caesarian, 50, to consulship of 49; unheard of during the civil war; perhaps an assassin of Caesar; last heard of, 43; end unknown
Vibius? **Sicca**	see Vibius
Spartacus	Thracian slave trained as gladiator; led escape of fellow gladiators which became a widespread revolt, 73; after many victories over Roman forces defeated by Crassus and killed, 71
Publius Cornelius Lentulus **Spinther**	see Cornelius
Lucius Cornelius **Sulla**	see Cornelius
Faustus Cornelius **Sulla**	see Cornelius
Quintus Minucius **Thermus**	see Minucius
Caius **Trebonius**	supported triumvirs as tribune of the people, 55; lieutenant commander with Caesar in Gaul, 54-49; commanded Caesarians forces at Massilia, 49; resisted radical actions of Caelius as praetor, 48; suffect consul, 45; complicit in assassination of Caesar, 44; killed in revenge, 43
Marcus **Tullius** Cicero	*novus homo*; leading orator and politician; suppressed Catilinarian conspiracy as consul, 63; failed to hold major leadership role because of the repercussions of the execution of citizens without trial during that conspiracy and in the face of the First Triumvirate's political domi-

	nance, 62-50; vacillating at the outbreak of the civil war, eventually joined Pompey in Greece, 49; took no part in important decisions and was not at Pharsalus, 48; pardoned by Caesar and returned to Rome, 48; not part of conspiracy to murder Caesar, 44; failed to secure leadership position in face of the Second Triumvirate, 43; murdered on orders of Marcus Antonius, 43
Caius **Valerius** Catullus	famous poet, representative of "gilded youth" of Rome who rejected traditional Roman ideals for those of the Hellenistic literary world
Vibius Curius	partisan of Caesar; commander of cavalry (*praefectus equitum*) for Caesar, 49; otherwise unknown
Vibius? Sicca	a senator?; noted as friend of Cicero, 58 and 44; emissary of Ahenobarbus at Corfinium to Pompey, 49
Marcus **Vinicius**	despite Tacitus' opinion ("mitis ingenio et comptae facundiae"), an important court figure under the emperor Tiberius; Velleius Paterculus dedicated his *History* to him; consul twice, AD 30, 45; married Julia Livilla, daughter of Germanicus, AD 33; killed by Messalina, AD 46

Appendix Two: Important Events from the Birth of Pompey to the Death of Cicero

Year BC	General Events	Caesar	Pompey	Cicero
106			born	born
105-101				
100	Saturninus killed	born		
99-92				
91	Social War			
90				
89			serves in Social War	serves in Social War
88				
87	Sulla seizes Rome I			
86				
85				
84		father dies		
83	M. Antony born		fights for Sulla	
82	Sulla captures Rome II	flees Rome		
81	Sulla dictator	remains in East	first triumph; called	
80			"Magnus"	defends Roscius
79	Sulla abdicates			studies in East
78	Sulla dies			
77			wars in Spain against	
76			Sertorius (77-71)	
75				quaestor
74				
73	revolt of Spartacus	pontifex		
72-71				
70	Pompey & Crassus consuls		consul I with Crassus second triumph	aedile; attacks Verres
69	Cleopatra born	quaestor		
68				
67	war against pirates		defeats pirates	
66	war with Mithradates VI		war with Mithradates VI	praetor
65		aedile		
64				
63	conspiracy of Catiline	pontifex maximus		consul; thwarts Catiline
62		praetor	returns to Rome; third triumph	
61		war in Spain		
60	first triumvirate	returns to Rome	first triumvirate	
59		consul I	marries Julia	
58	war in Gaul	command in Gaul I		exiled from Rome
57				returns to Rome
56	triumvirate renewed		first triumvirate renewed	mostly withdraws from public life to write
55		command in Gaul II	consul II with Crassus	
54		Julia dies	Julia dies;	
53	Crassus killed		Spanish command;	
52			remains in Rome	
51				governs Cilicia
50				returns to Rome
49	civil wars begin	invades Italy	final break with Caesar	joins Pompey in Greece
48		defeats Pompey at Pharsalus	defeated at Pharsalus; killed in Egypt	devotes self to writing
47				
46		dictator for 10 years		
45	civil wars end	battle of Munda		
44		dictator for life; killed		*Philippics* attacks Antony
43	second triumvirate			killed

Major Events in Roman History from its Founding to the Death of Cicero

Kings rule Rome	Expansion in Italy	1st War against against Carthage	War against Hannibal	Expansion into the East	Tiberius & Gaius Gracchus	Social War	Dictatorship of Sulla
753-509	509-264	264-241	218-202	202-146	133-120	90-89	82-79

Revolt of Spartacus	Conspiracy of Catiline	First Triumvirate	Caesar & Pompey break	Civil War begins	Battle of Pharsalus	Murder of Caesar	Murder of Cicero
73	63	60-53	53-50	49	48	44	43

Pompius Magnus

Marcus Tullius Cicero

Gajus Julius Caesar

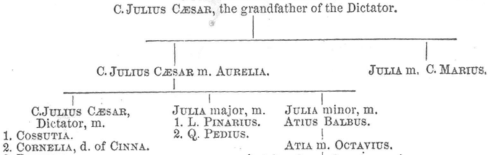

GENEALOGICAL TABLE.
C. Julius Cæsar, the grandfather of the Dictator.

C. Julius Cæsar m. Aurelia.   Julia m. C. Marius.

C. Julius Cæsar,   Julia major, m.   Julia minor, m.
    Dictator, m.   1. L. Pinarius.   Atius Balbus.
1. Cossutia.   2. Q. Pedius.
2. Cornelia, d. of Cinna.   Atia m. Octavius.
3. Pompeia.   C. Julius Caesar Octavianus a.k.a.
4. Calpurnia.   Augustus

Index One
Grammatical Material

Index Two
Vocabulary Glossed

a (ab before vowel or h): with abl.: from; by (living things only)

absens, -entis: absent, away

absum, abesse, afui, — (irreg.): be away, not to be there

abutor, abuti, abusum (dep.) (3): misuse (with abl.)

accedo, accedere, accessi, accessum (3): approach; to be added to (with ad, in)

accido, accidere, accidi, — (3): happen, occur

accipio, accipere, accepi, acceptum (3): receive

acer, acris, acre: sharp, fierce; adv: acriter: sharply

acerbitas, -tatis (f.): harshness, bitterness

acerbus, -a, -um: bitter; harsh; troublesome

ad: with acc.: for the purpose of; *also* to, toward, for, near

adduco, adducere, adduxi, adductum (3): bring forward, lead up; induce (with ut, etc.).

adeo ... ut: so ... that

adeo, adire, adii or adivi, aditum (irreg.): approach

adficio, adficere, adfeci, adfectum (3): move, impress; also "aff-"

adhuc: to this point (leading to a result clause); besides, moreover

adimo, adimere, ademi, ademptum (3): take away

aditus, -us (m.): approach, access

administratio, -onis (f.): management

administro, -are, -avi, -atum (1): conduct,manage

administro, -are, -avi, -atum (1): manage, govern

admoneo, admonere, admonui, admonitum: admonish, warn

adsum, adesse, adfui (irreg.): be near, at hand; be present

adulescens, adulescentis (m.): "the younger"; young man

adveho, advehere, advexi, advectum (3): carry, transport

adventus, -us (m.): arrival

adversarius, -i (m.): enemy

adversum (adv.): facing

aegre: scarcely; with difficulty

aequitas, -tatis (f.): fairness

aequus, -a, -um: calm, fair

aerarium, -i: state treasury

aestus, us (m.): heat

affero, affere, attuli, allatum (irreg.): bring

affinitas, -tatis (f.); relationship by marriage

ager, agri (m.): land or territory of a community; farm

agmen, agminis (n.): column, army (on march)

ago, agere, egi, actum (3): do; drive; discuss; live; spend

aio, ait: I say, he says

alienus, -a, -um: hostile; strange; another's

aliqui, aliqua, aliquod: some

aliquis, aliquid: someone, something

aliquot (adv.): several

alius, alia, aliud: different; (an) other (of more than 2)

alo, aluere, alui, alitum (3): nourish; support; promote

alter, -a, -um: the other of two, the other

alter...alter = the one ... the other

alteruter, -utra, -utrum: either

altus, -a, -um: high; deep

ambo, ambae, ambo: both, the two

amens, -entis: mad; foolish, stupid

amicitia, -ae (f.): friendship

amicus, -i (m.): friend

amitto, amittere, amisi, amissum (3): lose, mislay

amplius: more, more than

amplus, -a, -um: distinguished, honorable; glorious

angustiae, -arum (f.): narrow place, defile

animadverto, animadvertere, animadverti, animadversum (3): notice; realize

animus, -i (m.): feeling; mind, spirit; sometimes pl. = courage

annus, -i (m.): year

ante (adv.): previously, before (also prep. w/ acc.)

antea: previously

antecedo, antecedere, antecessi, antecessum (3): take precedence over, surpass

antecursor, -cursoris (m.): advance guard

anteeo, anteire, anteii, anteitum (irreg.): excel, surpass

antequam (or ante quam): before; *note*—ante and quam are often separated by another word

aperio, aperire, aperui, apertum (4): open; reveal

appello, -are, -avi, -atum (1): appeal to, call, name, address

appeto, appetere, appetivi, appetitum (3): strive after; claim for oneself; seek

apricatio, -onis (f.): place in the sun

apud: with acc: among; at the house of, near

aquila, -ae (f.): eagle (standard of a legion)

arbitror, arbitrari, -arbitratus (1) (dep.): think, consider

arcano: in secret, privately

arcesso, arcessere, arcessivi, arcessitum (3): summon

ardeo, ardere, arsi, arsum (2): burn

argentum, -i (n.): silver; money

armo, -are, -avi, -atum (1): arm

arx, arcis (f.): citadel, fortress, stronghold

asservo, -are, -avi, -atum (1): guard, watch over

attingo, attingere, attingi, attactus (3): reach, arrive in (+ acc.)

attribuo, attribuere, attribui, attributum (3): give, assign, allot

auctoritas, -itatis (f.): influence, power

audacia, -ae (f.): boldness, courage (in positive sense); recklessness, audacity (bad sense)

audacter (adv.): boldly

audeo, audere, -ausum (2): dare

audio, audire, audivi, auditum (4): hear

augeo, augere, auxi, auctum (2): increase

aut: or (mostly with contrasted alternative)

aut...aut: either...or

autem: but, however

auxilia, -orum (n.): auxiliaries (foreign troops)

auxilium, -i (n.): help

averto, avertere, averti, aversum (3): turn away; alienate

barbarus, -a, um: foreign, barbarian

bellum, -i (n.): war

bene: well

biduum, -i (n.): a period of two days

bonus, -a, -um: good

brevis, -e: short

caespes, -itis (m.): sod

cano, canere, cecini, cantum (3): sound [a horn]

capio, capere, cepi, captum (3): take; capture

caput, -itis (n.): head; capital

castellum, -i (n.): fortlet

castigo, -are, -avi, -atum (1): punish

castra, -orum (n. pl.): (military) camp

castus, -a, -um: pure; virtuous

causa, -ae (f.): reason for, cause (as in a political cause, faction, party); undertaking; constructed with the genitive = "for the sake of."

caveo, cavere, cavi, cautum (2): beware (ab = beware of)

cedo, cedere, cessi, cessum (3): yield; here accedo = come near, approach

celer, celere: quick; celeriter (adv.) = quickly

celeritas, -itatis (f.): speed, swiftness

censeo, censere, censui, censum (2): propose; believe; give an opinion

centurio, -ionis (m.): centurion

certiorem facere: to inform

certus, -a, -um: sure, definite

circiter: with acc: about; also adv.

circum: with acc.: around, about

circummitto, circummittere, circummisi, circummisum (3): send around to

circummunitio, -onis (f.): encirclement, circumvallation

circumscribo, -scribere, -scripsi, -scriptum (3): restrict; thwart the purpose of

circumsisto, circumsistere, circumsteti, — (3): surround

circumvenio, circumvenire, circumveni, circumventum (4): surround.

citatus, -a, -um: swift

citra: with acc.: this side of, the near side of

civilis, -e: civil

civis, civis, civium (m.): citizen

civitas, -atis, -atium (f.): community, state

clarus, -a, -um: clear, evident

classicum, -i (n.): battle horn, bugle

coepi, coepisse, coeptum (perf. tenses only) (irreg.): to have begun, begin

cogito, -are, -avi, -atum (1): think through, ponder

cognosco, cognoscere, cognovi, cognitum (3): find out, learn

cogo, cogere, coegi, coactum (3): bring together; compel, force

cohors, -ortis, -ortium (f.): cohort (a sub-unit of a legion; about 450-500 men)

cohortor, cohortari, cohortatum (dep.) (1): urge on, encourage

collegium, -i (n.): college, association

colligo, colligere, collegi, collectum (3): bring together, collect

colloquium, -i (n.): conference

colloquor, —, colloqui, collocutum (dep. 1): discuss

comitatus, -us (m.): troop (of cavalry)

comitia, -orum (n.): electoral assembly

commemoro, -are, -avi, -atum (1) (dep.): mention, relate

committo, committere, commisi, commissum (3): join; entrust

commodus, -a, -um: suitable, advantageous

commoror, commorari, commoratum (dep. 1): delay

commoveo, commovere, commovi, commotum (2): upset

communis, -e: general; common, shared

commutatio, -onis (f.): change

comparo, -are, -avi, -atum (1): gather together

comporto, -are, -avi, -atum (1): collect, gather

comperio, comperire, comperi, compertum (4): learn, ascertain; with dat. = known to...

compleo, complere, complevi, completum (2): fill

complures, complura (-ium): a considerable number of

compono, componere, composui, compositum (3): arrange, settle

compositio, -ionis (f.): reconciliation (of friends)

comprehendo, comprehendere, comprehendi, comprehensum (3): seize, arrest

concursus, -us (4): clash

condicio, -ionis (f.): terms, condition(s)

condo, condere, condidi, conditus (3): build, found (a city)

conduco, conducere, conduxi, conductum (3): bring together, assemble

confero, conferre, contuli, conlatum (irreg.): with se = go to, head for

confero, conferre, contuli, conlatum (irreg.): join, compare

confestim: immediately, suddenly

conficio, conficere, confeci, confectum (3): bring together; finish, complete

confido, confidere, confisum (semi-dep.) (3): be confident in; trust (with dat.)

confirmatio, -onis (f.): encouragement

confirmo, -are, -avi, -atum (1): strengthen; declare

confugio, confugere, confugi (3): flee; take refuge

conicio, conicere, conieci, coniectum (3): hurl, throw

coniecto, -are, -avi, -atum (1): guess, conjecture

coniungo, coniungere, coniunxi, coniunctum (3): unite

conor, conari, conatum (dep. 1): try, attempt

conquiesco, conquiescere, conquievi, conquietum (3): rest, take a nap

conquiro, conquirere, conquisivi, conquisitum (3): seek out

conscendo, conscendere, conscendi, conscensum (3): board (a ship), get on

consequor, consequi, consecutum (dep.) (3): pursue, overtake, get

consero, conserere, conservevi, consersitum (3): join, tie; manum conserere: fight hand to hand

consilium, -i (n.): advice, counsel; plan; meeting

consilior, -ari, -atum (dep. 1): take counsel, win over

consisto, consistere, constiti, constitum (3): take a stand

consolor, consolari, consolatus (1) (dep.): comfort, encourage, relieve

conspectus, -us (m.): sight, view

conspicor, -ari, -atum (dep. 1): catch sight of

constituo, constituere, constitui, constitutum (3): determine upon; decide, establish

consto, -are, constiti, -atum (1): (of facts): be well known

consuesco, consuescere, consuevi, consuetum (3): become accustomed

consuetudo, -inis (f.): custom, habit

consul, consulis (m): consul

consulatus, -us: consulship, the highest elective office at Rome

consulo, consulere, consului, consultum (3): consult; take thought for (with dat.); senatus consultum = decree of the senate

consumo, consumere, consumpsi, consumptum (3): waste

contendo, contendere, contendi, contentum (3): exert oneself, contend; hasten, march

contentio, contentionis (f.): dispute

continens, -entis (adj.): self-controlled

contineo, continere, continui, contentum (2): contain, restrain

contingo, contingere, contigi, contactum (3): be in contact; it happens (imper.)

contio, -ionis (f.): public meeting, rally

contionor, contionari, contionatum (dep.) (1): speak at a rally; speak before the troops; harangue

contra: with acc.: against

contradico, contradicere, contradixi, contradictum (3): oppose, speak against

contraho, contrahere, contraxi, contractum (3): draw together, assemble

contumelia, -ae (f.): insult

convenio, convenire, conveni, conventum (4): agree, coincide with; assemble; meet

conventus, -us (m.): gathering, assembly

convicium, -i (n.): insult; jeers; cry of protest

copia, -ae (f.): supply, abundance

copiae, -arum (f.) (pl.): troops, forces

coram: face-to-face; in the presence of

cornu, cornus (n.): horn; wing (of army)

corripio, corripere, corripui, correptum (3): attack; reproach

cotidianus, -a, -um: daily

cottidie: daily

crebo (adv.): frequently

credo, credere, credidi, creditum (3): believe; trust (with dat. of person)

crudelis, -e: cruel

crudelitas, -tatis (f.): cruelty

cum...tum (conj.): with tum below = both...and

cunctor, cunctari, cunctatum (dep.) (1): delay, hesitate

cunctus, -a, -um: the entire, altogether, all

cupiditas, -tatis (f.): desire, enthusiasm

cupidus, -a, -um: eager, enthusiastic

cupio, cupere, cupivi, cupitum (3): desire

cur: why

curo, -are, -avi, -atum (1): see to it; take care

custodia, -ae (f.): guard, surveillance

damno, -are, -avi, -atum (1): condemn

dare operam: exert oneself

de: with abl.: about, concerning; down from

debeo, debere, debui, debitum (2): owe, be obliged

decem (indecl.): ten

decerno, decernere, decrevi, decretum (3): decide, determine; decree, resolve

decerto, -are, -avi, -atum (1): fight it out; come to a decision

decet, decuit: it is proper, right (imper.)

decimus, -a, -um: tenth

decurro, decurrere, decurri, decursum (3): rush headlong to; pass over; have recourse to

dedo, dedere, dedidi, deditum (3): surrender

deduco, deducere, deduxi, deductum (3): withdraw, lead away

defendo, defendere, defendi, defensum (3): defend

defero, deferre, detuli, delatum (irreg.): carry away; report; grant, bestow

deficio, deficere, defeci, defectum (3): fail in, run out of

defugio, defugere, defugi, defugitum (3): avoid, evade, shy away from

deicio, deicere, deieci, deiectum (3): throw down into [the urn]

delector, -ari, -atum (dep.) (1): love, delight in (+ abl.)

delectus, -us (m.): conscription, levy

deligo, deligere, delegi, delectum (3): choose, select

demonstro, -are, -avi, -atum (1): point out, explain

denego, -are, -avi, -atum (1): deny

denique: finally

depono, deponere, deposui, depositum (3): deposit

deprecor, deprecari, deprecatum (1) (dep.): avert by prayer; intercede on behalf of

deprendo, deprendere, deprendi, deprendum (3): capture, seize

descendo, descendere, descendi, descensum (3): descend, sink

desero, deserere, deserui, desertum (3): desert

desidero, -are, -avi, -atum (1): lose (men as casualties)

desisto, desistere, destiti, destitum (3): stop, leave off

desperatio, -ionis (f.): despair

despicio, despicere, despexi, despectum (3): despise; express contempt for

destino, -are, -avi, -atum (1): determine, resolve

desum, deesse, defui, defuturus: fail; be missing; lack (with dat.)

detraho, detrahere, detraxi, detractum (3): remove

detrimentum, -i (n.): damage, harm

devinctus, -a, -um: strongly attached (to)

dico, dicere, dixi, dictum (3): express, say

dies, diei (m. or f.): day

diffido, diffidere, diffisum (3) (semi-deponent): lose confidence in (with dat.)

dignitas, -tatis (f.): dignity, reputation

dilectus, -us (m.): levy of troops, conscription

dimico, -are, -avi, -atum (1): struggle, fight

dimitto, dimittere, dimisi, dimissum (3): send away, dismiss

diripio, diripere, diripui, direptum: plunder

discedo, discedere, discessi, discessum (3): go away, depart

discepto, -are, -avi, -atum (1): settle, debate; decide

discrimen, -inis (n.): critical moment; crisis

disicio, disicere, disieci, disiectum (3): break up; scatter

dispono, disponere, disposui, dispositum (3): station, assign

disputatio, -onis (f.): argument, debate

dissensio, -onis (f.): conflict, dissention

dissentio, dissentire, dissensi, dissensum (4): disagree, be in conflict

dissimulo, -are, -avi, -atum (1): disguise; conceal, dissimulate

disto, -are, -avi, -atum (1): locate at a distance; stand apart

distraho, distrahere, distraxi, distractum (3): separate

diu: long, for a long time; diutius (adv.) = still longer, for a very long time

divulgo, -are, -avi, -atum (1): reveal, divulge, publicize

do, dare, dedi, datum (irreg.): give

doceo, docere, docui, doctum (2): reveal; teach

doleo, dolere, dolui, dolitum (2): hurt; take offence

dolor, doloris (m.): pain; distress; resentment

domus, -us or -i (f.): house, home

dubito, -are, -avi, -atum (1): hesitate; doubt

duco, ducere, duxi, ductus (3): consider; lead; take (someone) with you (along with many other meanings)

duo, duae, duo: two

durus, -a, -um: severe, harsh

duumvir, -i (m.): duumvir (local magistrate)

dux, ducis (m.): leader, general

e (ex before vowel or h): with abl.: out of

educo, educere, eduxi, eductum (3): lead out

efficio, efficere, effeci, effectum (3): produce; bring about

ego (pl. nos): I (we)

egredior, egredi, egressum (dep.) (3): go out; disembark

eicio, eicere, eieci, eiectum (3): throw out

enim: for

eo: to that place, there

eo, ire, ii (or ivi), itum (irreg.): go

eques, equitis (m.): equestrian, the second noble group at Rome; cavalryman; rider

equitatus, -us (m.): cavalry

equus, -i (m.): horse

erigo, erigere, erexi, erectum (3): arouse, inspire

eripio, eripere, eripui, ereptum (3): snatch, take away

eruptio, -ionis (f.): sortie, sally

et...et: both...and

et: and; also

etiam: also; even; still

etiam atque etiam: again and again

etsi: although

eventus, -us (m.): fortune; outcome

evocatus, -i (m.): recalled veteran soldier

exaequeo, exaequare, exaequari, exaequatum (1): equal

exanimo, -are, -avi, -atum (1): dishearten, scare a lot

exardesco, exardescere, exarsi, exarsum (3): flame up, flare up

exaudio, -audire, -audivi, -auditum (4): hear clearly

excedo, excedere, excessi, excessum (3): withdraw, depart

excipio, excipere, excepi, exceptum (3): receive; intercept

excusatio, -onis (f.): apology for; excuse (with gen.)

exeo, exire, exivi, exitum (irreg.): go out, go forth

exercitus, -us (m.): army

existimo, -are, -avi, -atum (1): think, believe; evaluate

expectatio, -ionis (f.): anticipation

expecto, -are, -avi, -atum (1): wait for, wait

expedio, expedire, expedii, expeditum (4): clear the way, arrange, settle

expello, expellere, expulsi, expulsum (3): drive out

expeto, expetire, expetivi, expetitum (4)): demand; long for

expleo, explere, explevi, expletum (2): fill out, fill up

explico, -are, -avi, -atum (3): set free, release

expono, exponere, exposui, expositum (3): declare, lay out

exposco, exposcere, expoposci, — (3): demand

exsisto, exsistere, exstiti, exstitum (3): arise, emerge

extorqueo, extorquere, extorsi, extortum (3): wrench, wrest (from); extort

extraho, extrahere, extraxi, extractum (3): waste (of time); draw, drag out

extraordinarius, -a, -um: extraordinary, special

extremus, -a, -um: most basic; outermost, last

facio, facere, feci, factum (3): do; make

factio, -ionis (f.): party, faction

facultas, -atis (f.): leave to do, opportunity (+ gen.)

fallo, fallere, fefelli, falsum (3): deceive; trick; let down, fail to live up to

falsus, -a, -um: false, incorrect, wrong

familiaris, -e: as adj., familiar, intimate; as noun, friend, companion

faveo, favere, favi, fautum (2) (with dat.): favor

fere: almost, practically; only

fero, ferre, tuli, latum (irreg.): put to a vote; bring; endure; assert

ferox, ferocis: fierce, savage, hostile

fides, fidei (f.): trust, belief; honor, loyalty; pledge, assurance

fiducia, -ae (f.): good faith; + gen. = with reliance upon

filius, -i (m.): son

fines, finium (m.): territory; boundary

finitimus, -a, -um: neighboring

fio, fieri, factum (irreg.): become; happen; be made

firmus, -a, -um: strong; firm

flagito, -are, -avi, -atum (1): demand

flumen, fluminis (n.): river

fortasse: perhaps

fortis, forte: brave; fortiter (adv.) = strongly, bravely

fortuna, -ae (f.): luck, fortune

fretum, -i (m): strait

frumentum, -i (n.): wheat, grain; plur. crops

frustra: in vain

fuga, -ae (f.): flight, running away

fugio, fugere, fugi, fugitum (3): flee (from), run away (from)

genus, -eris (n.): kind; lineage; tribe

gero, gerere, gessi, gestum (3): carry on, engage in; wear

gladium, -i (n.): or gladius, -i: sword

glorior, gloriari, gloriatum (dep.) (1): boast (about)

gratia, -ae (f.): favor; friendship; influence

gratias ago: give thanks (takes dat.)

gratulor, gratulari, gratulatum (dep. 1): give thanks to

gratus, -a, -um: pleasing, welcome

gravis, grave: serious, severe; heavy

graviter (adv.): severely

gravor, gravari, gravatum (1) (dep.): refuse; feel annoyed at

habeo, habere, habui, habitum (2): have; hold; consider

hedera, -ae (f.): ivy

hic, haec, hoc: this

hic (adv.): "on this side," here

homo, -inis (m.): man, human being, person

honor, honoris (m.): public esteem, repute

horreo, horrere, horrui, — (2): dread; shudder at

hortatus, -us (m.): urging, exhortation

hortor, hortari, — hortatum (dep.) (1): urge on, encourage

hospes, -itis (m.): friend; guest

hospitium, -i (n.): hospitality; friendship

hostia, -ae (f.): sacrificial animals

huc: to this place, hither

iacto, -are, -avi, -atum (1): boast, brag about

iactura, -ae (f.): loss, sacrifice

iam: (by) now; already

ibi: at that place, there

idem, eadem, idem: same

idoneus, -a, -um: suitable

igitur (adv.): therefore

ignoro, -are, -avi, -atum (1): fail to recognize, be ignorant of

ille, illa, illud: that

illic: there, (adv.) "on that side"

impedio, impedire, impedivi, impeditum (4): hinder

impeditus, -a, -um: difficult

impello, impellere, impuli, impulsus (3): stimulate; push, drive

imperator, -oris (m.): commander, general

imperium, -i (n.): command; chief power

impero, -are, -avi, -atum (1): order up; give orders (with dat.)

impetro, -are, -avi, -atum (1): to ask and gain the request.

implico, -are, -avi, -atum (1): envelope

imprimis: first and foremost, especially

improbo, -are, -avi, -atum (1): disapprove, reject

impudens, -entis: shameless

in: with abl.: during

inbecillitas, -tatis (f.): weakness

incido, incidere, incidi, incasum (3): (with in + acc.) fall in with, come upon unexpectedly

incipio, incipere, incepi, inceptum (3): take on, begin

incito, -are, -avi, -atum (1): urge on

incolumis, -e: unharmed

inde: from that place, thence

industrius, -i: diligent, industrious

ineo, inire, inii or inivi, initum (irreg.): begin; undertake

infamia, -ae (f.): disgrace, scandal

infectus, -a, -um: undone, unachieved

infero, inferre, intuli, illatum (irreg.): bring in or against

infirmus, -a, -um: weak; inconstant

informo, -are, -avi, -atum (1): form, shape

ingredior, ingredi, ingressum (dep.) (3): enter, undertake; begin

inimicus, -i (m.): enemy (personal)

iniquus, -a, -um: unfair, unjust

initium, -i (n.): beginning

iniungo, iniungere, iniunxi, iniunctum (3): join; inflict on; impose

iniuria, -ae (f.): injustice; injury

inopia, -ae (f.): shortage, lack

inquam: say (defective: see B 134 or AG 206b for forms)

insequor, insequi, insecutum (dep. 3): follow, pursue; attack

insolentia, -ae (f.): arrogance, insolence

instituo, instituere, institui, institutum (3): organize; equip

integer, -ra, -rum: whole; honest

intellego, intellegere, intellexi, intellectum (3): understand, recognize

inter: between; among (with acc.)

intercedo, intercedere, intercessi, intercessum (3): occur

intercludo, intercludere, interclusi, interclusum (3): cut off, blockade

interea: meanwhile

interficio, interficere, interfeci, interfectum (3): kill

interim: meanwhile

intermitto, intermittere, intermisi, intermissum (3): interrupt

internuntius, -i (m.): intermediary, messenger

interpello, -are, -avi, -atum (1): interrupt

interrumpo, interrumpere, interrupi, interruptum (3): break apart intersum, interesse, interfui (irreg.): take part

intervallum, -i: (n.): distance, interval

intra: with acc.: within

introitus, -us (m.): entrance

invado, invadere, invasi, invasum (3): rush upon; take possession

invenio, invenire, inveni, inventum (4): find, come upon

invidia, -ae (f.): envy

invitus, -a, -um: unwilling

iocor, iocari, iocatus (dep.) (1): joke

ipse, ipsa, ipsum: self; very

iracunia, -ae (f.): anger

irascor, irasci, iratum (dep.) (3): get angry (with dative)

is, ea, id: that; he, she, etc.

isdem, eadem, idem: the same

istuc: there

ita: so, thus, in such a way

itaque: and so

iter facere: to march

iter, itineris (n.): (a day's) journey; route, march

iubeo, iubere, iussi, iussum (2): bid, tell (to do something), order

iudicium, -i (n.): judgement, opinion

iudico, -are, -avi, -atum (1): judge

iuro, -are, -avi, -atum (1): swear; swear by

ius, iuris (n.): right(s), justice, law

iustus, -a, -um: just, right, fair, proper (+ iter = normal day's march)

iuvo, -are, iuvi, iutum (1): help, benefit; delight

iuxta: with acc.: next to, near to

labor, laboris (m.): toil, work, effort

laetitia, -ae (f.): joy, elation

languidus, -a, -um: weak, sluggish

largitio, -ionis (f.): bribery; generosity

lassitudo, -inis (f.): exhaustion

laudo, -are, -avi, -atum (1): praise

legatio, -onis (f.): mission, embassy

legatus, -i (m.): emissary; officer; lieutenant commander

legio, -ionis (f.): legion

legitimus, -a, -um: lawful, proper

lenis, -e: gentle; mild

levo, -are, -avi, -atum (1): lessen, lighten

lex, legis (f.): law

libens, -entis: free, willing

liber, -era, -erum: free:

liberaliter: generously

liberi, -orum (m.): children

libertas, -tatis (f.): freedom

liberus, -i (m.): child

libet, libuit: it pleases

licentia, -ae (f.): license, lack of restraint

licet, licuit (2): it is allowed (imper.)

litterae, -arum (f.): letter, message; literature

loca, -orum (n.): district, locality, place

longinquitas, -tatis (f.): length, duration

longinquus, -a, -um: distant

longus, -a, -um: long; far

loquor, loquari, —, locutum (dep.) (3): speak, say

luceo, lucere, luxi, —, (2): to dawn

ludus, -i (m.): training center for gladiators

lustro, lustrari, lustravi, lustratum: purify

lux, lucis (f.): light

magis: more

magis: more; rather

magistratus, us (m.): magistrate

magno opere (magnopere): greatly

magnus, -a, -um: significant; big, large, great

maior, maius: bigger, greater

maleficium , -i (n.): offense, harm, injury

malo, malle, malui (irreg.): want more, prefer; often constructed with quam

malus, -a, -um: bad, evil

mandatum, -i (n.): command; plural = instructions, communications

manus, -us (f.): hand; handful, band of people

mare, maris (abl. -i) (n.): sea

maximus, -a, -um: biggest, greatest

medeor, mederi (dep.) (2): heal, remedy (with dat.)

melior, -ius: better

memor, memoris: mindful

mendacium, -i (n.): lie

mens, mentis (f.): mind; heart

mensis, mensis (f.): month

mereor, mereri, meritum (dep.) (2): deserve; serve (in army)

metus, -us (m.): fear

meus, -a, -um: my

miles, -itis (m.): soldier, the soldiery

milia passuum: mile

milia, milium, milibus: thousands (with genitive)

miliens: a thousand times

minae, -arum (f.): threats

minax, minacis: threatening, menacing

minime: least of all

minimus, -a, -um = smallest, least

minor: smaller

miror, -ari, -atum (dep.) (1): wonder at; be amazed at

miser, -era, -erum: wretched, poor

miseret, miseruit: pity, feel sorry for (imper.)

mitto, mittere, misi, missum (3): send, let go

modo: only

moenia, ium (n. pl.): town wall

molior, moliri, molitum (dep.) (4): undertake, attempt

momentum, -i (n.): importance

moneo, monere, monui, monitum (2): warn, advise

mons, montis, montium (m.): mountain, hill

mora, -ae (f.): delay

morbus, -i: illness

morior, mori, mortuus (3): die

moror, morari, moratum (dep.) (1): delay

mors, mortis (f.): death

mortuus, -a, -um: dead

mos, moris (m.): custom, manner

moveo, movere, movi, -motum (2): move

multo, -are, -avi, -atum (1): fine

multus, -a, -um: much, many

municeps, municipis (m.): townsman, citizens of a municipium.

munio, munire, munivi, munitum (4): wall around, defend; make (a road)

munitio, -onis (f.): fortification

munus, muneris (n.): duty, public task

murus, -i (m.): (town) wall

muto, -are, -avi, -atum (1): change, alter

nam (namque mostly before a vowel): for

nanciscor, nancisci, na(n)ctum (dep.) (3): chance upon, obtain

navis, navis, navium (f.): ship

ne: lest, for fear that (with subjunctive)

ne: truly; indeed, certainly

ne ... quidem: not even; emphasizes the word between the ne and the quidem (B 347.1; 2)

-ne (enclitic): whether (introduces a question)

necessarius, -a, -um: necessary; related

necessarius, -i (m.): friend, close connection

necesse est: it is necessary (imper.)

necessitudo, -inis (f.): friendship, relationship; necessity, need; , bond

neco, -are, -avi, -atum (1): kill

negotiator, -oris (m.): businessman

negotior, -ari, -atum (dep. 1): do business

negotium, -i (n.): charge, assignment; business

nemo, nemenis (m./f.): no one

neque or nec: and ... not, nor

neque...neque: neither...nor

nequiquam (adv.): to no purpose, to no avail

nihil: nothing (often with gen.)

nimius, -a, -um: very much; excessive

nisi: unless, except

noceo, nocere, nocui, nocitum (2): harm (with dative)

nocturnus, -a, -um: nocturnal

nolo, nolle, nolui, — (irreg.): be unwilling, not to want

nomen, -inis (n.): name; reputation

non: not

nondum: not yet

nonnullus, -a, -um: some, many

noster, -ra, -um: our

noto, -are, -avi, -atum (1): repress; mark down; censure

notus, -a, -um: well known

novus, -a, -um: new, recent

nox, noctis, noctium (f.): night

nullus, -a, -um: no (irreg. adj. in -ius, -i)

numerus, -i (m.): number, quantity

nuncupo, -are, -avi, -atum (1): make (a vow); proclaim publicly

nuntio, -are, -avi, -atum (1): report, announce

nuntius, -i (m.): messenger; news, message

ob (with acc.): because of, on account of; quam ob rem, for which reason

obicio, obicere, obieci, obiectum (3): throw up, taunt

obsecro, -are, -avi, -atum (1): beseech, implore

observo , -are, -avi, -atum (1): observe, deduce

obsidio, -onis (f.): siege, blockade

obstringo, obstringere, obstrinxi, obstrictum (3): bind; put under obligation

obtempero, obtemperare, obtemperavi, obtemperatum (1): obey (+ dat.)

obtrectio, -onis (f.): disparagement

obvenio, -venire, -veni, -ventum (4): be alotted to; happen; it happens (imper.)

obviam prodire: go out to meet (with dat.)

occultus, -a, -um: hidden

occupo, -are, -avi, -atum (1): occupy; seize

octo (indeclinable): eight; octavus, -a, um: eighth

offendo, offendere, offendi, offensum (3): run up against; come upon

officium, offici (n.): allegiance

omitto, omittere, omisi, omissum (3): abandon

omnino: altogether, completely, wholly; (adv.) to be sure

omnis, omne: every; pl. = all

onus, -eris (n.): burden

opera, -ae (f.): assistance

opinio, -ionis (f.): expectation; opinion; reputation

oportet, oportere, oportuit (impersonal) (3): it is right, proper

oppidum, -i (n.): town

oppono, oponere, opponui, oppositum (3): oppose

opportunitas, -tatis (f.): suitableness; advantage

opprimo, opprimere, oppressi, oppressum (3): oppress, crush

oppugno, -are, -avi, -atum (1): attack, storm

optimus, -a, -um: best

opus est: there is need for (with abl.)

opus, -eris (n.): structure, building; product of work

oratio, -ionis (f.): speech

ordo, -inis (m.): order, rank

ornatus, -a, -um: adorned, illustrious, excellent

oro, -are, -avi, -atum (1): beg, beseech

os, oris (n.): mouth; lips

ostendo, ostendere, ostendi, ostentum (3): show, make clear

paene: almost, nearly, practically

paeniteo, paenitere, paenitui (2): to cause to regret

palam: openly

par, paris, parium: equal (to, with dat.)

parco, parcere, peperci, parsurum (3): spare

pario, parere, peperi, partum (3): win, get; give birth to

paro, -are, -avi, -atum (1): prepare; obtain

pars, partis, partium (f.): role, part, political faction

partim: partly

partio, partire, partivi, partitum (4): share

parvus, -a, -um: small, little

pastor, -oris (m.): shepherd

pateo, patere, patui (2): lie open, be open

pater, -tris (m.): father (pl.: senators)

patientia, -ae (f.): patience, long-suffering

patior, pati, passum (dep.) (3): endure; allow (with infin.)

pauci, -ae, -a: few

paulo: a little; (by) a little

pax, pacis (f.): peace

pecunia, -ae (f.): money

pello, pellere, pepuli, pulsum (3): drive back

penitus: completely

per: with acc.: through

perago, peragere, peregi, peractum (3): complete

percurro, percurrere, percucuri, percursus (3): travel through

perduco, perducere, perduxi, perductum (3): prolong, drag out

perfero, perferre, pertuli, perlatum (irreg.): endure to the end; bring news

periculum, -i (n.): danger

peritus, -a, -um: experienced, skilled

perlego, perlegere, perlegi, perlectum: read through, carefully

permaneo, permanere, permansi, permansum (2): remain, endure

permisceo, permiscere, permiscui, permixtum (3): confuse, mix up, throw into chaos

permitto, permittere, permisi, permissum (3): permit, entrust to (with dat.)

permoveo, permovere, permovi, permotum (2): affect deeply

pernicies, perniciei (f.): ruin, destruction

perpetuus, -a, -um: continuous, uninterrupted

persequor, persequi, persecutum (dep.) (3): take vengeance on

perterreo, perterrere, perterrui, perterritum (2): frighten, terrify

pertimesco, pertimescere, pertimescui, — (3): become afraid, alarmed

pertineo, pertinere, pertinui, pertentum (2): concern, have to do with (with ad)

pervenio, pervenire, perveni, perventum (4): come through; arrive

peto, petere, petivi (petii), petitum (3): ask for; attack

piget, piguit: it annoys (imper.)

placeo, placere, placui, placitum (2): please; seem right, proper

plane: clearly, evidently

plerique, pleraeque, pleraque: the majority of; most

plerumque: often

plurimus, -a, -um: most

plus: more (often with gen.)

polleo, pollere, — (2): be powerful, be strong

polliceor, polliceri, pollicitum (dep.)(2): promise

pondus, -eris (n.): weight; mass

pono, ponere, posui, positum (3): put, place

pons, pontis, pontium (m.): bridge

pontificus, -a, -um: pontifical, priestly

populus, -i (m.): the people of Rome; a tribe or nation

porta, -ae (f.): city gate; gate, entrance

portus, us (m.): port, harbor

possum, posse, potui, — (irreg.): be able, can

post: with acc.: after, behind; adv. = afterwards

postea: afterwards, later

posteaquam:after

posteritas, -tatis (f.): posterity, future generations

posterus, -a, -um: later, next following; in posterum = for the future

postremo: at last, finally

postulo, -are, -avi, -atum (1): demand

potens, potentis: powerful

potestas, -tatis (f.): power; permission

potior, potiri, potitum (with abl. or gen.) (3): get control of

potior, potius: preferable, more important (comparative of potis)

potius: rather, more; potius...quam = rather...than, more...than

praecipio, praecipere, praecipi, praeceptum (3): anticipate

praeda, -ae (f.): booty

praedico, praedicere, praedixi, praedictum (3): proclaim, assert

praedo, -onis (m.): pirate

praefectus, -i (m.): prefect (commander of allied troops)

praeficio, praeficere, praefeci, praefectum (3): put in charge (with acc. and dat.)

praemitto, praemittere, praemisi, praemissum (3): send ahead

praemium, -i (n.): reward, prize

praemoneo, praemonere, praemonui, praemonitum (2): foretell, forewarn

praesens, -ntis: present, at hand

praesentia, -ae (f.): present

praesidium, -i (n.): garrison post

praesto, -are, praestiti, praestitum (1): display; perform; offer

praesum, praeesse, praefui, — (irreg.): be in charge of (with dat.)

praeter: with acc.: past; besides; contrary to

praeterea: besides, moreover

praetereo, praeterire, praeterii, praeteritum (irreg.): pass over in silence, neglect

praetura, -ae (f.): praetorship

premo, premere, pressi, pressum (3): pursue

pridie: the day before (+ gen.)

primum: for the first time

primus, -a, -um: first

pristinus, -a, -um: earlier

priusquam: before (often the two words are separated in the text)

privatus, -i (m.): a private citizen, i.e., one not holding public office

privo, -are, -avi, -atum (1): deprive

pro: with abl.: on behalf of

probo, -are, -avi, -atum (1): approve

procul: at a distance

procurro, procurrere, procucurri, procursum (3): rush forward

proditio, proditionis (f.): betrayal

prodo, prodere, prodidi, proditum (3): betray

proelium, -i (n.): battle

proferro, proferre, protuli, prolatus (irreg.): bring out

proficio, proficere, profeci, profectum (3): accomplish

proficiscor, proficisci, —, profectum (dep.) (3): start, set out

profugio, profugere, profugi, — (3): flee, escape from

progredior, progredi, progressum (dep.) (3): advance

prohibeo, prohibere, prohibui, prohibitum (2): hinder, prevent

proicio, proicere, proieci, proiectum (3): betray, abandon

proinde: accordingly

pronuntio, -are, -avi, -atum (1): relate, announce

prope: with acc.: near (also adv. = nearly)

prope diem: very soon, presently

propere: quickly, hastily

propinquus, -i: relative

propius: near

propono, proponere, proposui, propositum (3): put forward, propose; report

propter: with acc.: because of

prosequor, prosequi, prosecutum (3) (dep.): follow

prosum, prodesse, profui (irreg.): be of advantage to (with dat.)

protinus: suddenly; immediately

provideo, providere, providi, provisum (2): foresee

provincia, -ae (f.): province

prudens, -entis: prudent, cautious

publicus, -a, -um: official, public

pudet, puduit: be ashamed (imper.)

puer, pueri (m.): boy, child; slave

pugna, -ae (f.): fight, battle

pugno, -are, -avi, -atum (1): fight

puto, -are, -avi, -atum (1): think, consider

qua (relative adv.): where

quaero, quaerere, quaesivi, quaesitum (3): try to get; inquire, seek

quaeso, quaesere, —, — (3): ask; beg

quam primum: as soon as possible

quam: as possible (w/superl.); than (w/ compar.), how (w/ adj. or adv. in question or exclamation), correlative after tam = as...as possible (w/ superl.)

quamquam: (conj.) although

quando (indefinite after "si"): ever, at any time

quantum: how much

quantumcumque: as much as

quantus, -a, -um: how big? ; as big

quartus, -a, -um: fourth

quaterni, -ae, -a: four each

quattuor (indecl.): four

-que: and (enclitic)

quemadmodum: how, in what way

queror, queri, questum (dep.) (3): complain

qui, quae, quod (interrogative): what? what kind of?

qui, quae, quod: (relative pron.) who, which, that

quicumque, quaecumque, quodcumque: whoever, whatever

quidem: certainly, indeed

quinque (indecl.): five

quintus, -a, -um: fifth

quis, quis, quid: who? what? (interrogative pron.)

quisquam, cuiusquam, quisquam, quidquam or quicquam: anyone, anything (with negatives)

quisque, quaeque, quidque and quodque: each, each one

quo...magis: all the more

quoad: until

quocumque: wherever

quod si (also quodsi): but if

quonam: where (i.e., whither); to what end

quoniam: seeing that; since

quoque: also

quotienscumque: however often

rapax, rapacis: grasping, insatiable

raptim: hurriedly, suddenly

ratio, -ionis (f.): reason; plan; account; candidacy for office ratus, -a, -um: established, approved

recipio, recipere, recepi, receptum (3): receive; take duly; retake, recover

recordor, -ari, -atum (dep.) (1): recall, recollect

recuso, -are, -avi, -atum (1): refuse

redire, redii, reditum: go back

reddo, reddere, reddidi, redditum (3): deliver

reduco, reducere, reduxi, reductum (3): lead back

refero, referre, rettuli, relatum (irreg.): put before the senate; bring back; report

reformido, -are, -avi, -atum (1): dread, shrink from

refugio, refugere, refugi, — (3): flee from

regio, -ionis (f.): district, region

regnum, -i (n.): kingship; kingdom, realm

religio, -ionis (f.): religious scruple

relinquo, relinquere, reliqui, relictus (3): leave aside or behind

reliquus, -a, -um: remaining

remaneo, remanere, remansi, remansum (2): remain

remitto, remittere, remisi, remissum (3): send back; slacken

renovo, -are, -avi, -atum (1): renew

renuntio, -are, -avi, -atum (1): report, announce

repello, repellere, repulli, repulsum (3): drive back, repel

repente: suddenly

reperio, reperire, repperi, repertum (4): find (by looking for)
repugno, -are, -avi, -atum (1): oppose

res, rei (f.): thing; affair

res publica (f.): government, state, constitution

rescribo, rescribere, rescripsi, rescriptum (3): write back

resisto, resistere, restiti, — (3): stand up (to), resist (with dat.)

respicio, respicere, respexi, respectum (3): look to; look at

respondeo, respondere, respondi, responsum (2): reply, answer

restituo, restituere, restitui, restitutum (3): restore

retineo, retinere, retinui, retentum (2): hold back

retraho, retrahere, retraxi, retractum (3): drag back

revertor, reverti, reversum (dep.) (3): return, go back

rex, regis (m.): king

rogo, -are, -avi, -atum (1): ask

ruo, ruere, rui, rutum (3): rush (to ruin)

rursus: again

sacerdotium, -i (n.): priesthood

sacramentum, -i (n.): military oath of allegiance

saepe: often

saltem: at least; in any event

salus, salutis (f.): health, safety, welfare

salvus, -a, -um: safe, unharmed

sancio, sancire, sanxi, sanctum (4): consecrate, make inviolable

sanguis, sanguinis (m.) or sanguen, sanguinis (n.): blood

satis (indeclinable adj.): enough; sufficient; with gen., enough of

scelus, sceleris (n.): wickedness, evil

scilicet: of course; (ironically) naturally; that is to say

scio, scire, scivi, scitum (4): know

scribo, scribere, scripsi, scriptum (3): write (to = ad)

se (pron.—reflexive): self

secessio, -onis (f.): withdrawal

secreto: in secret, in private

secundum: (with acc.): by (next to); alongside (of)

secundus, -a, -um: successful

sed: but

segnis, -e: slow, sluggish

semel: once

semestris, semestre: half a year

semper: always

senatus, -us (m.): senate

sentio, sentire, sensi, sensum (4): think, sense

septem (indecl.): seven

septimus, -a, -um: seventh

sequor, sequi, secutum (dep.) (3): follow, go (along) with

sermo, -onis (m): conversation, talk, discourse

sero: too late

servus, -i (m.): slave

sestertia, -orum (n. pl.): 100,000 sesterces

sex (indecl.): six

si: in case; if

sic ... ut (correlatives): such ... that

sic: so, thus, in such a way

significo, -are, -avi, -atum (1): signify, indicate

signum, -i (n.): standard (military); sign, signal

simul, simulque: at the same time (as)

simul atque (or ac or et) (conj.): as soon as

simulatio, -onis (f.): pretense

sin: but if

singularis, -e: outstanding, unparalleled

singuli, -ae, -a: one each

sino, sinere, sivi/sii, situm (3): allow

societas, -tatis (f.): business association, corporation

socius, -i (m.): ally

sol, solis (m.): sun

solacio, -ionis (f.): comfort (+ad = "for...")

sollicito, -are, -avi, -atum (1): stir up, incite, agitate, egg on

solum: only; non solum...sed etiam = "not only...but also"

soror, -oris (f.): sister

sors, sortis (f.): lot

spatium, -i (n.): time; space, room

spero, -are, -avi, -atum (1): hope; hope for

spes, spei (f.): hope(s) (often with gen. = "hopes of")

spolio, spoliare, spoliavi, spoliatum: destroy, plunder

statim: immediately

statio, -ionis (f.): guard station; pl. = sentries

statuo, statuere, statui, statutum (3): set up; decide

stipendium, -i (n.): pay for soldiers

studeo, studere, studui, — (2): be eager (with dat. or infin.)

studium, -i (n.): zeal, eagerness

subicio, subicere, subieci, subiectum (3): suborn

sublevo, -are, -avi, -atum (1): aid, support

subsequor, subsequi, subsecutum (dep.) (3): follow closely after

subsidium, -i (n.): reserve, support, help

subsisto, subsistere, substiti, — (3): take a stand

subvenio, subvenire, subveni, subventum (4): aid, relieve

summa, -ae (f.): chief point, substance

summus, -a, -um: greatest, highest, (the) top (of)

sumo, sumere, sumpsi, sumptum (3): take up, begin

sumptus, -us (m.): expense, cost

superior, superius: earlier; higher

supero, -are, -avi, -atum (1): overcome

supra: above, previously (adv. & prep.)

suscipio, suscipere, suscepi, susceptum (3): support, take up

suspicio, -ionis (f.): suspicion

sustineo, sustinere, sustinui, sustentum (2): withstand

suus, -a, -um: his (own)

taedet, taesus est: it irks (imper.)

tam: so (with adjs. and advs.)

tamen: nevertheless; yet, however

tamquam: just as if

tantum (adv.): so much

tantus, -a, -um ... quantus, -a, -um: as much ... as

tantus, -a, -um: so much, so great

tardus, -a, -um: slow

tego, tegere, texi, tectum (3): cover, hide

telum, -i (n.): weapon, spear, javelin (a weapon effective from afar)

tempestas, -atis (f.): storm; season, weather
tempto, -are, -avi, -atus (1): try, attempt; attack
tempus, -oris (n.): time
tenebra, -ae (f.): darkness, obscurity
teneo, tenere, tenui, tentum (2): hold
tenuis, -e: puny, insignificant
terni, -ae, -a: three (each)
tertius, -a, -um: third
testis, -is (m. or f.): witness
timeo, timere, timui, — (2): fear, be afraid
timidus, -a, -um: fearful
timor, -oris (m): fear
tollo, tollere, sustuli, sublatum (irreg.): take away; lift.
tormentum, -i: (n.): artillery
totidem: the same number, just so many
totus, -a, -um: (the) whole (of)
trado, tradere, tradidi, traditum (3): hand over
traduco, traducere, traduxi, traductum (3): lead...across
traho, trahere, traxi, tractum (3): draw, pull
transeo, transire, transii, transitum (irreg.): cross (over); in alia transit = voted against
transfero, transferre, transtuli, translatum (irreg.): transfer; go over (to)
trepido, -are, -avi, -atum (1): be jumpy, nervous
tres, tres, tria: three
triduum, -i: (n.): three-day period
tu: you
tueor, tueri, tuitus/tutus sum (dep.) (2): guard; watch
tum: with cum = both...and; (adv.) then
tuto (adv.): safely
tutus, -a, -um: safe
tuus, -a, -um: your
ubi: when; at what place, where
ullus, -a, -um: any
ulterior, -ius (adj.): further
ultro: of one's own accord; beyond
ultro citroque: back-and-forth
umbra, -ae (f.): shadow
una: together
undique: from (on) all sides
unquam (umquam): ever, at any time
unus, -a, -um: one; only
urbanus, -a, -um: of the city
urbs, urbis, urbium (f.): city
usus, -us (m.): use; experience
ut (conjunc.): as; although; when; in order that; that
uter, utra, utrum: each of two; also = uterque
uterque, utraque, utrumque: each of the two (i.e., both)
utor, uti, usum (dep.) (3): use (with abl.)
utrum...an: whether...or
vallum, -i (n.): rampart
vel: assuredly, indeed; or (mostly with similar alternatives)
venio, venire, veni, ventum (4): come
verbum, -i (n.): word
vereor, vereri, veritum (dep.) (2): fear, be apprehensive
vero: however; indeed, in truth
verto, vertere, verti, versum (3): turn
verus, -a, -um: true; vero = however; truly, certainly
vesper, vesperi OR vesperis (m.): evening
vester, vestra, vestrum: your
veteranus, -a, -um: veteran
vetus, veteris: old, long-standing
videor, videri, visum (2): seem, appear
vigilia, -ae (f.): guard, sentinal; watch of the night
vigilius, -i (m.): watchman, picket
viginti (indecl.): twenty
vinco, vincere, vici, victum (3): conquer

vindico, -are, -avi, -atum (1): set (in libertatem: set free)
vir, -i (m.): man; great man, hero; husband
virtus, -utis (f.): courage; merit
vis, vim (gen. not used) (f.): violence, force
vitium, -i (n.): fault; offense
voco, -are, -avi, -atum: call; invite; name
volo, velle, volui, — (irreg.): be willing, want, wish
voluntas, -atis (f.): intention, wish, inclination
voluptas, -atis (f.): sensual pleasure, indulgence
vox, vocis (f.): word; expression; voice; cry
vulnus, -eris (n.): wound
vultus, -us (m.): visage

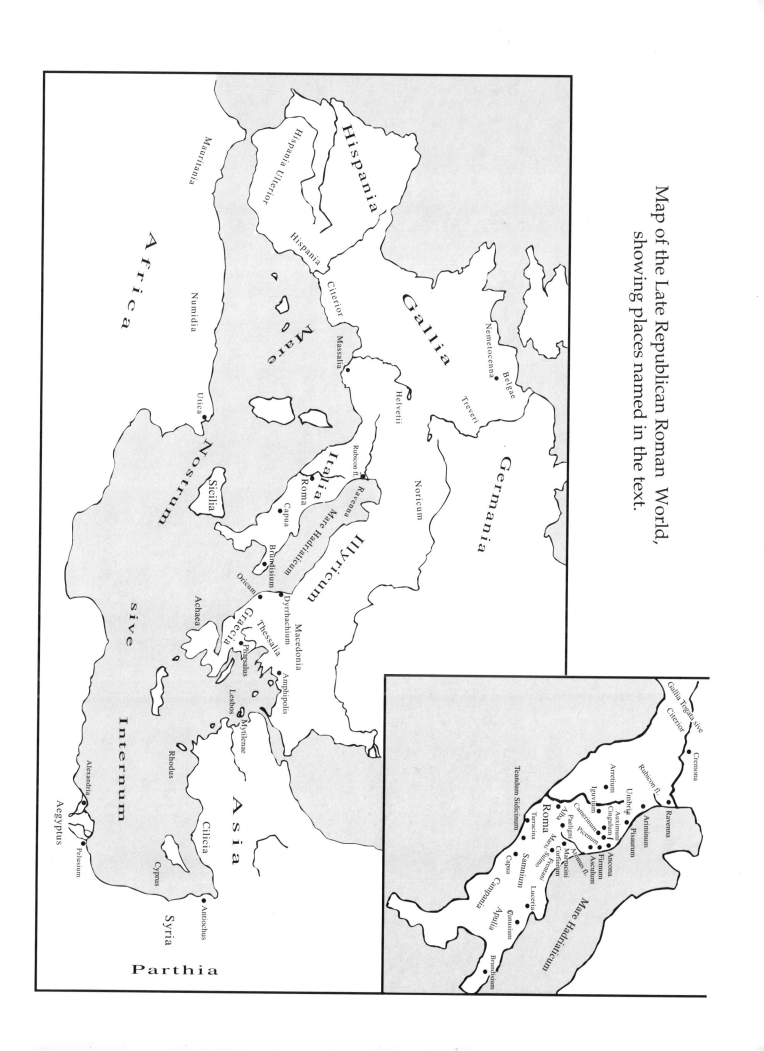

Map of the Late Republican Roman World, showing places named in the text.